Biracial in America

Biracial in America

Forming and Performing Racial Identity

Nikki Khanna

LEXINGTON BOOKS
Lanham • *Boulder* • *New York* • *Toronto* • *Plymouth, UK*

Published by Lexington Books
A wholly owned subsidiary of The Rowman & Littlefield Publishing Group, Inc.
4501 Forbes Boulevard, Suite 200, Lanham, Maryland 20706
http://www.lexingtonbooks.com

Estover Road, Plymouth PL6 7PY, United Kingdom

British Library Cataloguing in Publication Information Available

Library of Congress Cataloging-in-Publication Data

Khanna, Nikki, 1974–
  Biracial in America : forming and performing racial identity / Nikki Khanna.
    p. cm.
  Includes bibliographical references and index.
  ISBN 978-0-7391-4574-6 (cloth : alk. paper) — ISBN 978-0-7391-4576-0
(electronic)
  1. Racially mixed people—Race identity—United States. 2. Racially mixed
people—United States. 3. United States—Race relations. I. Title.
  E184.A1K434 2011
  305.800973—dc23

                                                                2011024917

Printed in the United States of America

To my loves, Michael and Olivia
and
to my parents, Leslie and Arun

Contents

A Note on Terminology

Because this is a book about biraciality, and ultimately race, various racial terms are used throughout, including *black*,[1] *white*, *monoracial*, *multiracial*, and *biracial*. I want to acknowledge up front that race has little meaning in biology; indeed, the validity of race as a scientific concept has been discredited by anthropologists, biologists, and geneticists alike (for examples, see Gould 1994, 1996; Graves 2004; King 1981; Lewontin, Rose, and Kamin 1984; Smedley 1993). Humans are genetically very similar to one another, sharing 99.9 percent of their genetic material despite visible physical differences (see Angier 2000). Of the 0.1 percent genetic variation that is observed in humans, more variation is found *within* so-called racial groups than *between* them (in other words, we are more alike than we are different, racially speaking; Cornell and Hartmann 1998; King 1981).[2]

Moreover, not only are these categories biologically indistinguishable, but they are socially constructed and arbitrarily defined. Racial categories vary across societies and have changed over time, which indicates that race is not as clear-cut and obvious as we tend to think it is. Blackness, for example, is defined differently in the United States and the United Kingdom. Whereas in the United States "blackness" is based on having African ancestry (Davis 1991), in the United Kingdom "black" is defined as anyone who is non-white; in this context, blackness includes those with African ancestry, but also East Indians, Pakistanis (Zack 1998), and other people of color.

Further, racial classifications and racial boundaries change over time. Looking at the United States, for instance, nearly every single census taken since 1790 has measured race using different criteria (Wright 1994)[3] and the inconsistencies in racial categories suggest that they are not scientific categories, but rather political categories constructed by society (in this case, by the federal government). Who has been included in and excluded from the category of "white" in this country has also varied over time: Jews, the Irish, and southern and eastern Europeans are today generally considered white, but were once excluded from this category (Cose 2000; Goodman 2001). The Irish, for example, were once deemed non-white and caricatured in racially inferior and demeaning ways (e.g., often with ape- and monkey-like characteristics[4]); they were also characterized as "niggers turned inside out," while blacks were sometimes referred to as "smoked Irish, an appellation they must have found no more flattering than it was intended to be" (Ignatiev 1995: 41). Arab Americans are currently defined as white according to federal classifications set forth by Congress,[5] but are arguably seen as non-white in their day-to-day lives.[6] East Indians, once considered white (at least according to the federal government), are today categorized as Asian,[7] further illustrating the socially constructed nature of race and the elasticity of the boundaries of whiteness (and of race itself).

Societies have also used arbitrary rules to classify people in terms of race, which further points to the social construction of race. In the United States, for example, the one drop rule (also known more loosely as the rule of hypodescent[8]) has been used to classify anyone with any "drop" of African ancestry as black (Davis 1991). According to the philosopher Naomi Zack, "A person is black if he or she has a black ancestor *anywhere* in family history" (1998: 5; emphasis added). Many notable "black" figures in American history have both black and white ancestry, but were labeled black due to the one drop rule. Famous examples include Frederick Douglass, Booker T. Washington, W. E. B. DuBois, Malcolm X, and Martin Luther King Jr. (Davis 2006; Spickard 2003; Wright 1994). In one now infamous case from the early 1980s, a Louisiana woman named Susie Guillory Phipps challenged the state's classification of her as black, arguing that "I never was black. I was raised white. . . . My children are white. Mother and Daddy were buried white. My Social Security Card says I'm white. . . . My birth certificate is the only thing that says I'm black" (Harris 1983). Nonetheless, the state argued that Phipps' great-great-great-great-grandmother had been a black slave (a black mistress of a Mobile, Alabama, plantation owner), which made her at least $3/32$ "Negro." Because Louisiana defined anyone with as little as $1/32$ black ancestry as black, she lost her case. In the eyes of the state of Louisiana, she was black and therefore defined as such on state documents.

The one drop rule is unique to the United States (Davis 1991) and completely foreign to most other countries, including Brazil, which defines blackness not by ancestry, but by physical appearance (e.g., having very dark skin). In fact, in Brazil, the categories of race are countless and vary from region to region; some basic categories include *branco* (white), *preto* (black), and *pardo* (brown),[9] which are descriptors of skin shade (Marger 2006). Because of these different conceptualizations of race, the same individual may be considered white (or *branco*) in Brazil (based on having light skin) but black in the United States (because of having some degree of African ancestry, no matter how distant) (Davis 1991; Goodman 2001).

Additionally, in the United States, the one drop rule was codified into state laws in various forms. The state of Virginia, for example, labeled as black anyone who had any "ascertainable" black blood; other states determined blackness by fractions of blood: $^1/_{32}$ black (e.g., Louisiana, as described above), $^1/_{16}$ black, $^1/_8$ black, $^1/_4$, or $^1/_2$ black. Because definitions of blackness varied from state to state, individuals could simply cross state lines to change their race from black to white (see, e.g., Valdez and Valdez 1998), further illustrating the arbitrariness of our racial categories and the social construction of race.

In this book, I frequently draw on terms such as *black* and *white*, but in doing so, I use these terms as social classifications, not as biological categories. While the categories of black and white are mere illusions (biologically speaking), they do carry significant social meaning, because, according to sociologist Howard Winant (1994), the illusion of race has taken on a life of its own. We continually create it and re-create it in our social lives, and in doing so, we give it meaning. Put another way, race itself may not be real, but prejudice, discrimination, and racism are.

I also use terms such as *biracial* and *multiracial* to describe the study participants who are quoted throughout this book. According to psychologist Maria Root (1996), a pioneer in the field of biracial and multiracial studies, *biracial* refers to "a person whose parents are of two different *socially* designated racial groups, for example, black mother, white father" (ix). *Multiracial* refers to "people who are of two or more racial heritages" (xi). Thus, the term *multiracial* may also apply to people who are biracial. I also use the term *monoracial*, which according to Root (1996: x), refers to "people who claim a single racial heritage" (e.g., white or black).

Taking a closer look at Maria Root's definitions, I want to draw attention to the artificial distinction between the terms *black* and *multiracial/biracial* (and *monoracial* and *biracial/multiracial*, for that matter). Race scholar Rainier Spencer argues that the distinction between black and multiracial/biracial is a false one given that the majority of black Americans are, in fact, multiracial (Spencer 1999, 2004, 2006a, 2006b). Because of centuries of interracial mixing and the one drop rule which for generation after generation defined them as black, most Americans identified as black are multiracial. Hence, to say that someone is biracial or multiracial because he or she has one black parent and one white parent is false because it selectively invokes the rule of hypodescent to label the parent, but not the child, as black. In Spencer's (1999) own words, it "deploy[s] the racist apparatus of hypodescent by perpetuating the idea that the extremely diverse people of African descent in the United States, the vast majority of whom possess

European and Native American ancestry as well, all constitute a single biological race" (194). The fact that the so-called monoracial black parent is likely multiracial also calls attention to the false demarcation between the terms *monoracial* and *multiracial* more generally. Given the centuries of mixing among Africans, Europeans, and the indigenous populations of the Americas, the majority of people labeled monoracial are likely multiracial. In fact, approximately 6 percent of all "whites" have some black ancestry, and an estimated 75 to 90 percent of American "blacks" have non-black ancestry (Nash 1995; Zack 1998).

Moreover, like the categories black and white, the terms *monoracial, biracial,* and *multiracial* are merely social constructs. Race is a social construction, and hence, so too are the terms *multiracial* and *biracial* because they are built upon the fictitious concept of race itself. This is not to say, however, that these terms are merely illusory—their reality is not rooted in biology or genetics, but rather in the social landscape of American society. Like the categories of black and white, we (as a society) frequently treat the terms *monoracial, biracial,* and *multiracial* as if they were "real" classifications, even though they have no biological meaning. Thus, as Rainier Spencer (2010) suggests in his own work, all racial terms in this book (*black, white, monoracial, multiracial,* and *biracial*) should always be read as if preceded by the words "so-called."

NOTES

1. The term *African American* is used much less frequently than *black,* simply to maintain consistency throughout the text.

2. For more information about "race," see the American Anthropological Association's "Statement on Race" (1998): http://www.aaanet.org/stmts/racepp.htm.

3. To see U.S. census categories over time (1790–1990), see Nobles (2000: 28, 44); see also the appendix in Nobles (2000) for instructions to census enumerators regarding definitions of each racial group.

4. For visual examples of Irish caricatures, see the online article by Michael O'Malley, associate professor of history and art history at George Mason University, at http://chnm.gmu.edu/exploring/19thcentury/alienmenace/pop_inhuman.html.

5. According to federal guidelines, a *white* person refers to "A person having origins in any of the original peoples of Europe, the Middle East, or North Africa." See http://www.whitehouse.gov/omb/fedreg_1997standards/ for the complete list of racial categories and definitions set forth by the Office of Management and Budget, the agency that determines federal categories of race and ethnicity.

6. Leading up to the 2010 Census, Arab American and Persian American groups mounted a campaign to tell their members to check the "other," not the "white" box on the U.S. Census form (Blake 2010). While late nineteenth-century immigrants from the Middle East identified themselves as white, many of today's Middle Eastern immigrants reject that classification because it does not reflect how they define

themselves or how other Americans have traditionally defined them. Often they are perceived in terms of their "otherness."

7. According to Wright (1994), Indians were classified as "Hindu" from 1920 to 1940, and then as "white" for three decades. In 1977, the Office of Management and Budget moved Indians to the "Asian or Pacific Islander" category.

8. The rule of hypodescent refers to the automatic assignment of children of mixed racial relationships to the racial group in their heritage that has the least social status (Root 1996). For example, anthropologist Madison Grant expressed the once commonly held belief that the offspring of interracial relationships take on the "lower" racial status: "The cross between a white man and an Indian is an Indian; the cross between a white man and a Negro is a Negro; the cross between a white man and a Hindu is a Hindu . . ." (Grant 1923: 18). In its most extreme form, hypodescent formed the basis of the one drop rule.

9. In Brazil, the most minute physical characteristics are often used to sort people out racially, and categories vary considerably from region to region. For examples of the detailed categories used in one region of Brazil (in Vila Reconcavo, a town in the state of Bahia), see Martin Marger (2006: 454–55). Some categories are as follows: *preto* refers to someone with "black shiny skin, kinky, woolly hair, thick lips and a flat broad nose." *Cabra* (male) or *cabrocha* (female) is "generally slightly lighter than the *preto*, with hair growing somewhat longer, but still kinky and unmanageable, facial features somewhat less Negroid, although often with fairly thick lips and flat nose." *Cabro verde* is "slightly lighter than the preto, but still very dark . . . has long straight hair, and his facial features are apt to be very fine, with thin lips and a narrow straight nose. He is almost a 'black white man.'" *Escuro*, "or simply 'dark man,' is darker than the usual run of mesticos, but the term is generally applied to a person who does not fit into one of the three types mentioned above. The *escuro* is almost a Negro with Caucasoid features." A *mulato* "has hair which grows perhaps to shoulder length, but which has a decided curl and even kink. . . .The *mulato's* facial features vary widely, thick lips with a narrow nose, or vice-versa." *Sarara* is someone who "has very light skin, and hair which is reddish or blondish but kinky or curled. . . . His facial features are extremely varied, even more so than the *mulato's*"; and the *moreno* "is light-skinned but not white. He has dark hair, which is long and either wavy or curly. . . . His features are much more Caucasoid than Negroid." These categories are literally tied to specific physical characteristics (e.g., skin shade, hair type, lip and nose shape). For Brazilian census categories and descriptions from 1872 to 1991, see Nobles (2000: 104).

1

Questions of Identity

On the night of November 4, 2008, Americans witnessed history unfold on their television sets as they watched a young Illinois senator, Barack Obama, defeat Republican hopeful, Senator John McCain, for president of the United States of America. Celebrating his presidential victory amidst thousands of his supporters in Chicago's Grant Park, Obama told the crowd, "It's been a long time coming, but tonight, because of what we did on this date in this election at this defining moment, change has come to America." The forty-seven-year-old senator made history that night, not because of his youth or campaign message of "change," but because of his racial background as the first African American to be elected to the presidency of the United States. Post-election newspaper headlines read "First Black President Makes US History" (*Miami Herald*), "The First Black President-Elect Wins" (*Los Angeles Times*), "Obama Makes History, US Decisively Elects First Black President" (*Washington Post*), and "African American Makes History" (*Baltimore Examiner*), to name a few.

The media and public perception of Barack Obama as black is both intriguing and, for some, perplexing, given that most Americans are aware of his biracial background. On numerous occasions, Obama has candidly described his family background and mixed racial ancestry: he was born in 1961 in Honolulu, Hawaii, to a white American mother (of predominantly English descent) from Wichita, Kansas, and a black African father from Nyang'oma Kogelo, Kenya. Despite widespread knowledge of his biracial background, Obama has been classified by the media and much of the general public simply as African American. This has hit a nerve for some Americans, often white or multiracial themselves, who have argued that this label is inaccurate and misleading. In response to all of those post-election head-lines that described Obama as black or African American, *Washington Post* columnist Marie Arana challenged the monoracial classification in her aptly titled column "He's Not Black." In it she wrote, "To me, as to increasing numbers of mixed-race people, Barack Obama is not our first black presi-dent. He is our first biracial, bicultural president" (November 30, 2008). Others, too, have challenged Obama's black identity, arguing, "Why does he refer to himself as black? Here is a man who is of mixed race, 50 percent black and 50 percent white . . . so why does this man identify himself as black and not white, or at least as mixed race?" (Sullivan 2008).

Despite his well-publicized biracial ancestry, his ascribed black classifica-tion may not be surprising, for two reasons—one, his personal identifica-tion (he self-identifies as black[1]), and two, his physical appearance (by most accounts, he looks black). How one self-identifies arguably shapes how we view him or her, although it is highly unlikely that Americans would have classified Obama as white or as biracial, even if he had self-identified as such. Clearly, physical appearance matters in our society when it comes to race. In response to those who wrote in to correct him for referring to then-senator Barack Obama as black, *Miami Herald* columnist Leonard Pitts, who is African American, cleverly quipped, "I've got two words of advice for those folks who are surprised to learn Barack Obama is black: Eye. Doctor" (February 4, 2007). His point? Obama looks black, therefore he *is* black. Theoretically, he could self-identify as biracial or even white, but the world would nonetheless perceive him as black because of his physical characteristics (e.g., dark skin)—including the stranger on the street, the potential employer interviewing him for a job, or the police of-ficer who pulls him over for a speeding violation (assuming, of course, he didn't have a famous face). Pitts adds, "You can be as 'biracial' as you want; so long as your features show any hint of Africa, the world is going to give you the treatment it reserves for 'black.'"

Further, Obama's classification as black may not be surprising given the unique rule that has traditionally defined blackness in the United States—the one drop rule. Used only in the United States and applied only to those with black ancestry, the rule classified black-white Americans (or anyone with any "drop" of black ancestry, for that matter) exclusively as black (Davis 1991; Lee 1993; Omi and Winant 1994; Williamson 1980; Wright 1994); biracial wasn't an option, nor was white. Further, one drop of black blood defined people as black regardless of their physical appear-ance—even those who looked stereotypically white, with light skin, blonde hair, and blue eyes.

The rule was rooted in slavery and southern segregation, and was a practi-cal tool whites used to maintain their superiority and position of privilege in the American racial hierarchy. It had several functions: (1) it provided an economic asset to slave owners during the slave era (any multiracial offspring born on the plantation, including those born to the white master, were classified as black and therefore were enslaved); (2) it kept the color line intact during Jim Crow segregation in the southern states (multiracial people were redefined as black preventing them from "muddling up" the carefully constructed system that segregated whites and blacks in public spaces and also denied basic civil rights to blacks); and (3) it was a useful tool to maintain white racial purity (black blood was seen as a "stain" that could never be removed; hence, whiteness was defined as having not even "one drop" of black blood running through one's veins). In attempting to explain Obama's black identity, we must situate it within this larger socio-historical context regarding race and blackness in the United States. According to the one drop rule, Obama may indeed have white ancestry, yet his whiteness is somehow negated by his black "blood." Being 50 percent black and 50 percent white is not a straightforward arithmetic calculation (as some might suggest when they argue he should identify as biracial or multiracial). According to the rule, 50 percent black plus 50 percent white simply equals black.

Barack Obama's experiences as a biracial person with black ancestry, although compelling because of his celebrity, are not unique and raise provocative questions about the black-white biracial experience in America today. For instance, how are black-white biracial people perceived by others with regard to their race? Are they generally seen as black or biracial? Can they be seen as white? Does their physical appearance take precedence today, or does the one drop rule continue to limit their identity options to black? If Obama had outwardly appeared white, for instance, would he have been seen as white by the American public (even if Americans were aware of his black father)? Or would the one drop rule have nonetheless defined him as black? Further, what other factors influence biracial Americans' identities, and what social psychological processes shape whether they identify as black, white, or biracial? These are just some of the many questions that this book seeks to address.

Examining racial identity (and how black-white biracial Americans racially self-identify) is important on multiple levels. At the individual level, racial identity is important because in race-conscious American society, race itself is important, and for many Americans (especially those with non-white ancestry in a white-dominated society), race arguably acts as a "master status"—an identity that overrides all others (Stephan 1992). Whether individuals self-identify (or are identified by others) as black, white, or biracial will influence how others interact with them, will likely shape their social networks (e.g., who they befriend, date, and marry), and will arguably affect their life chances and opportunities. For those biracial/multiracial people whose race is ambiguous, this may be problematic. In fact, race theorist Howard Winant claims that "U.S. society is so thoroughly racialized that to be without racial identity is to be in danger of having no identity" at all, and he draws a parallel with gender further arguing that "to be raceless is akin to being genderless" (1994: 16).

Racial identity (and external ascriptions of race) will likely affect an individual's life in profound and important ways, yet how biracial individuals identify themselves may also have effects beyond the personal; identities may also have implications for the racial communities to which they belong. How black-white biracial Americans identify arguably has reverberating effects on the larger African American community. Do they identify as black and align themselves with black Americans, or do they identify as biracial or multiracial and differentiate themselves from their black counterparts? Biracial and multiracial Americans have received increased attention in recent years largely because of these questions and concerns, especially as they pertain to the enumeration of race in the U.S. Census and the implications for African Americans as a community.

BIRACIAL OR BLACK: BROADER IMPLICATIONS

Historically, the one drop rule rendered black-white biracial (and multiracial) people invisible by redefining them as black, and in doing so, this population has largely been ignored by American society (see Cynthia Nakashima's 1992 discussion). This began to change, however, in the early 1990s with increased media attention due, at least in part, to very public and heated debates surrounding the 2000 U.S. Census. Every ten years, the Census Bureau collects data on race, although the methods for doing so have changed from decade to decade. Prior to 1960, census enumerators went door to door and determined a person's race based on what they could surmise from ancestry and physical appearance; since 1960, however, Americans have been able to self-identify their own race on census forms. From 1960 to 1990, Americans were instructed to "fill one" racial category (the one category that the person considered himself or herself to be): white, black, Asian or Pacific Islander, American Indian or Alaska Native, or other race (categories set forth in 1977 by Congress, which establishes the racial standards on all federal forms). Americans with multiple racial ancestries, who theoretically straddled multiple categories, were forced to choose the one box they felt fit them best. Many multiracial people argued that in doing so they felt confined or "boxed-in" to one category, and they began vocally challenging the way race data were collected in the U.S. Census (and other government forms). In the early 1990s, multiracial activist groups such as Project RACE (Reclassify All Children Equally) and the AMEA (Association of Multi-Ethnic Americans) argued for a new method of data collection that would give Americans the ability to identify themselves multiracially; their key argument was that the American system of monoracial classification was outdated and impractical in the face of a burgeoning multiracial population. The population was changing, they argued, and the census should be modified to accurately count the growing multiracial population.[2]

The media took notice and began to run stories about these so-called "new people," shedding new light on a population that had been hidden for years in plain sight. Heightened media interest was evident in the years and months leading up to the release of the 2000 Census, as stories about multiracial people surged. On November 18, 1993, for example, *Time* magazine ran an image of a multiracial woman on its cover with the caption "The New Face of America"; the future of America was a computer-generated image of a woman with Anglo-Saxon, Middle Eastern, African, Asian, southern European, and Latino roots, who was touted as "the new Eve" (see Root 1996; Streeter 2003; Wright et al. 2003). In 1996, the *New York Times* ran editorial pieces entitled "Multiracial People Must No Longer Be Invisible" (Ramona Douglass, Association of Multi-Ethnic Americans, July 12, 1996) and "Multiracial Americans Ready to Claim Their Own Identity" (Michel Marriott, July 20, 1996). In the same year, they ran an article written by multiracial author Lise Funderburg, who in response to the "choose one box" format of the census, asked, "I'm black and white. Can't the census reflect that?" (July 10, 1996). These stories and others drew new attention to biracial/multiracial people, their racial identities, and the difficulties they faced when trying to classify themselves on census forms.

The debate over the census, however, had fierce opponents. Because federal funding and government programs for minority groups are often dependent on group size, many activist civil rights groups (including the NAACP, ACLU, National Urban League, and Lawyers' Committee for Civil Rights Under Law) lobbied against the change, arguing that the addition of a multiracial category would diminish African American numerical strength as mixed-black Americans opted out of the monoracial black category. As Representative Thomas C. Sawyer, chair of the House Subcommittee on Census, Statistics, and Postal Personnel, said in 1993, "The numbers drive the dollars" (Wright 1994: 47). If multiracial blacks (an estimated 75 to 90 percent of African Americans) chose to check the multiracial instead of the black category, it could have a profound effect on federal programs and earmarks set aside for them. To illustrate the harm a multiracial category could cause, activist Charles Stewart argued at a National Association of Black Journalists symposium, "If you consider yourself black for political reasons, raise your hand." Most did. He then asked how many people in the room considered themselves to be of pure African descent. Not surprisingly, no one raised a hand. Stewart then added, "If you advocate a category that

includes people who are multiracial to the detriment of their black identification, you will replicate what you saw—an empty room. We cannot afford
to have an empty room" (quoted in Wright 1994: 54).

Further, minority activist organizations argued that race data collected via
the census are fundamental to monitoring and enforcing civil rights com-
pliance, not to validating one's personal identity. A multiracial category on
the census or other government forms would make it difficult to track and
combat racial discrimination, and would "pull the teeth of civil-rights laws"
(Wright 1994: 50). In 1991, for example, 35,000 people chose "Other"
on Home Mortgage Disclosure Act papers meant to track discrimination
in mortgage lending, illustrating the problems that a multiracial category
might cause (White 1997).[3]

Even beyond categories on forms, opponents argued that allowing
mixed-black individuals to classify themselves as multiracial could potentially fragment the African American community. Their key argument:
multiracial people with black ancestry, who have historically identified
as black, may separate themselves from other blacks by opting for a more
socially desirable middle position between black and white. They might
identify as multiracial as an escape from blackness and a way to avoid the
stigma historically associated with being black. Opponents also charged
that many of those leading the movement for a multiracial category were, in
fact, white mothers of multiracial children who did not want their children
to be classified as black; it was a way for them to be able to say to their children, "You're not black. You're better than that" (*Interrace* magazine editor
Candace Mills, as cited in Spencer 1999).[4] Opponents additionally argued
that a multiracial category was problematic because it would only create
further hierarchies and divisions among black Americans, and they needed
not look far into American history to make their point.

In some parts of the American South during colonialism and slavery,
like Louisiana for example, multiracial people with black ancestry (i.e.,
Creoles of color) worked hard to distance themselves from blacks in an
effort to hold on to what small racial privilege they had enjoyed under
French and Spanish rule (see G. Reginald Daniel's 2002 discussion). Once
the United States annexed Louisiana, they self-segregated and held tight to
French culture to distinguish themselves from American blacks (e.g., they
spoke French and practiced French cultural traditions), in an effort to maintain their elevated status. Daniel (2002) points to additional examples in
American history in which multiracial people with black ancestry worked
to separate themselves from their black counterparts in order to preserve
their special "buffer" status between black and white. As a consequence,
multiracial groups like those in Louisiana produced a black hierarchy that
many today do not wish to re-create, fearing it could come at the cost of
splintering the black community.

Nowhere has this sentiment become more evident than in the case of professional golfer Tiger Woods, who in 1997 proclaimed a multiracial identity on the *Oprah Winfrey Show*. Touted by the media as the first black golfer to win the prestigious Masters tournament, Woods surprised his audience, and many Americans watching from home, when asked whether it bothered him to be called African American. He replied, "It does. Growing up, I came up with this name: I'm a Cablinasian," a term he created in childhood to signify his white (Ca-), black (bl-), Native American (in-), and Asian ancestry (-asian). Asserting his multiracial identity caused a "mini-racial firestorm" and a backlash from many African Americans who perceived Woods as a race traitor (White 1997) and someone who was in self-denial about his blackness (Eason 1997 as cited in Thornton 2009). Further, if others, like Tiger Woods, opt for the multiracial box, they asked, what might this mean for the African American community?

Although the federal government nixed the multiracial category option, they did allow Americans for the first time in 2000 to check more than one racial box on the census form to signify their multiple racial backgrounds.[5] In doing so, approximately 2.4 percent of the American population, or 6.8 million Americans, chose two or more races; of the multiracial population itself, 12 percent claimed black and white ancestry (this was less than 0.28 percent of the total American population).[6] This change to the census allowed multiracial people to identify and be counted as such, and as part of the compromise, multiracial data were reaggregated to ensure minorities would not lose out in the process (e.g., someone who checked both the white and black boxes was counted as multiracial but also reclassified as black for purposes of funding and enforcement of civil rights laws; Williams 2005).

Despite the census change, however, the controversy over racial classification has not diminished. The battle continues at state and local levels as activist groups butt heads over racial classification policies in areas requiring racial data collection (e.g., schools, employment, medical forms, and even college admissions). Media attention to these battles, as well as the increased visibility of multiracial celebrities like Tiger Woods, have put multiracial Americans in the sociopolitical limelight, making the topic of multiracial identity highly relevant to today's ever-growing and increasingly diverse America. With increased awareness and visibility of this segment of American society has also come heightened scholarly interest.

RESEARCH ON BIRACIAL AND MULTIRACIAL AMERICANS

The 1990s saw a veritable explosion of scholarly research into biracial and multiracial people, and this book seeks to add to that body of work. Much of this work has centered on the census debate, experiences of multiracial people and, most relevant here, racial identity. Some of the earliest works included two anthologies by psychologist Maria P. P. Root, *Racially Mixed People in America* (1992) and *The Multiracial Experience: Racial Borders as the New Frontier* (1996); both consist of collections of essays by activists who lead groups advocating for multiracial issues (e.g., AMEA, Project RACE), as well as scholars in a variety of fields, including psychology, sociology, anthropology, literature, education, social work, ethnic studies, law, and philosophy. Both collections were groundbreaking for their time, yet for the most part, they are compilations of conceptual and historical essays. Both are light on empirical research and theory.

Other books published during this time or shortly thereafter also looked at multiracial issues; not surprisingly, they examined the multiracial movement, which was in full swing in the 1990s, and/or weighed in on debates over federal classifications of race. Jon Michael Spencer, author of *The New Colored People: The Mixed Race Movement in America* (1997), takes a civil rights approach to explain why biracial/multiracial people should be denied a multiracial category on the U.S. Census. He argues that a multiracial classification would only deepen Americans' racial consciousness, and would do nothing to alleviate discrimination. Rainier Spencer, author of *Spurious Issues: Race and Multiracial Identity Politics in the United States* (1999), also looks at multiracial activism and ultimately argues that a multiracial category is problematic because it is built upon the fallacious concept of race itself. Race is a socially constructed category, not a biological reality, and adding a multiracial category to the census only strengthens the concept of race rather than destabilizes it. This is because the new category of multiracial is dependent upon the existing racial structure to support it (e.g., we must have the categories of black, white, Asian, and Native American to have the category multiracial). G. Reginald Daniel, in *More Than Black? Multiracial Identity and the New Racial Order* (2002), provides insight into the history of multiracial Americans (in particular those with black ancestry), and looks at how the categorization of multiracial people has shifted over time. With regard to the debate over the 2000 Census, he argues that multiracial people have the potential to challenge the current binary black-white system of race in the United States.

While these books collectively engage the issues surrounding multiraciality and the debate over adding a multiracial category to the U.S. Census, other works more directly examine the experiences of biracial people today and, most relevant here, their racial identity choices. These studies have grown substantially in the last two decades, and to focus this discussion, I look only at scholarly books that specifically examine racial identity among biracial Americans with black ancestry. There is growing research on biraciality and multiraciality outside the United States (for examples of books, see Christian 2000; Song 2003; Tizard and Phoenix 2002; see also Aspinall 2003; Daniel 2003; Davis 2006; England 2010; Fernandez 1992; Mahtani 2001; Murphy-Shigematsu 2001; Oikawa and Yoshida 2007; Parker 2001; Song 2010; Song and Hashem 2010; Telles and Sue 2009; Twine 2004, 2006; Van Tuyl 2001). I exclude this work, however, because each society's unique history of race relations likely has different implications for its biracial and multiracial people and their respective identities. To further simplify the discussion, I focus on single-study books and I omit edited volumes, which often include a medley of studies by various researchers, with different samples and divergent methods of inquiry. However, for further reading and a more comprehensive list of contemporary scholarly and non-scholarly books on biracial and multiracial people in the United States and abroad, including both monographs and edited volumes, see appendix C. What follows is a brief summary of recent books that explore the topic of racial identity in the United States, with an eye towards the advances each have made in identity research.

Marion Kilson, in *Claiming Place: Biracial Young Adults of the Post–Civil Rights Era* (2001), addresses the experiences of biracial adults in that era, as well as issues of identity development. Drawing on forty-nine interviews with biracial Americans, she explores a range of themes, such as their relationships with their parents, relatives, and peers in childhood and adulthood; their dating and friendship patterns; and their experiences of being biracial today. Regarding identity in particular, she explores their identity choices (how they identify themselves to others), fluxes in their identities over time and situation, and the ways in which these identities impact their lives. This study moves the field forward by providing an eloquent descriptive analysis regarding the experiences of biracial Americans and the range of ways in which they identify themselves, yet provides little analysis with regard to identity formation and the factors and processes that shape those identities.

Moreover, although her respondents shared the experience of being born in the 1960s, they differed in many ways—in their physical appearances, regions of residence, incomes, and education. No doubt this variability allowed for broader generalizability to biracial Americans as a whole; however, respondents also differed with regard to racial ancestry. While the majority of her sample had a black parent (nearly 94 percent), the racial backgrounds of her interviewees ranged from black/white to Middle Eastern/ black, Asian/black, white/black/Native American, and Asian-white. I argue, however, that given the unique way in which blackness and the black-white binary have historically been defined in the United States, black-white biracial Americans have a distinct set of issues regarding identity development that set them apart from other biracial/multiracial groups. Thus, they merit their own analytic focus.

Kathleen Korgen does just this in her book *From Black to Biracial: Transforming Racial Identity among Americans* (1998), when she looks specifically at identity choices among black-white biracial Americans. Her work is particularly groundbreaking because she describes the transformation in racial identity of those with black-white ancestry over the last several decades. Drawing on interviews with forty biracial adults, she finds that those born before the civil rights era are likely to identify as black (because of the constraints of the one drop rule), while those born in the post–civil rights era identify as black, biracial, and sometimes white. Her work is innovative because it examines how identity choices have changed over time and addresses the declining impact of the one drop rule on shaping black identities, and the increasing importance of other factors, such as physical appearance. Further, the focus of her book is on changing trends in identity and factors shaping those trends; however, it is beyond the scope of her analysis to examine the underlying social psychological processes shaping these identities.

Adding to this work, Ursula Brown, in *The Interracial Experience: Growing Up Black/White Racially Mixed in the United States* (2001), draws on interviews with 119 young biracial adults to examine their experiences and identities; like Kathleen Korgen, she narrows her focus to those with black-white biracial ancestry. As a mental health professional, she devotes much of her attention to the experience of being biracial (or what she terms "interracial"), and she looks at self-esteem, acceptance by extended family members, racial labeling by parents, experiences of growing up in black or white communities, and experiences in dating (to name a few areas).

She also examines racial identity and finds that this varies among her sample: some see themselves as black, some as white, but the majority see themselves as interracial (or some related multiracial term). She also finds a compartmentalization of two identities—one public (how they publicly define themselves to others) and one private (their own racial self-perception), which adds a multidimensionality to racial identity that had previously gone unexplored. For instance, some people identify publicly as black, but privately as interracial, which reveals an inherent incongruity of identity. Moreover, Brown states her goal in this book is "to lay groundwork for more definitive studies" and not to offer "understanding into causal relationships" (27). Brown's focus, like some before her, is descriptive, and for the most part, atheoretical. Having said that, however, this work further illuminates many of the experiences biracial people face today, as well as allowed for the reexamination of how we examine identity. No longer can we look at identity as one-dimensional; in fact, Brown's work reveals that identity may have multiple layers.

Finally, one of the most recent and influential books in the field came in 2002 with *Beyond Black: Biracial Identity in America* by sociologists Kerry

Ann Rockquemore and David Brunsma (a later edition came in 2008). They, too, examine black-white biracial identity, but they do what few before had done—they draw on both interview and survey data (they interview 25 respondents and survey 117), and ground at least part of their work in broader identity theories. Their work corroborates studies, like that of Kathleen Korgen in *From Black to Biracial*, which show that black-white biracial Americans are increasingly identifying as biracial (or some related multiracial term) rather than as black. The majority of respondents in their sample (approximately 61 percent) identified as biracial, while only 13.1 percent identified as black. Rockquemore and Brunsma also add to the literature by identifying factors that influence racial identity (e.g., appearance, social networks, family context) and unlike those who came before, they begin to describe some of the processes shaping racial identity. In particular, they describe not just the "what," but also the "how" of racial identity development; for instance, going beyond simply describing the link between appearance and identity to explain *how* appearance shapes identity. Much of the work prior to *Beyond Black* focused on descriptions of biracial experiences and identity options, but Rockquemore and Brunsma propelled the field forward by illuminating some of the underlying processes of identity development.

In the present book, I add to Rockquemore and Brunsma's (2002a) work and to previous research by further examining racial identity among black-white biracial adults. I investigate how it is formed, and how biracial individuals negotiate their identities with others on a day-to-day basis. Unlike previous studies, which have largely been descriptive, exploratory, and light on theoretical frameworks to ground their studies, this book seeks to examine some of the *influencing factors* and *underlying processes* shaping their racial identities—something which has been missing from the vast majority of books examining racial identity among biracial Americans. Drawing from a distinctly social psychological perspective, I investigate racial identity among black-white biracial adults and in doing so, I draw links between biracial identity and broader social psychological theories and concepts to further illuminate *how* identity is formed.

Moreover, unlike previous studies, which for the most part examine racial identity as if it were one-dimensional (often measuring identity by what respondents check on a form), I draw on the work of Ursula Brown (2001) and conceptualize identity in two ways. Specifically, I look at how individuals publicly identify themselves to others, but also how they see themselves racially. Recent research suggests that different dimensions of identity do indeed exist and, in fact, they may not necessarily mesh (see Brown 2001; Brunsma 2006; Harris and Sim 2002; Tashiro 2002). Keeping this in mind, I examine different layers of identity and theorize on the social psychological processes that shape their development.

Additionally, what further distinguishes this study from previous books is that while I look at the processes by which larger society shapes individual identities, I also examine how individuals actively negotiate those identities with larger society. Many studies of biracial identity tend to focus on outside factors shaping identity; in contrast, I look at the role of individuals in shaping their race and the ways in which they "do race" to influence how others perceive them. Without a doubt, identity is not simply imposed by society, but is also created by individuals, and this study looks at the extent to which biracial people *perform* their racial identities in their day-to-day social interactions with others.

THE STUDY

In order to examine racial identity and the underlying processes shaping it, I draw from interview data with forty black-white biracial adults. For a period of twenty months in 2005 and 2006, I conducted face-to-face semi-structured interviews with individuals living in a large urban southern city—Atlanta, Georgia. Because locating biracial individuals within the general population is often difficult, I relied on convenience sampling. To recruit participants for interviews, I began by placing flyers at local colleges, universities, and places of worship. To target black-white biracial individuals, the flyers read, "Do you have one black parent and one white parent?" I omitted terms such as *biracial* or *multiracial* from flyers aware that some individuals may not perceive themselves as such, and hence may not have responded to my advertisement.

Further, because the majority of non-clinical studies examining racial identity among biracial people have looked at college students attending predominantly white colleges and universities, my goal was to also recruit respondents outside the college/university setting (e.g., places of worship) and to look beyond predominantly white schools. In order to seek some degree of variation in the racial composition of respondents' social networks, for example, I advertised at majority white colleges and universities (Emory University, Georgia Tech, University of Georgia, Georgia State, and Mercer University), as well as several historically black colleges and universities in the area (Spelman College, Morehouse College, and Clarke Atlanta University). I also asked interviewees to pass along my contact information to others with similar racial backgrounds.[7]

Sample Population

To participate in the study, respondents had to meet two basic criteria. First, they had to have biological parents who identify with two separate racial groups (i.e., one parent as white, the other as black). Because of the prevalence of interracial mixing in American history, it is estimated that the majority of so-called blacks have some non-black ancestry (e.g., Native American or white ancestry); hence, many of the supposedly black parents could theoretically label themselves as multiracial (see Spencer 1999, 2006a). However, because of the historical legacy of the one drop rule, many of these individuals self-identify exclusively as black. Thus, for the purpose of this study, a biracial individual refers to a person whose parents claim different socially designated racial groups (e.g., the mother self-identifies as black and the father as white). It must be acknowledged, however, that racial identities of respondents' parents are based solely on the respondents' perspectives.

Second, participants had to fall between eighteen and forty-five years of age. I chose this range for two reasons: (1) I used eighteen years as the baseline age in order to omit from the sample children and adolescents who may have relatively limited experiences regarding race and their biraciality and are likely still forming their racial identities; (2) I used forty-five years as the upper limit because respondents in this age range spent the bulk (if not all) of their formative years in the 1970s, 1980s, and 1990s. Korgen (1998) notes a divergence in experience between those growing up before the civil rights era versus those growing up in the post–civil rights era. In short, those who grew up before the civil rights era are more likely to identify exclusively as black because one drop norms constrained their racial identity choices. In contrast, those born after the civil rights era have more racial choices available to them as the one drop rule has waned in importance (Korgen 1998). To control for cohort effects and differing racial climates for this study, I chose not to interview those born before 1960.

The Interviews

My research questions are best answered by in-depth interviews that allow respondents to describe in rich detail how they think about their identity and how others influence the ways they see themselves. Survey methods (such as those used by Brunsma 2005, 2006; Campbell 2007; Harris and Sim 2002; Khanna 2004; Qian 2004; Roth 2003; Saenz, Hwang, and Anderson 1995; Xie and Goyette 1997) allow for a relatively larger sample than other methods and are useful for identifying broad patterns regarding racial identity. Qualitative methods, such as interviewing (as used here), allow for further understanding of how these processes unfold in social interactions and how they affect the formation and negotiation of identity. According to Toby Jayaratne and Abigail Stewart (1991), one of the great strengths of qualitative methods is the ability to get close to the respondents' perspectives. Shulamit Reinharz (1992) would agree, claiming that "interviewing offers researchers access to people's ideas, thoughts, and memories in their own words rather than in the words of the researcher" (19). From the respondents' own perspectives and words, we can further understand *how identity processes play out* in social interactions with others.

The interviews were semi-structured to allow me to focus on specific questions I had regarding identity among biracial people, while at the same time allowing for some flexibility to probe participants' responses. Often new questions and themes arose during the course of each interview, and I remained flexible in order to be able to incorporate these new topics and ask additional questions as necessary. I did, however, begin with a pre-set list of questions (see appendix A) to guide the interview process.

The interviews took place in a variety of settings. Of primary concern was the issue of privacy and making sure respondents felt comfortable providing honest responses to the questions posed. As much as possible, I allowed respondents to choose where we met, all the while informing them that they should choose a place in which they would feel comfortable discussing their private thoughts. We met in a variety of places, including my office, their workplace offices, college/university student centers, restaurants, coffeehouses, bookstores, public or university libraries, and church spaces.

I read with each respondent a consent form approved by the Institutional Review Board (IRB) at my university, which explained the study and detailed their rights as participants. This form briefly describes the study and indicates to respondents that their participation is voluntary, their responses are confidential, and their names are to be changed in any publications. In addition, it informs them that they may skip any uncomfortable questions or stop the interview at any time. Respondents signed the form, indicating their consent, before beginning the interview process. After signing the consent form, I turned on the audiotape and began the formal part of the interview. Interviews ranged from 45 to 165 minutes, with the bulk of the interviews lasting approximately 60 to 90 minutes. All interviews were audio-recorded and later transcribed verbatim.

During and after the interview, I also took notes on respondents' nonverbal cues (pauses, facial expressions, etc.), physical appearance (dress, skin color, racial appearance, etc.), and my feelings about the interview process. At the end of the interview, I allowed participants to ask any additional questions (about myself, the project, etc.) or speak on topics that they perceived as relevant or important. Finally, after each interview was completed, I wrote a brief memo that highlighted and summarized some of the major points brought up during the interview.

Defining and Measuring Racial Identity

Whereas much of the research on racial identity among biracial people draws on a one-dimensional view, often focusing on how people label themselves to others or what race box they check on forms, Ursula Brown

(2001) (as described earlier) draws a distinction between two types of identities —public identity, or how one publicly defines oneself to others, and private identity, which refers to one's own racial self-perception. While public and private identities might mesh, Brown finds that they often do not—some people identify publicly one way and privately another. David Brunsma (2006) also notes a distinction between public categorization and private racial identification, arguing that, with regard to his sample, "a disjuncture does exist between the ways in which these black-white biracial people understand themselves racially *and* the ways that they wish to present and manifest themselves in other contexts" (573).

Keeping in mind the research that suggests racial identity is multifaceted (see also Harris and Sim 2002; Tashiro 2002) and the potential mismatches among different layers of identity, I chose to take a multidimensional approach to racial identity. Specifically, I defined and measured identity in two ways: (1) as a *"public" identity*, the way in which these respondents labeled themselves to others, and (2) as an *"internalized" identity*, referring to how they internally identified (i.e., how they saw themselves). It is important to note that these identities may be contextual and fluid, depending upon the situation and audience.

Regarding public identities, I looked at the descriptors respondents used to describe or identify themselves to others (e.g., as biracial, multiracial, mixed, interracial, black, white). Using an open-ended format so as not to influence respondents' answers, I asked, "How do you tend to identify yourself to others?" This dimension of identity, the social labels individuals use to describe themselves, mirrors how multiracial identity has often been studied in quantitative research. To move beyond a one-dimensional portrait of identity, however, I also defined and measured identity as an internalized identity. To assess internalized identity, I asked two closed-ended questions: "How strongly would you say you identify with being black? Would you say very strongly, somewhat, very little, or not at all?" I then repeated the same format to ask how strongly they identified as white. With both questions, I gave respondents the opportunity to explain their responses.

I then asked a third question, "Is there a racial group, whether white or black, with which you more strongly identify?" I used these three closed-ended questions to gauge internalized racial identity. For the majority of respondents, responses were consistent between questions. Nine respondents, however, gave the same answer (e.g., "somewhat") when asked how strongly they identified as white and as black, indicating that they might have identified equally with both racial groups. When this occurred, I used the question, "Is there a racial group, whether white or black, with which you more strongly identify?" to further gauge whether, in fact, respondents identified more closely with one racial group over the other. Of the nine respondents, two chose one racial group when further probed, while seven indicated that they identified with both groups equally. These seven respondents were coded as internally identifying with both racial groups (i.e., as biracial).

Profile of the Participants

My data collection efforts resulted in a sample of forty black-white biracial individuals (see appendix B for an overview of the sample). As described previously, their ages ranged from 18 to 45 (the lower and upper age limits were intentionally set). The average age was a little more than 24 years. More than half of the respondents, 57.5 percent, fell between the ages of 18 and 22, which is typical college age; this is not surprising considering that my recruitment efforts began at local postsecondary institutions. Of the remaining respondents, 27.5 percent fell between the ages of 23 and 30, and 15 percent were over the age of 30. Regarding gender, 22.5 percent were men and 77.5 percent were women. I found that women were much more likely to answer my advertisements, and an imbalance of gender appears to be a common problem in qualitative research on biracial and multiracial people. Other studies on biracial people similarly show a disparity that favors women over men (or girls over boys) (see Brown 2001; Kilson 2001; Korgen 1998; Rockquemore and Brunsma 2002a; and Tizard and Phoenix 2002 for examples). Further, most respondents in this study (85 percent) were single and had never been married. Six respondents (15 percent) were married, and four respondents had at least one child.

These respondents grew up in a variety of contexts. Regarding family of origin, the majority were raised with both biological parents (57.5 percent). Thirty percent were raised solely by one biological parent: nine respondents were raised by their biological white mothers, two were raised by their biological black mothers, and one was raised by her biological black father. The remaining 12.5 percent were adopted. One was adopted by two black parents, one by two white parents, one by a single white woman, and two by interracial black-white couples. While respondents were all recruited in the South and all were currently living in northeast Georgia, many had lived in various parts of the country, as well as outside the United States.

Additionally, the racial makeup of their social networks varied considerably, which was likely due to the recruitment methods. When asked about the racial compositions of their neighborhoods, schools, churches, and workplaces, 60 percent of respondents described racially mixed networks and significant contact with both blacks and whites (and often other racial groups as well). The remaining respondents described one-sided racial networks: 30 percent described predominantly white networks embedded in white communities, while 10 percent described minority networks, in which they were surrounded primarily by blacks and Latinos.[8] Of the thirty-two respondents in college or graduate school, nearly 72 percent were attending colleges or universities with majority white populations, while a little more than 28 percent were attending predominantly black schools (historically black colleges and universities in Atlanta).

In terms of socioeconomic background, the majority had a middle-/upper-middle-class background, as measured by their educational backgrounds and those of their parents. All respondents were either enrolled in college or college-educated—67.5 percent being current college students and 32.5 percent having completed a bachelor's degree. In addition, 15 percent of respondents were pursuing advanced degrees in astronomy, nursing, psychology, or social work. Further, the majority of respondents (82.5 percent) were currently in school pursuing undergraduate or graduate degrees, but 20 percent held full-time jobs and careers (as a store manager, a scientific researcher, teachers, nurses, and social workers). While respondents often had limited information about their parents' incomes, they frequently described their parents as highly educated. Most had at least one parent with some college (87.5 percent) or a bachelor's degree (75 percent), and almost half of all respondents (47.5 percent) had at least one parent who held an advanced degree. The middle-/upper-middle-class status of the sample was further evidenced by the professions of many of the parents (e.g., doctors, entrepreneurs, college professors, teachers, lawyers, nurses, as well as a dentist, scientist, college dean, accountant, airline pilot, judge, and minister).

Finally, with regard to physical appearance, this sample showed wide variation in skin color, facial features, and hair texture and color. After each interview, I coded each respondent in terms of my subjective view of his or her racial appearance: as "white" (looks white with few, if any, physical features that would indicate otherwise), as "black or multiracial black" (has physical features/skin coloring that indicate black ancestry), or as "racially ambiguous" (difficult to ascertain racial ancestry). I coded "black" and "multiracial black" together because most black Americans have white ancestry; so distinguishing between black and multiracial black is difficult given the wide range in physical appearance among black Americans, and furthermore, distinguishing between the two likely has little meaning considering the multiracial background of most so-called black Americans. While this coding method is quite subjective and others may have perceived these individuals quite differently, I include it *only* to give the reader an idea of the range of physical appearance; it does not figure in the analysis.

The majority of the sample I perceived as black or multiracial black (75 percent), but the range of skin tone varied widely from very dark to very light. Those with light skin might be perceived as biracial or multiracial, rather than black, by most observers. Of the remaining respondents, six (15 percent) were classified as racially ambiguous, meaning that it was difficult for me to categorize them racially. If I saw them in another context, I would have had a difficult time placing them racially. The remaining four respondents (10 percent) were categorized as white. These respondents often described how they sometimes "passed" as white or were "mistaken" for white. One example was John. When I first met John for the interview, we almost missed each other, in part because I didn't recognize him as biracial. When I first saw him in the coffeehouse where we had agreed to meet, he was already sitting at a table. Assuming the seated man was white, I continued to wait for him by the door. We did eventually find each other—once he figured out that I was waiting for *him*. Furthermore, his own perception of his physical appearance surfaced throughout the interview. On several occasions, John described himself as looking like a "regular white guy."

Limitations of the Study

Before continuing, two key limitations of this study must be addressed. First, a major challenge in studying biracial people is locating a representative sample (Tizard and Phoenix 2002). The respondents who participated in this study were gathered by means of convenience sampling and the sample is, in fact, biased with regard to gender (most participants were women), social class (the sample was skewed towards those of middle-/upper-middle-class backgrounds), and region (all were recruited from the South). As such, the data gathered from this project cannot be generalized to all biracial people, and care must be taken when interpreting the findings in this book. In *Challenging Multiracial Identity* (2006), Rainier Spencer argues that scholars of biraciality must acknowledge the limitations of their samples, and refrain from generalizing biased samples to the entire population of biracial people. Heeding his concern, I am careful throughout this book to remind the reader that I am describing trends and processes within *this* sample; I am not generalizing these results to the larger population of black-white biracial Americans.

The southern sample is particularly important to bear in mind because at various points throughout this book, I consider the present-day influence of the one drop rule on their racial identities. Because the one drop rule flourished under slavery and Jim Crow segregation in the South, its force may be strongest in this region. Indeed, recent research points to the continued influence of the one drop rule—*especially in the South*. David Harris and Jeremiah Joseph Sim (2002), for instance, find that black-white adolescents living in the South were significantly less likely to identify as white as compared with black-white adolescents living in other regions of the country, which may be explained by the lingering influence of the one drop rule in the South. Similarly, David Brunsma (2005, 2006) finds evidence of the one drop rule in the South in two empirical studies of black-white biracial Americans. Findings from survey data on kindergarten-aged children show that parents in the South are more likely than parents in other regions to identify their children exclusively as black (Brunsma 2005). He also finds that biracial college students in the South are least likely to identify as white and most likely to identify as black as compared to students in the Midwest and East (Brunsma 2006). The uniqueness of the southern sample is, according to Brunsma (2006), "somewhat expected" given the "impact of the one drop rule in the South" (568). Therefore, it is imperative to keep in mind that while this sample is not representative of all biracial southerners, the findings (particularly with regard to the one drop rule) may differ from what would be found in other regions of the country. The strength of this study, however, is that it looks at a region rarely examined in qualitative research on black-white biracial Americans (for an exception, see Rockquemore and Arend 2003). Moreover, the purpose of these findings is not to describe the broader biracial population in the United States (or even in the South), but rather to illuminate the *processes and mechanisms* by which identity is shaped.

A second limitation of this study is that, as an Asian Indian-white woman, I was uniquely positioned as *both* an insider and outsider with regard to respondents. In particular, I share a white-minority biracial background with them, but I do not share their black ancestry. To partially position myself as an insider, I shared information about my own biracial background before each interview. Often respondents were curious about my background before I divulged it (some said it was because they wondered why I was interested in this research), and I believe that sharing this information "broke the ice" in many cases. For instance, they often appeared more enthusiastic about the interview, more open to answering my questions, and much more talkative once this information was shared.

While I share a biracial background (as well as some degree of white ancestry) with my respondents, however, some respondents may have nonetheless perceived me as an outsider since I do not share their same racial "mix," and this may have affected their responses. Further, I am biracial but I outwardly appear white, and this may have also affected how they responded to some of the interview questions. For instance, some respondents may have been less open with me because of my white appearance and non-black ancestry. This was apparent in an interview with one respondent, Jack, who at the end of his interview admitted that his responses might have differed had I been black. He said, "I'll be honest. I was thinking this whole interview would be different if you were black. Because I don't mean to be two-faced, but . . . I was thinking, 'Well, if she's gonna be black, I'm going to have to be more sensitive.' I might not have said so much." Whereas Jack explained that he was more open with me because I was not black, certainly there may have been other respondents for whom the opposite was true.

Nevertheless, while some respondents may have perceived me as an outsider, no interviewer can completely escape this status when doing face-to-face interviews. France Winddance Twine (2000) argues that while having a shared racial background may grant one an "insider status" with interviewees when doing race-related research, she says, "race is not the only relevant 'social signifier'" (9); my gender, age, status as researcher, education, racial appearance, and respondents' own perceptions of my racial identity (e.g., as white or non-white) could have positioned me as an outsider for some respondents even if I shared their black-white biracial background. Despite these limitations, however, I remain confident that respondents were forthcoming in their interviews, as evidenced by their candor and the richness of their responses. I think the interview excerpts speak for themselves in showing the high-level rapport that was established between myself and the respondents in this study.

STRUCTURE OF THE BOOK

In order to give historical context to the study, chapter 2 ("Black and White in America: Then and Now") provides historical background regarding black-white interracial mixing and traces the history of black-white Americans in the United States from colonial America to today. Furthermore, this chapter examines how evolving black-white relations and intra-racial tensions within the African American community have likely shaped the experiences, and hence the identities, of black-white Americans today. Understanding that biracial Americans' contemporary experiences cannot be divorced from their broader historical experiences, this chapter focuses on how their racial options have evolved over time, with a particular focus on the influence of the one drop rule in shaping racial identity.

Chapters 3, 4, 5, and 6 consist of the findings of this study. Chapter 3 ("'From the Outside Looking In': Reflected Appraisals and the One Drop Rule") explores how others (e.g., family members, peers, friends, and society more generally) influence one's racial identity. Drawing on Charles H. Cooley's concept of the "looking glass" self (1902), this chapter examines how individuals *think* they appear to others, and how this perception shapes their racial identities. Of the black-white biracial men and women I interviewed, the majority described how "others" or "society" have influenced their racial identities. Often viewed by others as black, they frequently identify more strongly with being black than white. Further, participants describe a fascinating discrepancy between how they believe they are perceived by whites and by blacks—put simply, most participants believe that blacks often recognize their biracial/multiracial backgrounds, while whites tend to think they are black. Here, I explore the implications for these different perceptions for their racial identities and explore how the one drop rule continues to shape their racial identities even today.

Chapter 4 ("'Blacks Accept Me More Easily Than Whites': The Push and Pull of Day-to-Day Interactions") examines participants' experiences in everyday interactions that shape their racial identities. Drawing on Kerry Ann Rockquemore and David Brunsma's (2002a) conceptualization of "pull" and "push" factors, this chapter examines respondents' interactions with blacks and whites, which pull, push, or pull and push biracial individuals towards and away from particular racial identities (whether as black, white, or biracial). Specifically, I look at how perceived acceptance by a racial group (i.e., a positive experience) pulls individuals towards that identity, while perceived discrimination and rejection by a group (i.e., a negative experience) functions to push them from the identity. I examine these push and pull factors (discrimination, acceptance, and rejection) within the context of social interactions between these biracial respondents and (1) whites and (2) blacks. These respondents tend to describe experiences of discrimination and rejection by whites, yet they often describe feeling accepted by blacks as black (at least for the most part). In looking at biracials' experiences with both whites and blacks, I also examine the role that gender plays in influencing these experiences of rejection and acceptance, and its subsequent impact on racial identity.

Chapter 5 ("'I'm Not Like Them At All': Social Comparisons and Social Networks") examines the role of social comparisons and social networks in shaping racial identity among black-white biracial Americans. Social psychologist Leon Festinger (1954), the first to use the term *social comparisons* and the first to propose a systematic theory of social comparisons, argued that individuals learn about themselves and assess themselves through comparisons with other people. Searching for a sense of racial identity, participants compare themselves with others on a number of dimensions. These dimensions include: (1) phenotypic comparisons (they compare their skin color, hair, facial features, and body types with those of black, white, and biracial others); (2) cultural comparisons (they compare themselves to black, white, and biracial others based on perceived cultural similarities and differences regarding language/dialect, clothing styles, food, musical tastes, participation in various sports, and values); and (3) experiential comparisons (they compare their experiences of privilege, prejudice, and discrimination with those of other black, white, and biracial others). More importantly, this chapter also looks at how the racial composition of their social networks (i.e., predominantly white, predominantly black, or racially mixed) influences these social comparison processes, furthering our understanding of how social networks shape racial identity among biracial people.

Whereas previous chapters examine how others influence one's racial identity, chapter 6 ("'I Was Like Superman and Clark Kent': Strategies and Motivations of Identity Work"), focuses on how biracial individuals actively manage their preferred racial identities in everyday situations. Building on David Snow and Leon Anderson's (1987, 1993) concept of "identity work," I explore both the range of strategies that biracial individuals draw upon and their motivations for negotiating their identities in various situations. This chapter highlights not only individual agency in presenting preferred identities, but also the fluidity of race. These participants often describe moving between categories, depending upon the immediate context or situation. In the final chapter, chapter 7, I conclude with a discussion of the key findings of this study and their implications for the future study of racial identity.

Barack Obama is a visible example of someone with black-white ancestry who identifies as black, but there are hundreds of thousands of other Americans with similar biracial backgrounds.[9] Previous research suggests that some will identify as black, others as biracial or multiracial, and others as white, and their identity choices exemplify the different ways in which biracial people self-identify in America today. Ultimately, this book seeks to better understand how and why people identify the way they do and the underlying processes influencing their identities. Identity is complex and multidimensional, and is influenced by a multitude of factors all working simultaneously to shape it on a day-to-day continuous basis. It is beyond the scope of this book to explain every factor shaping individual identity; rather, the purpose of this book is to identify some of the most important factors and begin to explain some of the mechanisms by which identity is formed.

NOTES

1. When asked to declare his race in the 2010 Census, Obama checked "Black, African American, or Negro" as his race of choice (Roberts and Baker 2010).

2. Collectively, there were many options that were suggested to amend the race question in the 2000 Census including: (1) a multiracial category (a catch-all classification for all people of mixed-racial heritage), (2) a multiracial category with a write-in (this allowed multiracial people to specify their specific racial ancestries), (3) an open-ended race question (all Americans would simply write in their race), and (4) a "check all that apply format" (Americans would be given the option of checking as many racial categories that applied to them).

3. For more information on the debate, see Elliott Lewis' book, *Fade: My Journeys in Multiracial America* (2006: 205–28); Rainier Spencer's book, *Spurious Issues: Race*

and Multiracial Identity Politics in the United States (1999: chap. 4); and Kimberly Mc-Clain DaCosta's (2003) book chapter "Multiracial Identity: From Personal Problem to Public Issue" (2003; chapter 4 in *New Faces in a Changing America: Multiracial Identity in the 21st Century,* edited by Loretta I. Winters and Herman L. DeBose).

4. This includes, for example, Susan Graham, the founder and director of Project RACE and the white mother of two biracial children. Her organization fights for multiracial classifications on federal, state, and local forms. Accused of having ulterior motives for pushing for multiracial classifications, she says, "People have said all kinds of things to me, that we're part of a Nazi movement, that I just want my kids to be white and that's why I'm doing this. . . . I've always said that until we can stop counting by race, what I want is for my biracial kids to be counted accurately" (quoted in Lewis 2006). She argues that she does not want her children to be classified as black because she believes that the label is an inaccurate description of their race.

5. Directions for the race question in the 2000 Census read, "What is person (X's) race? Mark one or more races to indicate what this person considers himself/herself to be." Categories included white; black, African American, or Negro; American Indian or Alaska Native; Asian Indian; Chinese; Filipino; Japanese; Korean; Vietnamese; Native Hawaiian; Guamanian or Chamorro; Samoan; Other Pacific Islander; Other Asian; and Some Other Race.

6. These data were gathered from CensusScope at http://www.censusscope.org/us/chart_multi.html.

7. I was able to find four respondents through this method (a half-sister, a friend, a coworker, and an acquaintance of the initial interviewee).

8. Regarding social networks, I was interested in the *racial composition* of respondents' networks in childhood and adulthood (up to this point in their lives). To gauge network composition, I asked the following series of questions: "How would you describe your social networks growing up?"; "Were you primarily surrounded by other blacks, other whites, another group altogether, or diverse racial groups?"; "What about in your neighborhood(s)? Church? School(s)? College?" I then repeated these questions with regard to the racial composition of their networks at the time of the interview: "How would you describe your social networks today?"; "Are you primarily surrounded by other blacks, other whites, another group altogether, or diverse racial groups?"; "What about in your neighborhood? Church? College? Workplace?" Based on the responses to these questions, I then coded each respondent into one of three network categories: "White" (one who had experienced predominantly white social networks), "Black" (one who had experienced predominantly black social networks), or "Mixed" (one who had experienced racially mixed networks and contact with both blacks and whites). For the majority of respondents, this was a relatively straightforward process because they described growing up in one-sided racial networks (black or white) and living in similar networks as adults. Kate and Caroline, for example, described growing up in small, predominantly white southern towns and attending predominantly white public schools and colleges. Kate also described currently attending a predominantly white university while pursuing an advanced degree. In their interviews, both also conveyed limited contact with other black people. They were both coded into the "White" network category. In contrast, Georgina and Anthony both described

growing up in predominantly black neighborhoods, attending public schools with disproportionately high percentages of minority students (black and Latino), and currently attending historically black colleges and universities (HBCUs). Both were coded into the "Black" network category. The majority of respondents who were coded into the "Mixed" network category grew up in racially mixed communities and attended schools where they had significant contact with both blacks and whites. Two in this category (of twenty-four respondents), however, lived in predominantly black neighborhoods yet attended predominantly white schools; they were also coded into the "Mixed" category. Further, two respondents described situations in which they were embedded in predominantly white networks, but moved to an HBCU (i.e., predominantly black network). Because many of the respondents described how their experiences in college continued to shape their identities, as did these two individuals, these respondents were also coded into the "Mixed" network category. A final note here: because network type (whether black, white, or mixed) is based on respondents' *perceptions* of their networks growing up and today, it is plausible that their perceptions of the racial composition of their social network(s) may not match reality (e.g., they may think their networks were predominantly white, but in fact there was more racial variation than they recall). I argue, however, that *perception* is what matters most here, and other studies similarly rely on respondents' perceptions to measure the racial composition of their social networks (see Rockquemore and Brunsma 2002a). Furthermore, biracial individuals, who often face the challenge of identity negotiation, may be more cognizant of their racial identities than their monoracial counterparts. Therefore, they may be more aware of their networks, and relatively more accurate in reporting the racial composition of their networks than others. I also argue that because the interview questions regarding network composition were broad (e.g., who were you "primarily surrounded" by?), misperception is likely not an issue of concern. Had I asked more detailed questions (such as, What percentage of your school was black?), there would arguably have been more room for error, but I remain confident that the broad wording of the questions yielded relatively accurate responses.

    9. Nearly 785,000 Americans checked both "black" and "white" boxes on the 2000 Census form. However, this figure does not necessarily reflect the number of black-white biracial Americans in the United States because (1) it is likely they did not all identify as both black and white on the form (it is very probable that many biracial people identified themselves solely as black); and (2) the census figure probably also includes individuals who have some degree of white and black ancestry in their family trees, but do not necessarily have one black and one white parent.

2

Black and White in America

Then and Now

Interracial mixing, also known as *miscegenation*,[1] has been a part of American history since the first Europeans landed on American shores. Early contact between diverse groups such as Europeans, Africans, Native Americans, and Asians led to interracial romantic, sexual, and marital relationships—and as a direct result, children born with multiple racial backgrounds. With heightened media and scholarly attention given to interracial relationships and multiracial people in the last decade (see Kahn and Denmon 1997; Rockquemore, Brunsma, and Delgado 2009; and Shih and Sanchez 2005, 2009 for comprehensive reviews of the scholarly literature), it may appear that multiraciality is a relatively recent phenomenon and that multiracial people are a newly emergent group in America. While frequently misdescribed as "new people,"[2] multiracial Americans have long been a part of the American landscape.

In this chapter, I provide a historical overview of interracial mixing in the United States and of multiracial Americans from colonial times to the present day, with a focus on black-white relationships and the racial classification of the offspring of these unions. For much of American history, white society classified black-white multiracial Americans simply as black, and like their black counterparts, they were enslaved, denied basic civil rights, and generally subjected to the same social indignities, second-class treatment, and negative stereotypes. While they occasionally derived some advantages from having white phenotypic characteristics (e.g., light skin) and white ancestry, especially during slavery, whites for the most part saw them as black. Their racial options were limited and arguably nonexistent, although some scholars argue that in the aftermath of the civil rights movement for racial equality, this began to change. Whereas their predecessors were once constrained to identify exclusively as black, biracial people born in the post–civil rights era appear to have more racial options by comparison—they identify as black, biracial, and sometimes even white. In this chapter, I pay particular attention to the role of the one drop rule in defining blackness, and the implications of this rule regarding the social status of black-white multiracial people at various points in American history.

EARLY MISCEGENATION

Early records show that the first significant mixing between blacks and whites in America occurred in the seventeenth and early eighteenth centuries, primarily in colonial Virginia and Maryland (Williamson 1980). In 1619, the first African slaves arrived in Virginia to cultivate tobacco, and miscegenation occurred frequently between these African slaves and European indentured servants (Zack 1993). Indentured servitude was common in Europe, and an estimated 80 percent of English immigrants in the early years came as indentured servants (Russell, Wilson, and Hall 1992). During the colonial period, interracial relationships were not uncommon between white servants and enslaved Africans who worked and lived side-by-side on large plantations (Rockquemore and Brunsma 2002a; Russell, Wilson, and Hall 1992; Williamson 1980).

Because of a gender imbalance whereby white male servants outnumbered their white female counterparts, white men often married African slaves, and though less common, white women also married black men (Russell, Wilson, and Hall 1992). Mixing between black and white at this time was viewed as "abhorrent or morally repugnant" (Herring 2004: 4), yet these relationships were tolerated as a vice of the underclass. It was in this context that the first generation of mixed black-white Americans was born (otherwise known as "mulattoes"). According to Cedric Herring (2004), these children were typically poor and were treated in the same way as blacks.

Not long after interracial mixing began, condemnation followed. During the seventeenth century, Virginia and Maryland were the first colonies to condemn interracial sex and interracial marriage by law. A little more than two years after the first Africans arrived, Virginia proclaimed that a "sexual union between Whites and Blacks was twice as evil as fornication between two whites, and that sex with Negroes was equivalent to bestiality" (Russell, Wilson, and Hall 1992: 13). According to historian Joel Williamson (1980), the earliest colonial record of punishment was of Hugh Davis of Virginia, who in 1630 was sentenced to be "soundly whipped . . . for abusing himself to the dishonor of God and shame of Christians, by defiling his body in lying with a Negro" (7).

By 1661, Maryland passed a statute that is generally considered the first anti-miscegenation law. It was designed to discourage white women, free white indentured servants in particular, from crossing the color line. Women who entered into interracial marriage with black slaves were enslaved and sentenced to serve the masters of their husbands during the husbands' lifetime (Williamson 1980). Any offspring were also condemned to slavery (Zabel 2000). Because of the patriarchal structure of slavery, white men who crossed the color line faced few repercussions during this time, and most notably, did not face any fear of enslavement for their sexual transgressions with black women. This law, however, was repealed after it became apparent that planters were forcing their white female servants to marry slaves in order to take advantage of their (and their future children's) enslavement (Teo 2004).

A year after the passage of Maryland's statute, Virginia passed its own law. To discourage miscegenation, mulatto children of slave mothers were automatically to take on the slave status of the mother. Mulatto children of white mothers posed more of a dilemma, but by 1691 Virginia decided that those children would be sold into servitude until age thirty. English women were strongly discouraged from interracial sex and marriage, and white women who gave birth to a "bastard child by a negro" would endure a heavy fine (fifteen pounds to the church) or five years of servitude (Scales-Trent 2001: 272; Sickels 1972). While Maryland and Virginia were the first to create anti-miscegenation laws, similar statutes would soon be found in nearly all colonies (Zabel 2000).

SOUTHERN SLAVERY

During the slave era, southerners perceived race mixing even more harshly than that of their northern counterparts. The institution of slavery was built on a strong white supremacist ideology of white racial superiority and black inferiority. Because of the careful racial hierarchy constructed on the plantation, interracial intimacy was considered taboo. Many whites feared that mixing with black slaves would "taint" the purity of their pure white ancestral line (Rockquemore and Brunsma 2002a; Zack 1995) and degrade the superior biology of the white race. Further, to justify the plantation hierarchy and slavery itself, blacks were characterized in subhuman ways—as barbaric, savage, heathen, and ugly (Hunter 1998). These negative stereotypes were also useful tools to discourage interracial intimacy: because blacks were seen as less than human, interracial sex was perceived as sexually deviant and was likened to bestiality (Korgen 1998).

Despite the growing number of anti-miscegenation laws and fears of miscegenation, white men nonetheless practiced it with regularity (Rockquemore and Brunsma 2002a). During this period, the plantation system brought whites and blacks in close physical proximity to each other, and it was during this time, more so than any other in American history, that black-white interracial sex occurred (Kennedy 2003). Most often, interracial sex on the plantation occurred through the rape of black female slaves by their white masters. According to F. James Davis (1991), "Ownership of the female slave on the plantations generally came to include owning her sex life" (38). Because of the white patriarchal structure governing the southern states, white slave owners often used their black female slaves at will and even allowed their adolescent sons to use slave women as acceptable sexual outlets (Gardner 2000). Thus, many mulatto children of this era were conceived within the context of rape, brutal force, and sexual domination (Daniel 1996).

While little has been written about interracial sexual relationships between white women and black men during this time, Kathy Russell and her colleagues (1992) argue that there were white women who regularly crossed the color line, and a few who even left their husbands for black men. Some had affairs with their black slaves and others with free men of color (Russell, Wilson, and Hall 1992; see Kennedy 2003 for examples). Although especially taboo because it threatened the white patriarchal structure on the southern plantation, it was not uncommon for white mistresses to bear mulatto children (Williams 1996). However, while white men faced few repercussions for their sexual transgressions, black men faced whipping, castration, and even murder for their sexual involvement with white women (Russell, Wilson, and Hall 1992).

With the reality of miscegenation in the slave era, mulatto offspring posed a problem to the strict color line separating black and white. Where did they belong? Free or enslaved? To deal with the growing number of these children, an informal "one drop" rule was born in the South—anyone with any known trace of black blood would be considered black (Davis 1991). Thus, mulatto children of enslaved mothers were classified as black and hence enslaved, which provided an economic asset to white plantation owners. Slave owners wanted to perpetuate as many slaves as possible (Daniel 1996), making their sexual exploitation of slave women economically beneficial. Further, because slavery was built upon the assumption that whites were a superior race and could not be enslaved, the one drop rule became increasingly important to justify the enslavement of a growing number of slaves with white skin and appearance (Zack 1993).

In fact, mulatto slaves made up about 10 percent of the slave population before the Civil War (Russell, Wilson, and Hall 1992). Though defined by the one drop rule as black, they were viewed as more valuable in comparison to black slaves. Indeed, in some parts of the South, such as New Orleans and Charleston, some mulattoes were actually bred and sold for huge profits (Russell, Wilson, and Hall 1992). Because they brought the highest prices on the slave block (often bringing in twice the price of "pure" black slaves; Gardner 2000), they held high status among slaves. They were often seen as more intelligent and capable than monoracial or "pure" blacks, and were often given advantages unavailable to their black counterparts because of their white ancestry, and often because they were the offspring of white slave owners. Some of these advantages included opportunities for manumission, less violent treatment by overseers, opportunities for skilled labor, access to education, and less physically demanding work (Hunter 1998, 2005). For instance, they were often assigned the desirable indoor jobs (e.g., cooks, seamstresses, housekeepers, drivers, valets) instead of the physically demanding outdoor jobs (e.g., picking cotton in the hot sun).

Being in the house in such close proximity to whites, however, had its own dangers—especially if one was female. Working close to white masters was especially risky, and some female slaves faced sadistic treatment by white wives who were retaliating for their husbands' affairs (Russell, Wilson, and Hall 1992). Nonetheless, the "special treatment" that mulattoes received created envy and resentment among other slaves, generating deep and lasting divisions among the slave community (Russell, Wilson, and Hall 1992).

Additionally, free people of color in the South, many of whom were mulatto,[3] also benefited from their special status. Because of the educational opportunities available to them and their mulatto enslaved ancestors, many became educators, businessmen, doctors, lawyers, and early leaders of the black community (Hunter 1998; Russell, Wilson, and Hall 1992). As a result of their elevated status, free mulattoes rejected the one drop rule and often separated themselves from the black masses (Korgen 1998). Southern whites often perceived them as constituting a "buffer class" between whites and blacks, which created a three-tiered system of race in some parts of the South (Russell, Wilson, and Hall 1992): blacks, whites, and the intermediate class of mulattoes. This three-tiered system found its way into South Carolina and Louisiana, and here free mulattoes, who were often allied with whites, were not considered to be black (Williamson 1980).

In South Carolina, for example, mulattoes "could become white by behavior and reputation and could marry into white families" (Davis 2006: 17). In Louisiana, Creoles of color, many of whom were of European and African descent, also resisted the one drop rule in favor of the three-tiered racial hierarchy. French colonists had granted them an intermediate status and given them privileges unavailable to other blacks as a strategy to maintain their loyalty against the threat of the black slave majority. Once France transferred Louisiana to the United States in 1803 with the Louisiana Purchase, however, their status was threatened by the American one drop rule and the two-tiered American system of black and white. Having clearly benefited from their intermediate status under French rule, Louisiana's

Creoles of color worked to maintain their racial privilege. To do so, they physically and socially segregated themselves from other blacks and even arranged marriages so that their "bloodlines" could be maintained (Russell, Wilson, and Hall 1992).

As the Civil War approached, however, southerners became increasingly defensive of slavery and began to question the loyalties of their mulatto slaves (Fernandez 1996). In response to increasing fears regarding the abolition of slavery, white southerners rallied together in firm support of the one drop rule—southern whites' common interest in preserving slavery spurred a movement to identify all persons as either white *or* black (Davis 1991; Karthikeyan and Chin 2002). The privileged position held by mulatto slaves would deteriorate as whites began to view all those with *any* trace of black blood as one and the same. The three-tiered system in the South, in particular in places like New Orleans and Charleston, further eroded into a binary classification of black and white.

Additionally, in reaction to the threat of abolition and in defense of slavery, "scientific racism" (science used to "prove" the biological superiority of whites and inferiority of blacks) was increasingly called upon to justify slavery in the South. Blacks and mulattoes alike were characterized as inferior and childlike, and according to some pro-slavery scholars like Dr. Samuel Cartwright from Louisiana, they actually benefited from slavery. Cartwright, for instance, concluded that their biological inferiorities (such as a smaller brain, excess nervous matter, and insufficient supply of red blood cells) could be improved if they were forced to work, and "slavery . . . improved blacks in 'body, mind, and morals'" (Tucker 1994: 14). Formerly aligned with whites, enslaved and free mulattoes increasingly felt alienated from whites, and what few privileges they had once enjoyed began to dissipate as the line between black and white hardened. Feeling bitterness towards whites, whom they felt had turned their backs on them, mulattoes began to turn towards an alliance with blacks (Daniel 1992).

RECONSTRUCTION AND JIM CROW SEGREGATION

Despite white southern efforts to hold on to slavery, the Civil War (1861–1865) brought an end to three hundred years of involuntary servitude. Once blacks were freed from slavery in the South, white southerners sought new ways of re-strengthening the boundary between black and white. To keep the color line intact, a system of forced and legally sanctioned separation was created in the form of Jim Crow segregation. Newly freed blacks were now seen as potential competitors for jobs, land, and political power (Davis 1991), and segregation was one tool used by white southerners to re-solidify the line between blacks and whites in the former slave states.

Further, with the emancipation of black slaves, white males worried that sexual relations between newly freed black men and white women would run rampant (Davis 1991), and they looked for ways to curb these unions. Despite the fact that daily contact between whites and blacks became less frequent with the fall of slavery and the plantation system (Williamson 1980), as did interracial intimacy between the two groups (Davis 1991; Kennedy 2003), numerous anti-miscegenation statutes were passed in southern states during this time. Physical separation was mandated by state laws (e.g., separate public facilities for blacks and whites), but whites also constructed laws to maintain sexual separation between blacks and whites in an effort to preserve white racial purity. Through these formal methods of segregation and sexual control, southern society continued its pattern of white racial domination.

Moreover, legislation separating blacks and whites in physical spheres and laws prohibiting interracial sex and marriage further necessitated legal definitions of who was black and who was white. It was during this time in southern American history that the once-informal one drop rule was codified into law (Rockquemore and Brunsma 2002a). The informal rule maintained that any "drop" of black blood made one black, but legal definitions of blackness varied from state to state: some states defined as black anyone who was ½, ¼, ⅛, or even ¹/₃₂ black. States such as Alabama, Arkansas, Georgia, and Virginia defined a Negro as anyone who had *any* known black ancestry (Zabel 2000); thus, they literally invoked the notion that one drop of black blood made one black. Nonetheless statutory inconsistencies from state to state literally meant that one could be defined as black in one state and white in another.

Not only did these laws vary by state, but state laws defining who was black often changed over time, and in most cases, became more restrictive with each new permutation. For instance, the state of Virginia defined anyone with a black grandparent as black until 1910, then changed the definition to include anyone with a black great-great-grandparent, and in 1930 legally defined anyone with any black ancestry at all as black (Zack 1993). Booker T. Washington commented on the one drop rule prevailing at the time: "It is a fact that, if a person is known to have one percent of African blood in his veins, he ceases to be a white man. The ninety-nine percent of Caucasian blood does not weigh by the side of the one percent of African blood. The white blood counts for nothing. The person is a Negro every time" (Zack 1993: 83).

The nation's courts, including the U.S. Supreme Court, would also play a role in upholding state statutes defining blackness. In 1896, Homer Plessy challenged the state of Louisiana's Jim Crow statute, which required racially segregated seating on Louisiana's trains. Refusing to leave the white car of the East Louisiana Railroad, Plessy, who was "black," was arrested and fined. The Louisiana judge in his case ruled against him and argued that he was in violation of Louisiana's Separate Car Act. On appeal, the U.S. Supreme Court ruled that separate facilities for blacks and whites were acceptable, as long as they were equal; thus, this case upheld Jim Crow legislation under the premise of "separate, but equal." Most relevant here, however, is that Homer Plessy was a Louisiana Creole, was considered an *octoroon* (one-eighth black and seven-eighths white), and by some accounts, was light-skinned enough to be able to pass as white (Daniel 2002). In describing the implications of this case, Davis (1991) notes, "Without ruling directly on the definition of a Negro, the Supreme Court briefly took what it called 'judicial notice' of what it assumed to be common knowledge: that a Negro or black is any person with any black ancestry" (8). The *Plessy* decision set a legal precedent for future court rulings on laws defining blackness; even if Plessy was only one-eighth black, he was black. This ruling would drive the final nail in the (racial) coffin, so to speak, for Louisiana's multiracial Creole population, who had for nearly a century waged a battle to maintain their intermediate racial status. The Supreme Court, via the *Plessy* ruling, upheld the one drop rule and America's black/white binary system of racial classification. Being one-eighth black did not grant one an intermediate or special status (as it once did under French rule); Homer Plessy was black and therefore required to sit in the black car of the East Louisiana Railroad.

The one drop rule also found its way into state courts. For instance, in 1948, Davis Knight was sentenced to five years in prison for violating Mississippi's anti-miscegenation statute prohibiting marriage between whites and blacks. He argued that he was white, but the court proved that he had one black ancestor (a great-grandmother); thus, accordingly, he was black and in violation of state law (Davis 1991). In some cases, juries used the one drop rule to determine whether a person was black and, as authorized by a statute in Missouri, juries could decide whether a person was black or white based on his or her appearance (Zabel 2000). In these cases, any noticeable so-called black physical characteristics indicated some degree of black ancestry, and automatically, the individual was classified as such.

As the one drop rule found its way into state laws and court decisions, it would also appear in the U.S. Census. Prior to 1850, each person was categorized as black *or* white. Census enumerators were instructed to make a decision, based on physical observation, and choose one or the other category. The instructions for the 1850 census, however, told enumerators to classify everyone as white, black, or mulatto; this was the first time in American history that a multiracial category appeared in the census. Because enumerators were not given any direction regarding how to classify mulattoes, sociologist Ann Morning (2003) argues that census takers may have assigned all people of mixed-race ancestry to this category (not just those with black-white backgrounds).

In 1890, the categories further expanded and multiracial categories became more detailed. The categories included white, black, Chinese, Japanese, Indian, mulatto, quadroon, or octoroon, with careful instruction on how to classify blacks, mulattoes, quadroons, and octoroons. According to the instructions of the 1890 Census, "The word 'black' should be used to describe those persons who have three-fourths or more black blood; 'mulatto,' those persons who have from three-eighths to five-eighths black blood; 'quadroon,' those persons who have one-fourth black blood; and 'octoroon,' those persons who have one-eighth or any trace of black blood" (Nobles 2000: 188). Although the classifications mulatto, quadroon, and octoroon were differentiated from the category of black, it must be noted that they were always seen as a type of black, never as a type of white, which suggests that despite the addition of these multiracial categories, the one drop rule was still implicitly at work.

Nevertheless, by 1930, multiracial classifications such as mulatto, quadroon, and octoroon were removed from the census and replaced by one category—black. Census enumerators were instructed to enter "Negro" for any person of "mixed white and Negro blood," irrespective of how small "the percentage of Negro blood." Thus, while the majority of the black population at this time had a mixed-race background (the Census Bureau estimated that three-quarters of all blacks in the United States at this time were multiracial; see Wright 1994), the one drop rule redefined them simply as black.

Some historians argue that this period was marked by a new alliance of mulattoes with blacks, yet Russell, Wilson, and Hall (1992) argue that some lighter-skinned mulattoes still struggled to preserve their elevated status within the black community. To do this, they began to segregate themselves into separate communities by creating their own elite social clubs, neighborhoods, churches, preparatory schools, colleges, business organizations, and even vacation resorts (Daniel 1992; Russell, Wilson, and Hall 1992). Using their white ancestry and physical characteristics to distance themselves from the black masses (Daniel 1992), they limited membership only to those with the appropriate skin shade, physical features, and European cultural manners.

Often qualifying tests were used to grant entrance and membership into their various organizations. For instance, "Blue vein" societies were elite social groups that granted membership only to those whose skin was so light that their blood was visibly seen running through the veins of their hands. According to Russell, Wilson, and Hall (1992), it has been alleged that some of the most prestigious historically black colleges and universities, such as Spelman College in Atlanta, required applicants to pass a color test before being admitted. Even some historically black fraternities and sororities allegedly maintained partiality for those with European physical traits (Daniel 2002). Some highly color-conscious black organizations and institutions used various tools to keep the black masses out: the paper bag test (to deny entry to those darker than a paper bag), the comb test (to refuse admittance to those whose hair would snag the comb), and the door test (to discourage the entrance into church of those whose skin was darker than the light shade of brown painted on the church doors) (Daniel 2002; Russell, Wilson, and Hall 1992).

Moreover, members of this multiracial elite practiced endogamy, encouraging their children to marry others from the same elite circles; it was taboo for a member of the multiracial elite to marry a darker-skinned black. They also segregated themselves in exclusive neighborhoods, and most U.S. urban centers had sections where predominantly multiracial, light-skinned blacks resided—including cities such as Los Angeles, Chicago, and Harlem. Many cities were also well known for their "blue vein" societies, such as Atlanta, Charleston, New Orleans, Nashville, Philadelphia, Louisville, Boston, New York, and what has been described as the "capital" of the multiracial elite, Washington, D.C. (Daniel 2002). In Washington, D.C., members of the multiracial elite were perceived, in comparison to the larger black community, as wealthier, better educated, more professional (often working in the professions of law, medicine, and education), and most importantly, lighter skinned. A prominent example is Pinckney Pinchback, the first "black" governor of Louisiana, who moved to Washington, D.C., in 1893. He and his family quickly earned a place among the multiracial elite because of his wealth, political power, light skin, and near-white appearance (Daniel 2002).

While intra-racial tensions continued, the weight of Jim Crow segregation and the one drop rule soon weighed heavily on the black community as a whole. Skin shade continued to play a significant role among blacks, but whites had little reason to distinguish mulattoes from blacks (or light skin from dark skin). They saw only two colors: black and white. Whether you were a dark-skinned or a light-skinned Negro, you were still a Negro. No matter the skin shade or degree of white ancestry, any black ancestry relegated one to the back of the bus or the back of the restaurant. This attitude soon was internalized by whites and blacks alike, and over time, black-white multiracial individuals with light skin gradually came to regard themselves less as multiracial (i.e., mulatto) and more as light-skinned blacks (Daniel 1992). As they watched their privileged position erode, they moved towards a greater alliance with blacks. This is evident in Louisiana in the relationship between multiracial Creoles of color and their black counterparts. According to G. Reginald Daniel (2002), once Creoles lost their privileged intermediate status, many began collaborating with black Americans in the civil rights movement, and even in the creation of the musical genre jazz.[4]

In broader society, too, multiracial blacks who had once self-segregated themselves from black Americans, now joined them in the fight for civil rights and often emerged as leaders within the African American community. Some of the most notable "black" leaders at this time were, in fact, multiracial with white ancestry, including (to name a few examples) Booker T. Washington and Frederick Douglass (both of whom had white fathers), and W. E. B. DuBois (Davis 2006; Spickard 2003; Wright 1994). Further, social barriers against marriage with darker-skinned black Americans began to dissipate, and marriages between multiracial blacks and blacks began to increase (Korgen 1998; Williams 1996; Williamson 1980). As a result, miscegenation between these two groups increasingly eroded the line between black and mulatto.

At the same time, sexual relations between blacks and whites dwindled during this era. The history of frequent rape of black women by their white masters under the repressiveness of southern slavery was often overlooked and ignored by white southerners, yet interracial transgressions during the Jim Crow era became increasingly taboo because of the perceived "stain" on white racial purity. Black blood was seen as a taint that corrupted and defiled white blood. Once it infiltrated one's white line, it could never be washed away, and it was believed that even one proverbial single drop of black blood "kinks the hair, flattens the nose, thickens the lip, puts out the light of intellect, and lights the fires of brutal passions" (Dixon [1902] 1994). In addition to the racial taboo concerning interracial sex, declining spatial propinquity also contributed to the decline in sexual relations between blacks and whites. Unlike the slave era, when blacks and whites lived in close proximity to one another on the plantation, the Jim Crow era of racial segregation increasingly kept them apart.

Further reflecting the taboo of interracial relationships during the Jim Crow era, anti-miscegenation laws sprung up around the nation. At one time or another, thirty-eight states had anti-miscegenation statutes, and all prohibited black-white marriage (often these laws were broadened to also ban interracial relationships between whites and other non-white groups) (Farley 1999; Zack 1993). Penalties for the violation of anti-miscegenation statutes varied from state to state and ranged from having the marriage voided, paying fines, facing expulsion from the state, to in some cases, even imprisonment (Kennedy 2000).

The state of Mississippi even criminalized the publication of "general information, arguments or suggestions in favor of social equality or of intermarriage between whites and Negroes" (Zabel 2000: 58). In Alabama, the fear of interracial marriage was clearly palpable when a children's book, *The Rabbits' Wedding* (Williams 1958), was removed from the shelves of the public libraries because the illustration portrayed one rabbit as white and the other as black (Tucker 2004). The taboo of miscegenation during this era was also evidenced in Hollywood when the Motion Picture Association of America completely forbade the theme of miscegenation from the 1930s until the late 1950s (Courtney 2005; Sickels 1972).[5] Moreover, vigilante groups, such as the Ku Klux Klan, had also emerged to keep the races separate (Russell, Wilson, and Hall 1992), and Kennedy (2000) argues that "fear of lynching probably played a more influential role in [black men's] conduct towards white women than fear of enforcement of anti-miscegenation laws" (146). Formal and informal methods of forced endogamy appeared to be working, and the one drop rule was increasingly internalized by whites, blacks, and multiracial black Americans alike.

G. Reginald Daniel (1992) argues that during this era most black-white individuals identified themselves as black, although it must be noted that some individuals, those who outwardly appeared white, resisted black classification, the one drop rule, and the racial status quo of the Jim Crow era by "passing" (see also Williamson 1980).[6] The Jim Crow era has been described as the "great age of passing" (Daniel 2002: 52) as individuals passed as white to gain access to privileges and opportunities unavailable to them as African Americans (e.g., access to schools, universities, jobs, and "white only" public facilities), and to escape the social stigma associated with blackness during this era.

Some scholars have estimated that the number of blacks who were passing into the white population was approximately 10,000 to 20,000 people per year from 1900 to 1920 (Williamson 1980); others have put the figure significantly higher, at more than 100,000 people annually (Daniel 2002). Although an attractive option for those wanting to gain access to privileges and opportunities—and the only strategy for those wanting to cross the impervious color line—this option was unavailable to the majority of the population. The ability to pass depended upon one's skin shade and facial features (Bradshaw 1992), and on having close physical approximation to whiteness (Day 1932 as cited in Daniel 1992). For those who did not outwardly appear white, the one drop rule restricted to them to only one racial option: black; they identified and were identified by others as black.

CIVIL RIGHTS AND BLACK NATIONALISM

In 1954, *Brown v. Board of Education*,[7] a case that challenged racial segregation in public schools, was the first prominent Supreme Court decision to begin to reverse years of southern Jim Crow laws. The Court struck down *Plessy*'s (1896) "separate but equal" ruling as unconstitutional, and ordered schools to integrate. This was the first step paving the way for the dismantling of Jim Crow laws across the South. According to Joel Williamson (1980), "the white South went into shock" (139). White resistance to racial integration through riots, violence, and overt anger led to even more strained race relations between whites and blacks in the South. White backlash to the civil rights movement strengthened black support for the one drop rule, and lighter-skinned blacks felt increased pressure to identify as black (Davis 2006). Further, to counter subjugation wrought by the one drop rule, black Americans began to embrace this powerful rule as a way of resisting white racism: they began to invoke the rule as a tool of inclusivity to promote unity and numerical strength among the black community (Perlmann and Waters 2002; Williamson 1980).

Additionally, the civil rights movement and the rise of black nationalism stirred a sense of pride in black Americans. Slogans such as "Black is beautiful," "Black pride," and "I'm black and I'm proud" (Russell, Wilson, and Hall 1992; Williamson 1980), emerged in the late 1960s and elevated blackness, which was once denigrated under southern slavery and Jim Crow, to a new level. Within the black community, value was increasingly placed on "dark skin, wide noses, thick lips, and kinky hair" (Rondilla and Spickard 2007: 12), and according to Russell, Wilson, and Hall (1992), the sixties saw a revolution in black hair. For the first time, black women stopped straightening their hair, and instead opted for more natural styles to further assert their black identities. Shifting attitudes about skin color and hair reflected the message of the time—"Black is in." Young black-white multiracial Americans increasingly defined themselves as black and took pride in their blackness (Korgen 1998). Just as larger society had labeled them solely as black for generations, they began to more strongly embrace that identity with a new sense of pride.

Additionally, interracial tensions between blacks and whites and the racial upheaval of the 1960s kept interracial sexual relations between the two groups low. While the civil rights era did see an upsurge in interracial dating and marriage, likely due to increased integration and interracial contact, the numbers remained very small (Williamson 1980)—especially between blacks and whites. Interracial marriage was still prohibited in many states, especially in the South, and interracial relationships were curbed by means of social control in both white and black communities. Interracial sex and marriage were looked down upon by whites and blacks alike—whites saw it as polluting the purity of the white race (Karthikeyan and Chin 2002) and blacks saw it as a rejection of blackness (Korgen 1998).

At the same time, marriage between multiracial blacks and darker-skinned blacks continued, further blurring the boundary between the two groups. Yet, Russell, Wilson, and Hall (1992) claim that, "While the black community appeared united on the surface, undercurrents of colorism still rippled below" (35). Light-skinned blacks continued to hold a special status in the black community, and studies published in the 1960s and 1970s reported that skin tone remained an issue in the black community;

lighter skin continued to have an impact on stratification outcomes such as education, occupation, and income (for examples, see Edwards 1972; Freeman et al. 1966; Ransford 1970; Udry, Bauman, and Chase 1971). Because lighter-skinned individuals continued to enjoy a privileged status amongst black Americans, their loyalties were often called into question. Darker-skinned leaders questioned their lighter-skinned counterparts, arguing that they had benefited from their light skin for so long that they could never really understand the oppression felt by black Americans (Russell, Wilson, and Hall 1992). While they increasingly identified as black, light-skinned blacks were now being challenged for "not being black enough" (Williamson 1980).

As the civil rights movement continued, Jim Crow laws lingered in many southern states. Anti-miscegenation laws, in particular, remained on the books in many states and continued to prohibit interracial marriages between whites and blacks. This would begin to change in 1958, when Mildred Jeter (a black woman) and Richard Loving (a white man) fell in love and married in Washington, D.C. When they returned to their hometown in Caroline County, Virginia, where they had spent most of their lives, they were arrested for violating the state's anti-miscegenation statute. After pleading guilty to the charges, they were sentenced to one year in jail. The trial judge, however, suspended their sentence on the condition that they leave the state of Virginia for twenty-five years (Zabel 2000). In his opinion, the judge stated, "Almighty God created the races white, black, yellow, malay and red, and he placed them on separate continents. . . . The fact that he separated the races shows that he did not intend for the races to mix" (Sollors 2000: 28). Mildred Jeter and Richard Loving left their home in Virginia, but soon filed suit against the state, claiming that prohibition of marriage on the basis of race violated the Fourteenth Amendment to the U.S. Constitution.

In *Loving v. Virginia*, the Virginia Supreme Court upheld the state's anti-miscegenation laws, stating that it is a state's right "to preserve the racial integrity of its citizens" and to prevent a "mongrel breed of citizens" (Sollors 2000: 31). However, the case would soon be appealed to the U.S. Supreme Court. In 1967, after nearly ten years of marriage and the birth of three children (Sickels 1972), the U.S. Supreme Court reversed the earlier decision that criminalized the Lovings' interracial marriage. The Court ruled anti-miscegenation laws unconstitutional, overturning Virginia's anti-miscegenation law as well as similar laws still on the books in fifteen other states (Harrison and Bennett 1995; Zack 1993): Alabama, Arkansas, Georgia, Kentucky, Louisiana, Mississippi, Missouri, Tennessee, Texas, West Virginia, North Carolina, South Carolina, Florida, Oklahoma, and Delaware.

THE POST–CIVIL RIGHTS ERA

Some scholars have argued that interracial marriage increased as legal restrictions were lifted subsequent to the 1967 *Loving* ruling (Kennedy 2003;
Root 2001),[8] as did the number of multiracial children born in the United
States (Root 1996). According to Smolowe (1993), the birthrate of multiracial children increased from the 1970s to 1990s to twenty-six times higher
than any other measured group, leading to what has been termed the
"biracial baby boom" of the 1970s (Root 1992). Rainier Spencer (2006a),
however, questions the link to *Loving* and claims that there is no evidence
of a "cause-and-effect relationship between the *Loving* decision and a subsequent increase in interracial marriages" (65). He argues that interracial marriage was already legal in thirty-four states prior to *Loving*, and the rate of
intermarriage was already on the rise in those states. He further argues that
the sixteen states where anti-miscegenation laws were overturned should
have shown the greatest increase in interracial marriage if *Loving* were a
factor, but rates of intermarriage still remain relatively low in those states.
Further challenging that a "biracial baby boom" even occurred, he argues
that the real baby boom occurred in the colonial Chesapeake region three
hundred years ago.

Nonetheless, the *Loving* decision may have had a lasting influence on
American popular thought about interracial unions. With regard to interracial relationships, Russell, Wilson, and Hall (1992) argue that attitudes
have become more tolerant over time. Surveys conducted by the National
Opinion Research Center of the University of Chicago indicate that attitudes among whites and blacks towards interracial marriage have become
more relaxed. In 1972, 39 percent of whites believed that interracial marriage should be illegal, but these numbers dropped to 17 percent by 1991.
Attitudes among blacks showed a similar but stronger shift—in 1980, 20
percent of blacks believed that interracial marriage should be banned as
compared to 7 percent in 1991. More recently, a 2007 Gallup poll showed
the highest public approval rating for marriages between blacks and whites
since the question was first asked some fifty years earlier; 77 percent of
Americans approved.

Additionally, the 1990s witnessed the emergence of the multiracial movement, which may reflect the biracial baby boomers who came of age during this time period. Newly formed multiracial activist groups lobbied for
changes on local, state, and federal forms that collected race data. The most
visible fight centered around the format of the race question on the 2000
Census. Instead of the instructions to "check only one box" to signify one's
race (in place prior to 2000), organizations such as Project RACE and the
Association for Multiethnic Americans argued for some sort of multiracial

option in the 2000 Census. The Census Bureau ultimately decided to forgo a single, catch-all "multiracial" category, and instead allowed Americans the option of checking more than one racial category on census forms.

In consequence, 2.4 percent of the American population identified with two or more races in 2000. Those who claimed black-white ancestry, however, made up only 0.41 percent of the total American population—certainly a gross underestimation given that most African Americans have some degree of white and/or Native American ancestry. This suggests that the one drop rule may still be at work, because despite having the opportunity to identify with multiple racial groups, most of those with black-white ancestry (not just those who are biracial black-white) self-identified simply as black on the 2000 Census. Jennifer Lee and Frank D. Bean (2004) argue that the low percentage of Americans who chose black and some other race is evidence of just how rigid the black/non-black racial divide remains in the United States.

Indeed, many scholars argue that the one drop rule remains a powerful force even today. For instance, anthropologist Michael L. Blakey claims that the one drop rule is "still operative today," and legal scholar Julie C. Lythcott-Haims argues that the one drop rule "still exists today; Americans who are part-Black are considered Black, and only Black by most Americans. . . . The one-drop rule is so ingrained in the American psyche that Blacks and Whites do not think twice about it" (as cited in Sweet 2005: 271–72). Mary Campbell (2007) further argues, "There is a widespread consensus that the 'one-drop rule' is such a powerful force in the United States even today" (922), and recent studies suggest that the one drop rule remains salient in shaping racial identity for those with black ancestry (Bratter 2007, 2010; Davis 1991; Doyle and Kao 2007a; Herman 2010; Lee and Bean 2007; Oware 2008; Song 2003; Waters 1990, 1991; Zack 1996). Mary Waters, for instance, argues that "Black Americans . . . are highly constrained to identify as black, without other options available to them, even when they believe or know that their forbearers included many non-blacks" (1990: 18). In a 1991 study, Waters found that half of her subjects knew their personal ancestries were not purely black, but all racially identified as black. She also found that the majority of her black sample believed that multiracial black-white children should identify as black, which further points to the continued influence of the one drop rule.

Other quantitative studies parallel Waters' (1990, 1991) claims. Zhenchao Qian (2004), for example, looked at how intermarried couples (black-white, Asian-white, Latino-white, and Native American-white) racially identified their biracial children on the 1990 U.S. Census, and found that black-white children were more likely than any other group to be identified solely as non-white (59 percent were identified as black). While children were not selecting their identity themselves, Qian (2004) draws on the one drop rule to explain the trend towards identifying as black and argues that "African American communities generally include descendants of every racial group, regardless of their physical appearance. Individuals with mixed racial backgrounds are often labeled black" (764).

These studies show that the one drop rule remains a powerful force shaping black identities, but studies also suggest that more racial options are available to black-white people today. Kathleen Korgen (1998), for example, finds that black-white biracial Americans have more choice in identity today and a greater range of racial options than in previous decades. In particular, she finds that those born before the civil rights era are likely to identify exclusively as black, whereas those born in the post–civil rights era identify as black, biracial, and sometimes white. Wendy Roth (2005) looks at how parents identified their children in the 1990 and 2000 Censuses and finds that despite the fact that their identity choices "have traditionally been limited in America by the one drop rule, which automatically designated them as black . . . options in racial identification are now available" (35). In the 1990 Census, when parents could only select one race for their child, she finds that parents identified their children as black (60.6 percent), white (25 percent), and "other" (14 percent). (She hypothesized that selecting "other" was an option that parents used to indicate interracial identity; see Roth 2003.) In the 2000 Census, when they had the option to check "all that apply," she again finds many options: parents identified their children as both white and black (53.1 percent), black (25 percent), white (11 percent), and "other" (9.6 percent). Similarly, Kerry Ann Rockquemore and Patricia Arend (2003), in a multistate study of black-white biracial individuals, find they self-identify in at least five different ways: as (1) black; (2) white; (3) biracial; (4) black, white, and biracial depending upon the social setting; and (5) no racial identity at all. Taken together, these studies clearly suggest that the one drop rule does not constrain racial options as it once did.

Collectively, these studies show that the one drop rule remains prevalent in American society, yet at the same time, multiracial people have more racial options than in previous decades. Moreover, despite the growing range of racial choices, some argue that a "color complex" still exists among those with black ancestry (Russell, Wilson, and Hall 1992). Color divisions that began during slavery continue to mark the experience of light-skinned blacks within the African American community, granting them an elevated status while simultaneously creating resentment and envy towards those who might benefit from having light skin. For today's biracial individuals, skin color—and other features such as hair texture, hair color, eye color, and facial features—continue to play a significant role in shaping their experiences and relationships with their black counterparts.

CONCLUSION

In this chapter, I provided an overview of black-white people in the United States, beginning in colonial America and ending with a look at black-white people today. While once constrained by the one drop rule to identify exclusively as black, particularly in the slave and Jim Crow eras, this population has more racial options today. It is within this post–civil rights context that I examine black-white biracial identity and the underlying processes and factors shaping their racial identities. However, in order to appreciate and understand black-white Americans and the issues they face in forming and negotiating their racial identities, we cannot divorce their contemporary experiences from their broader historical experiences in America. How these biracial individuals relate to whites and blacks, and how they perceive themselves racially, is rooted in a long and ever-evolving history of black-white race relations in American society, as well as in intra-racial tensions within the black community.

Keeping in mind the historical and contemporary influence of the one drop rule on black identity, I now turn to investigating the one drop rule today. In the next chapter, I explore the racial options available to black-white people by examining how biracial people in this study racially identify and why. In particular, I examine the role that the one drop rule plays in their racial identities, and I argue that while it affects identity differently than in decades past, its legacy remains. Most respondents label themselves as biracial or multiracial to others, which suggests a weakening of the one drop rule. However, the majority also more strongly identify as black rather than white when probed further about their racial identities. When asked to explain their black identities, they frequently describe how both blacks and whites perceive them as black. I argue that the one drop rule still shapes racial identity, namely through the process of reflected appraisals (i.e., how they think others see them).

NOTES

1. Many people today reject the term *miscegenation* (Tizard and Phoenix 2002). Because it has historically been used in the context of laws banning interracial marriage (called *anti-miscegenation* laws), some view the term as offensive and outdated. The word itself comes from the Latin words *miscere* (to mix) and *genus* (race) (Tucker 1994).

2. See Ann Morning's (2003) discussion in which she argues, "Multiracial Americans have often been heralded as 'new people' and in fact have been rediscovered as such more than once in the last century" (41). They have been described, for example, as "the new Negro" and "Neo-Americans," which according to Morning, conveys the false sense that multiraciality is a recent phenomenon.

3. "In 1850, mulattoes or mixed bloods constituted 37% of the free Negro population" (Frazier 1957: 32 as cited in Hunter 1998).

4. Those Creoles who did not want to be classified as black left Louisiana for northern states or left the United States altogether for Mexico or the Caribbean, where racial lines were more fluid (Daniel 2002).

5. In 1927, the Motion Picture Producers and Distributors of America (MPPDA) (which later became the Motion Picture Association of America; MPAA) adopted a list of "Don'ts and Be Carefuls." One of "those things [that] shall not appear in pictures" targeted "Miscegenation (sexual relationships between the white and black races)" (Courtney 2005: 113). Variations of this clause were incorporated into the more elaborate and enforceable Production Codes of 1930 and 1934, in an effort to appease city- and state-level censor boards and growing calls for federal censorship on Hollywood movies (Courtney 2005). In addition to prohibiting themes of interracial sexual relationships, these codes also banned (among other things) nudity, suggestive dancing, the ridicule of religion, the depiction of illegal drug use, offensive words, and scenes of passion (if not essential to the plot). The 1934 code required that all films released on or after July 1, 1934, obtain a certificate of approval before being released; thus, the code was enforceable.

6. The concept of "passing," not the act itself, is racist in origin (Russell, Wilson, and Hall 1992; see also Williamson 1980) because it is entwined with the racist one drop rule. Even if a person has white ancestry and looks white, he is considered "really" black because of his black ancestry (no matter how distant); white identity is perceived as somehow "fraudulent" (Daniel 2002: 83). Further, because the concept of passing rests on the American one drop rule, passing is difficult to explain to those outside the United States. According to F. James Davis (1991), people from other countries typically ask, "Shouldn't Americans say that a person who is passing as white *is* white, or nearly all white, and has previously been passing for black?" or "To be consistent, shouldn't you say that someone who is one-eighth white is passing as black?" (13–14).

7. *Brown v. Board of Education* (1954) was a landmark U.S. Supreme Court decision which declared that segregating public schools on the basis of race was unconstitutional because it was in violation of the Fourteenth Amendment to the U.S. Constitution. *Brown v. Board of Education* actually combined five separate cases, but was headlined by a class-action lawsuit brought in the state of Kansas by Oliver Brown for his daughter, Linda Brown (an African American third-grader who was denied entry to the white elementary school near her home). The victory directly affected Kansas, Delaware, South Carolina, Virginia, and Washington, D.C. (regions named in the original case), but it also overturned school segregation laws in twelve other states. Interestingly, one of the chief objections to the *Brown* decision and school integration was the fear of interracial mixing (see Tucker 2004).

8. The number of interracial couples in the United States increased from 150,000 in 1960 to more than one million in 1990, and interracial marriages tripled from 1970 to 1992. Further, while the number of marriages between blacks and whites remains small compared to other interracial marriages, black-white marriages increased 414% from 1960 to 1990 (see Roth 2005).

3

"From the Outside Looking In"

Reflected Appraisals and the One Drop Rule

I am
I am not what I think I am
I am not what you think I am
I am what I think you think I am

—Unknown

Scholars studying biracial identity, especially sociologists, have relied heavily on symbolic interactionism as a theoretical frame (Blumer 1969; Cooley 1902; Mead 1934; for examples, see Khanna 2004; Rockquemore and Brunsma 2002a; Tashiro 2002; Williams 1996).[1] According to symbolic interactionists, identities are created by the give-and-take in shared meaning between self and society,[2] and a central concept within the symbolic interactionist perspective is the "looking glass self," or reflected appraisals (Cooley 1902). According to Charles H. Cooley's concept of the "looking glass self," self-concepts are formed as reflections of the responses and evaluations by others in the environment. In the process of constructing the "looking-glass" self, individuals first imagine how they appear to others. Second, they imagine others' judgments of that appearance. Finally, they develop some sort of self-feeling or self-concept from this process. In short, individuals come to see themselves as they perceive others to see them. Their self and identity is formed, at least in part, by this reflective process.

Later theorists and researchers further substantiate Cooley's notion that the self develops out of the reflected appraisals of others (for examples, see Felson 1981, 1985; Mead 1934; Schlenker 1980; Sullivan 1947). According to Richard Felson (1981), "self-perception does not occur in a social vacuum" (79); whether based on the actual responses of others, or perceptions of those responses, individuals' conceptions of themselves can be strongly influenced by others. Felson (1981) further suggests that reflected appraisals are likely to be important in instances where there are no clear criteria or objective feedback as a basis for self-evaluations. In the absence of "objective" criteria (e.g., IQ tests to measure one's intelligence, for instance[3]), people may instead rely on reflected appraisals—how they *think* others see them. For example, physical attractiveness is socially constructed and there are no objective measures for self-evaluating it. Therefore, in order to judge their physical beauty, people must rely on their perceptions of how others judge them—do people tell them that they are good-looking? Like physical attractiveness, race is socially constructed and lacks objective measures (i.e., there is no test or marker that definitively determines one's race). In fact, because race is socially constructed and biologically unfounded (see "A Note on Terminology"), racial classification can be fuzzy and unclear, especially for biracial people. As a consequence, they may turn to reflected appraisals to decide where they belong racially, relying on others' perceptions of their race—or more precisely, their *perceptions* of others' perceptions of their race.

Additionally, Israel (1956) and Backman, Secord, and Pierce (1963) claim that others' appraisals exert more influence when the subject is in a state of uncertainty. This may especially pertain to biracial individuals, who are arguably more likely to encounter ambiguity about their race as compared to individuals with monoracial backgrounds. According to George Kitahara Kich (1996), "ambiguity is part of the territory" of being biracial (273), and indeed, in an earlier study I found reflected appraisals to be important in shaping racial identity among Asian-white multiracial individuals (see Khanna 2004). How they believed they were perceived by others (whether as Asian, white, or some other race) strongly influenced their racial identities. More specifically, their perception of how others viewed their phenotype (i.e., their racial appearance) was the strongest influence on their racial identity. Asian-white individuals who believed that others saw them as white in physical appearance, for example, were more likely to identify as such. It remains unclear, however, if and how reflected appraisals affect other biracial groups—including black-white biracial individuals.

In this chapter, I extend previous research on reflected appraisals and racial identity by looking at black-white biracial individuals, a group historically defined as black based on the one drop rule. While phenotype is particularly important in the reflected appraisal process for Asian-white adults, phenotype may be relatively less important for black-white biracial adults. Whether by law or prevailing social norms, black-white Americans have historically been defined as black in order to maintain the strict color line separating black from white under southern slavery and Jim Crow segregation. Because ancestry defined one as black, physical appearance had little consequence for racial identity for black-white biracial people (having light skin, blonde hair, or blue eyes, for instance, did not preclude a black identity[4]).

I propose that the one drop rule no longer trumps physical appearance, but nonetheless it continues to influence racial identity today. In particular, the one drop rule affects how black-white biracials' physical appearances are *perceived* by others. Despite the range in their physical appearances (e.g., some have dark and others light skin), black-white biracial Americans are frequently raced as *black*. This is because the legacy of the one drop rule has shaped how Americans (of all racial and ethnic backgrounds) perceive normative "black" phenotypes. According to Russell, Wilson, and Hall (1992), black Americans show a "kaleidoscope of skin tones" (9), due both to the long history of interracial mixing between blacks and whites and to the broad definition of "blackness." Under the one drop rule, individuals with any degree of black ancestry were classified as black; thus, the normative phenotypic image of a "black" person became broad, and we can see today that black phenotypes vary widely in skin tone and other physical characteristics (e.g., nose shape, hair texture). Even today, having some "white" phenotypic characteristics—such as light skin, blue eyes, and straight hair—does not necessarily conflict with Americans' image of blackness. For example, actress Vanessa Williams and recording artist Beyoncé Knowles are both "black" with some degree of white ancestry and "white" features. While Williams and Knowles do not outwardly appear white (i.e., they could not pass as white), they do have some physical features that reflect their white ancestry; Vanessa Williams has light skin and blue eyes, and Beyoncé Knowles has light skin and long, straight hair.[5] Having these "white" normative physical characteristics, however, does not necessarily conflict with Americans' image of what it looks like to be black.

This broad image of blackness not only influences how Americans view blacks, but also how they view *biracial* black-white Americans. Regardless of any "white" physical characteristics biracial individuals may have, others tend simply to classify them as black because their perceptions of what a "black" person looks like do not preclude normative "white" physical characteristics. For instance, a biracial person may have straight, long hair, but so do many black Americans (either because of white ancestry or because of hair straightening/"relaxing" techniques common among black women today). As a consequence, many Americans are unable to distinguish between black and biracial phenotypes. Thus, appraisals of these phenotypes (both real and reflected) are influenced by the historical legacy of the one drop rule, which continues to shape black identities even today.

To illustrate the effects of the one drop rule and reflected appraisals on racial identity, I first examine how participants identify themselves with regard to race, paying particular attention to public and internalized identities.

The majority of individuals in this study publicly identify as biracial (or some related multiracial term), but most more strongly identify as *black* than white when describing their internalized racial identities. Second, focusing on internalized identities, I show how reflected appraisals shape the racial identities of these black-white respondents. Individuals in this sample frequently explain their internalized identities by pointing to how they believe they appear to *others*; for instance, some identify strongly as black, in part, because they believe "larger society" or "others" see them as black (often based on their physical characteristics). Finally, I take a closer look at reflected appraisals by examining how respondents' perceptions differ depending upon the race of the observer. Respondents often draw a distinction in how they think they are perceived racially depending upon whether the observers are white or black. More than a third of respondents argue that while blacks are likely to recognize their multiracial background, whites simply perceive them as black. These conflicting perceptions have the potential to shape different "racial reflections" (i.e., biracial or black), yet I show how the one drop rule affects the entire reflected appraisal process, subsequently shaping black identities in these biracial respondents.

IDENTITY: PUBLIC AND INTERNALIZED

An interesting pattern emerges among this sample with regard to both public and internalized racial identities (see appendix B). Regarding public identities, or the ways in which these respondents label themselves to others, an overwhelming majority (82.5 percent, or 33 respondents) label themselves using multiracial descriptors (e.g., biracial, multiracial, mixed, interracial). In comparison, only 17.5 percent of respondents label themselves monoracially: six respondents label themselves exclusively as black/African American and only one labels herself as white. That these respondents more often identify as biracial (or some related multiracial term) than as black parallels recent empirical work showing similar trends (see chapter 2).

Although the majority of respondents label themselves using multiracial terms, there is considerably more variation in internalized identities.[6] Interestingly, the majority of respondents said they more strongly identified with being black (60 percent, or 24 respondents) and only 22.5 percent (9 respondents) more strongly identified with being white. The remaining seven respondents, 17.5 percent, claimed to identify with both racial groups equally (e.g., as biracial) (see table 3.1 for a detailed breakdown of both public and internalized identities). I focus the remainder of the chapter on internalized identities and investigate the trend towards identifying as black.

Table 3.1. Public and Internalized Racial Identities

Public Identity	Internalized Identity			
	White	*Black*	*Biracial*	*Totals*
White	1	0	0	1
Black	0	6	0	6
Biracial	8	18	7	33
Totals	9	24	7	40

REFLECTED APPRAISALS AND RACIAL IDENTITY

In this section, I examine how others' perceptions of a respondent's race influence his or her internalized racial identity. Many individuals, for example, more strongly identify as black (than white) because they believe that is how they are perceived by others. When asked about their racial identities, the majority of respondents (26 of 40) describe their identities in relation to how they think they are perceived by "others" or "larger society" (without being directly prompted or probed by me).

According to Michael, who labels himself as biracial but who internally identifies strongly as black, his identity is heavily influenced by how he thinks he is perceived by "society." When asked to explain his self-described strong black identity, he says:

> I would say I identify very strongly [as black] only because I think part of how you define yourself is the category that society puts you into. And when people look at me, they're not going to see a white person, you know? And they definitely see me as a person of color. . . . So I definitely feel like I identify more with my black side because that's how I'm perceived, rather than being [white]. I'm perceived as African American. So that's kind of where I identify most.

Michael identifies as black because he believes that "society" perceives him as such. Further, he links his phenotype with others' perceptions of him, noting the dominance of his black features: "I think all groups kind of throw me into the black category because those are my dominant features. . . . I think it's a visual thing . . . black features are just more dominant over all races. . . . I think the only reason I identify more with being black is because society's kind of labeled me as that." According to Mary Waters (1990, 1996), multiracial people with black ancestry are largely constrained to identify as black. She argues that certain ancestries are "essential" and become a defining aspect of a multiracial person. This is because in American society, a non-black identity (i.e., biracial or white) will likely not be accepted if one looks black "according to the prevailing social norms" (1996: 447).

Like Michael, Alicia labels herself as mixed and internally identifies more strongly as black than white. When explaining her strong internalized black identity, she describes how she thinks others see her, similarly noting her "dominant" black features:

> [My black features are] kind of more dominant. I look more black than I do white. At some point, like sophomore year [or] junior year of high school, I kind of realized I was black and I guess now I more associate with being black than being white. And like, how other people see the way I look. . . . I feel like black is such a dominant race. Because it shows up so much on your skin that you kind of at some level have to associate with being black very strongly. People who just see me don't really take the time to ask me what I am. They just assume I'm black.

Alicia points to the importance of her racial appearance, but most notably, she describes her physical appearance in the context of how "other people" see her. According to Alicia, they assume that she is black, not biracial, because of her visible black characteristics (e.g., dark skin).

Angie labels herself as black and internally identifies strongly as such. To explain her black identity, she also emphasizes how she believes she is perceived by others. Describing her experiences growing up in Germany (her mother is German), she says:

> Well I only identify as what people see me. So I'm black. Black foremost. I remember when I was growing up in Germany, it was obvious that I wasn't German . . . from the outside looking in and even now when I meet someone that's German, they'll bend over backwards to try to speak the most broken English that they can muster up. . . . Like me, personally, I know I'm darker. I can't pass for white. I know what I am.

Daily interactional experiences confirm to Angie how others see her—as black (not German, not white). Like others, she points to her physical characteristics to explain why she thinks others perceive her as black. And, according to Angie, her physical appearance prevents her from identifying as white, since she cannot "pass for white."

Similarly, Nick labels himself as mixed and internally identifies more strongly as black than white. When asked to explain this identity, he also describes how he thinks he is perceived by others: "Well, my features and qualities are more with blacks anywhere . . . you know, just from the outside looking in, people don't really see anything but a black guy." Notably, both Nick and Angie draw on the same phrase ("from the outside looking in") to explain their internalized black identities, drawing focus to how they think they are perceived from the outside by *others*.

Cherise labels herself as African American and internally identifies strongly as black. When asked why, she replies:

I think it's just because when I get out into the real world and I'm looking for a job and I'm looking for an apartment and, you know what I'm saying, and the person that is looking to hire me looks at my face, they aren't going to see a white person . . . and they're not going to know if I'm biracial or if I'm just a light-skinned African American. They're just going to see a black person.

She notes that because people cannot differentiate between biracial and light-skinned black, she is perceived as black. This is not surprising given the long history of interracial mixing in America and the fact that the majority of African Americans are, in fact, multiracial.[7] Further, some Americans who are classified as black may, like their biracial counterparts, have light skin and other white normative physical characteristics because they, too, have white ancestry. Because distinguishing between black and biracial physical characteristics is arguably difficult (if not impossible in some cases), many biracial people are seen as black (see also Herman 2010; Lee and Bean 2007). Hence, they more strongly identify as such.

Michael, Alicia, Angie, Nick, Cherise, and other interviewees more strongly identify as black, in part, because of how they believe they are perceived by larger society. In rare cases, respondents identify more strongly as white because they believe that larger society sees them as such. Kate, for instance, internally identifies very strongly as white because she believes others, including her friends and peers, see her as white. The few occasions when she has asserted a black identity, she has faced challenges from her white peers, whom she says see her as a "white girl":

Like whenever people would be telling racial jokes and they are doing all those little black people jokes or whatever, I would be like, "Wow, hey, I am black." . . . I would say I am black. And they were like, "You are not black. You are a white girl.". . . I would think I have black in me . . . but they would say I am white. Oh, "You are not a black girl" or whatever. [*NK: How did that make you feel when they said that you were not black?*] In my head I would think, "Yeah, I'm a white girl." . . . I mean I would think, "Yeah I am part black," but then again I would be like, "Yeah, you are right. I am a white girl."

Unlike the majority of respondents, Kate outwardly appears white and, by her own account, can pass as white because of her light skin, curly hair, and light-colored eyes. Because she does not show any visible black traits, her white peers have challenged her when she has attempted to claim a black identity. When her black identity is challenged by others, Kate admits that they are right ("Yeah, you are right. I am a white girl"). Thus, their perceptions of her as white have, in part, influenced her white identity.

These findings parallel previous research that finds reflected appraisals important in shaping racial identity in other biracial groups, such as Asian-white individuals (Khanna 2004). Additionally, some respondents draw links between their phenotypes (e.g., their "black features") and their black identities, which further supports previous work suggesting that phenotype is important in shaping racial identity (Khanna 2004; Korgen 1998). While reflected appraisals appear to be linked to internalized identities, I now turn to investigating how external perceptions of biracial phenotypes may differ depending upon the audience. Maria Root (1990) suggests that multiracial people may be perceived differently by different people. Because how they see themselves is influenced by how they think they appear to others, the racial reflection they see in their "looking glass" may differ depending upon *who* is looking at them—for instance, whether the observers are white or black.

RACIAL PERCEPTIONS: BLACKS VERSUS WHITES

David Brunsma and Kerry Ann Rockquemore (2001) find that how biracial people think others view them is moderated by social context: the black community distinguishes among shades of color, whereas whites see only black and white. Thus, how individuals see themselves may vary depending upon the racial background of the observer. In this section, I explore respondents' perceptions of how they appear to whites and to blacks. Many respondents (again, without being directly prompted by me) describe how they believe that white people perceive them exclusively as black, yet black people often recognize their biracial/multiracial backgrounds. In particular, they argue that their light skin, straight hair, or white facial characteristics often indicate their mixed racial background to black people, yet the same characteristics often go unnoticed by white people, who label them simply as black.

Differing Perceptions

In this sample, more than a third of respondents draw a distinction between how they think they are perceived racially by whites and by blacks. Olivia is one of these. When asked how she thinks people in general characterize her racially, she says:

> Some people just see me as a black woman. But there's other people who are just like "What are you?" . . . it just depends on the background of the person who's approaching me. [NK: How so?] Blacks always know that I'm mixed with something else. They always know that. They see me as a black woman that's mixed with something else. They don't know what that something else is, but they know it's something else. [NK: What about whites?] Whites, I think, most of the time see me as a black woman.

Michael similarly notes differences in how he believes he is perceived by whites and blacks. Earlier he described how "society" sees him as black, but later in the interview he clarifies that statement by adding, "With black people, I think when I say I'm black, they want to know what I'm mixed with, because they know I'm not solely black. You know, with white people they just keep it, 'Oh you're black' and they just leave it at that." From his perspective, blacks tend to recognize that he is multiracial, whereas whites assume he is black.

Similarly, other respondents believe that whites perceive them as black. For those embedded in predominantly white social networks, being perceived exclusively as black on a daily basis frequently shapes a black identity. Kendra, for instance, publicly identifies as black and internally identifies strongly as such. In her early years, she grew up in a predominantly white community, and she says that whites often assumed she was black. To explain her strong black internalized identity she says, "Because of my physical appearance. Like when people see me, they pretty much think I'm African American . . . it's more likely to be I'm black to a white person." Highlighting her physical appearance to explain her identity, she believes that others (whites in particular) perceive her as black.

Likewise, Cherise grew up in a predominantly white community and identifies as black (both publicly and internally). When asked to explain her identity, she says, "Just because on the outside that's how the world is going to view me. I mean, if I were lighter—well, no, I'd probably still [identify as African American]." Cherise identifies as African American because that is how she believes the "world" views her. She also maintains that she would identify as African American even if she had lighter skin, suggesting that perhaps it is not her skin color alone that influences how the world sees her; other characteristics and traits also identify her as black to the "world" (e.g., her hair and facial features). Further, this statement suggests that having light skin does not rule out a black identity, and in fact, it shouldn't, since many black Americans also have light skin.

But what Cherise means by "the world" at this point in her interview is unclear: is she referring to a white world or the world more generally? Later in her interview, she answers this question when asked how she identifies herself to others: "I think that when a white person asks me what I am, I will say African American and when a black person asks me what I am, I'll say biracial. [NK: Why is that?] Because the white person is always going to see me as black." Thus, when Cherise asserts that the "world" sees her as black, she is, not surprisingly, referring to a world that is white. Similarly, Alicia more strongly identifies as black than white. When explaining her black identity, she describes how "people" assume she is black (see above). Later in her interview, however, she qualifies this statement by adding, "Black people never assume I'm black. Black people always will ask me what I'm mixed with. Like, they always know I'm black and something. I think white people assume I'm black more often than not."

Other respondents similarly describe how they think whites perceive them as black. Carrie, who attended predominantly white schools growing up, notes that she was always referred to as the "black girl" in school. Natasha, who grew up in a predominantly white community, describes being similarly labeled as "black," "the black girl," and "the black friend" by her white peers. Whites, according to Natasha, primarily saw her as black, even if they were aware of her biracial background. Likewise, even though she claims that most of her white peers were aware of her biracial background, Beth says, "Growing up [my white peers] saw me as black Beth. Not biracial Beth. And certainly not white Beth."

While these respondents argue that whites often perceive them as black, some respondents describe how whites often assume they are *white*. In fact, a handful of respondents (5 of 40) claim that they outwardly appear white (based on their own self-assessment) and that they are often perceived, by whites in particular, as white (most often in cases when their black ancestry is unknown). This finding parallels Brunsma and Rockquemore's (2001) claim that whites see only black and white; there appears to be little "middle" ground for these respondents. Kim, for example, describes how black people tend to recognize her biracial background, while whites assume she is white. She says, "A lot of times some people, it tends to be white people, think I'm just white with a really great tan . . . and then a lot of black people do know [that I am biracial]—it's more common that a black person would know that I'm biracial. Usually [they ask], 'What are you mixed with?'" While black people tend to recognize (or "know") that she is biracial, she believes that whites assume she is white—likely because they are unable to detect any black physical characteristics. They assume her darker skin is the result of having a "really great tan," rather than a physical manifestation of her black ancestry.

Similarly, Kristen notes a distinction in how she is perceived by whites and blacks. Like Kim, Kristen claims that black people "know" that she is biracial, whereas whites tend to think she is white. She says:

> If people want to know who I am, then I'm very open and tell them I'm biracial. "Yeah, my mom's white" and they're kind of like, "Okay." I guess most black people know. They're like, "Well, that girl isn't white. . . . She's something else, but she's not white," whereas white people always assume I'm white. . . . I guess it's because my skin's a little bit lighter, my hair's lighter, my eyes are lighter, and so, yes, people just assume that [I'm white]. I guess white people usually. But then when I tell them [that I am biracial], I've had white people that are totally shocked and are like, "What? You're what?"

According to Kristen, whites assume she is white based on her white physical characteristics, and when she reveals her biracial background, some openly express surprise and shock. Why? Likely because they could not readily detect any visible characteristics that would indicate black ancestry. Put another way, Kristen could easily pass as white, and her white peers are surprised when they learn of her black ancestry. Whites see both Kristen and Kim as white because they do not detect *any* black phenotypic characteristics.

Even more interesting, Kristen describes numerous interactions with white peers and their parents when her biracial background is revealed. She says not only are they shocked, but she argues that they begin to see her differently—as black (not white or biracial). She describes instances where whites have remarked, "Oh, I didn't know you were black!" or "Really? You're black?" This is particularly interesting given her white outward appearance and the fact that only moments before the revelation, she was perceived as white. Thus, according to Kristen, she can easily pass as white, but once her biracial background is revealed, she is redefined as black. Three of the five respondents who claim they can pass as white argue that once they reveal their black ancestry, whites look at them and respond to them differently. In short, whites interact with them as if they are black.[8] In these rare cases, we can see the explicit invocation of the one drop rule— they appear white in physical appearance, but any revelation of their black ancestry leads to their reclassification as black.

We can also see the rule operating implicitly as well. Its implicitness is apparent in that many whites assume that many of these biracial individuals are black; it is rare, they claim, for whites to recognize they are biracial or multiracial. As Cherise noted earlier, most people are "not going to know if I'm biracial or if I'm just a light-skinned African American. They're just going to see a black person." *Any* visible black physical characteristic (in terms of skin color, hair texture, or facial features) compels many whites to assume these biracial individuals are black simply because it is difficult for them to distinguish between black and biracial based on phenotype alone. This, I argue, is the legacy of generations of the one drop rule. While the one drop rule may trump physical appearance in some cases, the real effect of the one drop rule in contemporary America is its continued influence on shaping (white) Americans' perceptions of what black looks like today. Since black people, like their biracial counterparts, can have light skin and straight hair, it may be challenging for many white Americans to distinguish those who are biracial from those who are black.

Black Americans, on the other hand, appear to have relatively less difficulty distinguishing biracial from black (or at the very least, recognizing when a respondent has non-black ancestry). It's unclear why this is, but it is plausible that black people are more attuned to even the slightest variations in physical appearances among those with black ancestry because of the history of colorism within the African American community. Since those with light skin and European features have historically gained some measure of status and privilege within the black community, blacks may be more conscious of the physical differences between themselves than are whites. Conversely, many whites are unaware of colorism within the black community, and hence they may be comparatively less perceptive of and sensitive to the phenotypic variations among those with black ancestry.

Perception of Race by Blacks: A Closer Look

Because respondents often describe how blacks more readily recognize their multiracial backgrounds as compared to whites, one might conclude that in contexts where observers are white, reflected appraisals will shape black identities (and in rare occasions, white identities), while in contexts where observers are black, reflected appraisals will shape biracial (or multiracial) identities. Upon closer examination, however, this is not the case. While these biracial respondents believe that black people frequently recognize their multiracial backgrounds, they simultaneously describe how they nonetheless pigeonhole them as black. In particular, a quarter of respondents describe how black people invoke the one drop rule, both explicitly and implicitly, to label them as black even when aware of their biracial backgrounds. Respondents often feel that blacks categorize them as black as if to say, "Yes, you may be biracial, but *really* you're black."

For example, Monique describes the messages she receives from blacks, both friends and strangers, regarding her race. Describing some of the comments that she has received from complete strangers, she says, "I've heard comments [about my race], especially in passing. Every once in a while, a total stranger will ask me what I am. Or they say, 'You must be mixed' or 'There's something about you.' I get that a lot from black people." Black people recognize that she is "mixed" or, at the very least, they notice her physical appearance enough to ask her about her racial background. Despite this recognition, however, Monique also notes, "I've also heard the comment so many times that 'if you've got a little in you, it's all in you' from other blacks." According to Monique, when black people make this comment, they are referring to her black ancestry: if she has a little blackness, then she is black. Here the use of the one drop rule is implicit; black people recognize her multiracial background, but nonetheless draw on the one drop rule (that one drop of black blood somehow weighs more heavily as compared to white blood) to label her as black.

Like Monique, Michelle believes that black people perceive her as black, despite her outward white physical appearance. To explain her strong internalized black identity, she describes interactions she has had with black people and says, "It goes back to that whole, 'If you have one drop of black blood in you, then you're black.' . . . And, you know, [black people have said], 'Oh, she's black' and, 'She's not mixed. She's black. She's black.' They just kind of overlooked everything." Because of the one drop rule, Michelle perceives that black people see her as black and tend to "overlook" her biracial background and white appearance. Later in the interview, she adds, "You know, they always say now that you're never really 100 percent black. If you've got some Indian in you, [black people will] say that, but at the end of the day, you're still black."

Denise publicly and internally identifies as black, and she describes how black people label her as black despite knowing about her biracial background. Further, she feels her identity choices are somewhat constricted by blacks who implicitly draw on the one drop rule. When asked how she identifies herself to others, she says: "If I'm in a group of blacks, I would definitely say I'm black. I would say black first. [If they ask] 'What are you?' [I would say] 'I'm black, but I'm also half white.' [*NK: Why is that? Why do you say black first?*] [Black people] have said, 'Why don't you just say black? If you're half black, you're just black. You're not really white. You're not a mix.'" Directly told that "if you're half black, you're just black," Denise has learned to identify exclusively as black when with her black peers (or at the very least, to identify as black first) to avoid any potential confrontation or conflict over her identity.

Finally, John describes himself in his interview as looking like a "regular white guy," and I was initially surprised to find that despite his white phenotype, he internally identifies more strongly as black than white. To explain, he describes how black people draw on the one drop rule to label him as black:

> Historically, it's kind of a one drop rule . . . just about all black people have relatives who are mixes or partial races. Got a grandparent or something. So black people are pretty familiar with how [the one drop rule] will work . . . when [my biracial background has] come up, [black people] tend to say, "You're black." And they're okay with that because, again, it goes back to how society generally sees things, and there have been a million examples of people who have been excluded or discriminated against because they are a quarter black or because they're an eighth [black] sometimes. We will use that rule because it's been a pretty big part of history. So if anything, [black people] just say, "Yeah, you're black." . . . They consider me black and that's it. There's no discussion. Yeah, "You're black." That's it.

According to John, black people frequently draw on the one drop rule to label him as black despite his white outward appearance, and, as a consequence, he more strongly identifies as black than white. While he may not literally see a black person when he looks in the mirror, figuratively he does; because his social interactions with black people communicate to him that black people see him as black, he can see a black reflection in his "looking glass."

Thus, while these biracial respondents perceive that black people are more likely than whites to recognize their biracial/multiracial backgrounds, they also believe that black people nevertheless race them as black, often drawing on the one drop rule. For those who believe they appear black to black people, their reflected appraisals (i.e., how they imagine they appear to others) frequently shape black identities in contexts where the observers are black. Even those with racially ambiguous or white racial appearances describe how black people see them as black. Hence, respondents in this sample frequently describe how they believe that *both* whites and blacks see them as black.

DISCUSSION AND CONCLUSION

This chapter illustrates the importance of reflected appraisals in shaping racial identity (i.e., how people *think* others see them), but more importantly, these findings also show how reflected appraisals are (still) fundamentally shaped by the one drop rule for black-white Americans. Few studies examine reflected appraisals as a determinant of racial identity, and I find that biracial respondents frequently explain their internalized black identities as due in part to how they believe they are viewed by "others" and by "larger society."

Interestingly, however, respondents in this study draw a distinction between how they think they are perceived by whites versus blacks. White people, they argue, see them as black (not biracial, and certainly not white), while black people are more likely to recognize their biracial/multiracial backgrounds. These conflicting perceptions have the potential to shape different "racial reflections" (e.g., as black or biracial), yet I find that the one drop rule affects the entire reflected appraisal process, subsequently shaping internalized black identities for the majority of respondents in this study.

Blacks, they argue, are more likely to recognize their biracial/multiracial ancestry than are whites. According to these respondents, blacks appear relatively more adept than whites at distinguishing between black and biracial (or at the very least, more able to recognize when someone has non-black ancestry), which perhaps may be explained by the long history of colorism within the black community. According to Russell, Wilson, and Hall (1992), black Americans have a "color complex"—an arguably heightened sensitivity to variations in skin color that can be traced back to the slave era. Light skin has historically conferred privileges and advantages unavailable to their darker skinned counterparts (e.g., more opportunities for education, less stressful work, and manumission during slavery), and even today, research shows that lighter skin continues to have an impact on one's educational attainment, occupation, and income: lighter-skinned blacks are likely to have more years of schooling, higher-status occupations, and higher incomes than darker-skinned blacks do (Allen, Telles, and Hunter 2000; Herring, Keith, and Horton 2004; Hughes and Hertel 1990; Hunter 1998, 2005; Johnson, Bienenstock, and Stoloff 1995; Keith and Herring 1991; Russell, Wilson, and Hall 1992).

Possessing "white" physical features has also been equated to beauty in American society, especially for women (Hall 1995; Hill 2002; Hunter 1998). Lighter-skinned women with more European features are viewed by most Americans as "the most physically appealing" (Hall 1995: 177) and as "superior" (Hunter 2005: 71) to those with darker skin. I argue that the societal privilege awarded to light skin, light eyes, straight hair, and anglicized facial features has heightened blacks' attention to even the slightest variations in skin color within the "black" community; this may explain, at least in part, why black Americans *may* be relatively more skilled in recognizing mixed racial ancestry as compared to whites. It is imperative to keep in mind, though, that blacks' perceptiveness of these biracials' non-black ancestry is based on the *perceptions* of *these* respondents and may or may not actually reflect (1) what is actually going on (their perception may not necessarily match reality) or may not reflect (2) the larger pattern in the United States (keep in mind that this sample is not generalizable to blacks and whites in the larger American population). However, it was undoubtedly a very noticeable trend within this sample.

Regardless of blacks' recognition of their non-black ancestry, however, this sample of respondents describes how blacks often cite the one drop rule (explicitly or implicitly) to say: "Yes, you may be biracial, but you know, you're *really* black." F. James Davis (1991) argues that this rule, once used by whites as a tool of oppression, now serves as a positive strategy to resist white racism by unifying black Americans, and other scholars similarly claim that the black community has embraced the rule arguably as a means of promoting black unity and inclusiveness (Perlmann and Waters 2002; Williamson 1980). Orlando Patterson (2007: 44), in a recent *Time* magazine article, writes that the one drop rule was:

> invented and imposed by white racists until the middle of the 20th century. As with so many other areas of ethno-racial relations, African Americans turned this racist doctrine to their own ends. What to racist whites was a stain of impurity became a badge of pride. More significantly, what for whites was a means of exclusion was transformed by blacks into a glorious principle of inclusion.

Whites created and utilized the one drop rule to subjugate black Americans, but black Americans appropriated the rule for their own means. By saying things like, "Hey, you know, you're one of us" or "Come over here, we'll accept you," they are able to unite together by embracing even those individuals with a "little" or "part" African/black ancestry.

Blacks may also draw on the one drop rule as a way to "lay claim" to biracial and multiracial people whom they believe *should* identify as black. A notable example is Tiger Woods, who (as described in chapter 1) publicly claims a multiracial identity. This has incensed some black Americans who arguably want to claim the phenomenal golfer as black. In fact, some have charged that Woods is a race traitor for not identifying as black, and this has most certainly opened up debate both within and outside of the black community regarding his race. The pressure Tiger Woods has felt to identify as black is arguably also shared to some degree by other biracial and multiracial people. Michelle (as described earlier), for example, notes that even though she is not a "superstar making half a million dollars or anything like that," she feels, too, that black people want to claim her as black.

Additionally, some biracial respondents in this study believed that some blacks invoked the one drop rule and labeled them as black as a way of subtly or not so subtly reminding them, "You're no better than me because you're biracial. You're *just* black, too." This may well be a strategy used by some black Americans to counter the intra-racial hierarchy that has historically privileged biracial over black (or light skin over dark skin). While Louisiana's Creoles of color and the multiracial elite of the Jim Crow era (as described in the previous chapter) worked to separate and elevate themselves above the black masses, some blacks may label biracial people as black in order to remind them that they are "just black"; they are not "better" or superior for having a white parent.

From this set of findings, it appears that the one drop rule trumps physical appearance—especially for those who outwardly appear white but feel that blacks nevertheless see them as black. At first glance, this suggests that phenotype may have little consequence for racial identity for black-white biracial Americans, contradicting previous work linking phenotype and identity in other multiracial groups. Comments from other biracial respondents, however, who point out their "black features" to help explain their black identities, indicate otherwise. Clearly phenotype does have some relationship with identity, although it is a highly complex one. This complex relationship is evident in how respondents believe they are perceived by whites.

Regarding whites, the majority of respondents describe how they believe white people see them simply as black. Some respondents who can easily pass as white claim that any revelation of their black ancestry leads whites to reclassify them as black. This finding again suggests that there may be some trumping of ancestry over phenotype, at least among these respondents. I argue, however, that phenotype also shapes racial identity; this is evident in the majority of respondents who do not outwardly appear white, but rather appear black, multiracial, or even racially ambiguous. These respondents describe how white people see them as black, and often any visible "black" characteristic (in terms of skin tone, hair, facial features) leads to the assumption that they are black, not biracial (and certainly not white). Even if these biracial respondents have phenotypic characteristics considered normative for whites, *any* noticeable black physical characteristic(s) continue to take precedence and often lead to a black classification by whites. This finding is echoed in the recent words of Vice President of Communications for the NAACP Leila McDowell, who commented on her own biracial ancestry: "If you have any identifying [black] characteristics, you're black" (Washington 2010). This statement reveals the importance of phenotype and others' perceptions of that phenotype in shaping one's identity; having dark skin or any features associated with Africa for that matter, often means people see you as black.

These statements also parallel Mary Waters' (1990, 1996) argument, as described earlier, that certain ancestries are "essential" and become a defining aspect of a multiracial person. In American society, she argues, a non-black identity (i.e., biracial or white) will likely not be accepted if one looks black "according to the prevailing social norms" (1996: 447). What shapes "prevailing social norms" regarding black phenotypes? Put simply—years of the one drop rule. Generations of interracial mixing between blacks and whites and the broad definition of "blackness" as defined by the one drop rule have created a wide-ranging phenotypic image of blackness (Russell, Wilson, and Hall 1992); possessing normative white physical characteristics does not necessarily conflict with this image. Hence, while biracial Americans may inherit certain physical traits from their white parent, such as light skin, these traits do not necessarily contradict the "prevailing social norm" of what it looks like to be black. Any black traits, however, do contradict notions of what it looks like to be white.

Thus, while previous studies show a link between phenotype and racial identity for other multiracial Americans (see Khanna 2004), I find that for black-white Americans, the link is not as clear-cut and straightforward; rather, the link is complex and arguably asymmetric. In short, "white" phenotypic characteristics may not preclude a black identity (because black people invoke the one drop rule as an inclusive tool or because "white" characteristics do not necessarily conflict with Americans' image of blackness), yet it appears that having any "black" phenotypic characteristics automatically rules out a white identity. Because the one drop rule has functioned in part to maintain white racial purity, having any "black" characteristics conflicts with the concept of whiteness, and arguably conflicts with our image of whiteness even today. Thus, the relationship between phenotype and racial identity is still influenced by the *legacy* of the one drop rule. This one drop legacy influences how black phenotypes are perceived even today ("black" includes a broad range of phenotypic characteristics), which in turn affects reflected appraisals (biracial respondents often think others see them as black) and hence racial identity (often as black) (see figure 3.1).

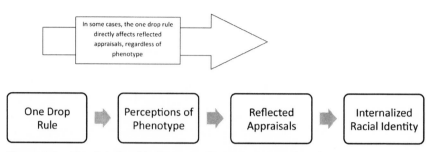

Figure 3.1. The Relationship between the One Drop Rule, Phenotype, and Racial Identity

Finally, while this study shows that the one drop rule continues to shape internalized black identities (via reflected appraisals), it also shows a simultaneous rejection of the rule with regard to public identities. Only six respondents identify exclusively as black or African American, while the majority of respondents publicly identify as biracial or multiracial. The widening range of racial options available to these biracial respondents undoubtedly points to the declining power of the one drop rule, which parallels the findings of recent studies (Brunsma and Rockquemore 2001; Korgen 1998; Roth 2005). I find, however, that the one drop rule continues to operate via societal ascriptions that nonetheless tell the respondents that they are black. David Harris and Jeremiah Joseph Sim (2002), in explaining why black-white adolescents in their sample identified as multiracial but often identified as black when asked to choose their single best race (black or white), similarly argue, "Given the enduring power of the one drop rule, we suspect that many white/black adolescents are socialized to understand that *even if they identify as multiracial, they are 'really' black*" (621; emphasis added). These findings further support their claim—black-white biracial people may publicly identify as biracial or multiracial, yet societal ascriptions, via reflected appraisals and the one drop rule, continue to tell them that they are black, hence shaping internalized black identities. Thus, racial labels such as biracial and multiracial may, indeed, be becoming more frequent in contemporary America (as recent research shows), yet the world still views these individuals as black. Whether this will change as people increasingly claim biracial and multiracial identities, however, remains to be seen.

A final note: while the majority of respondents in this sample internally identify as black, the remainder internally identify as white (22.5 percent) or biracial (17.5 percent). This is quite remarkable, given that this was a southern sample and some studies suggest that the one drop rule may be strongest in this region. This raises an important question: How do the experiences of white- or biracial-identified respondents differ from those who identify as black? I find that these respondents describe the *same pat-*

terns as black-identified respondents regarding how they believe they are perceived by others; they too describe thinking that blacks and whites see them as *black*. However, these respondents appear to resist these appraisals, which suggests that other factors may affect or even buffer the influence of reflected appraisals on racial identity. Clearly, multiple factors and processes are shaping racial identities, and more work is needed to better understand the development of non-black identities. In the next chapter, I examine how day-to-day interactional experiences with others also work to shape racial identities. In particular, I focus on interviewees' interactions with both blacks and whites, and I look at how their perceptions of acceptance, discrimination, and rejection operate to push and pull them towards various racial identities.

NOTES

1. An amended version of this chapter appears in 2010 in the *Sociological Quarterly* 51: 96–121 ("'If You're Half Black, You're Just Black': Reflected Appraisals and the Persistence of the One-Drop Rule").

2. According to symbolic interactionists (see Blumer 1969), (1) human beings act towards things on the basis of meanings that the things have for them; (2) the meanings of such things arise out of social interaction; and (3) these meanings are modified through social interaction.

3. IQ tests may be seen as an objective measure of intelligence, but in reality, there are no objective measures of intelligence. In fact, there is a growing body of literature which claims that IQ tests are culturally biased and only measure certain types of intelligence (see Mensh and Mensh 1991).

4. An example is Walter Francis White, civil rights activist and executive secretary of the NAACP (National Association for the Advancement of Colored People) from 1931 to 1955. White was "fair-skinned, blue-eyed, and blond-haired, the son of light-complexioned Negroes who were stalwarts of Atlanta's black middle class" (Kennedy 2003: 287). Even though he outwardly appeared white, his black ancestry nonetheless defined him as black and early experiences of discrimination led him to reflect, "I was a Negro, a human being with an invisible pigmentation which marked me as a person to be hunted, hanged, abused, discriminated against, kept in poverty and ignorance." (Kennedy 2003: 288). Another example is Anita Hemmings, the first "black" graduate of Vassar College. Although she outwardly appeared white and enrolled in Vassar College as a white student, evidence of her black ancestry was revealed by a suspicious roommate who had her father investigate the Hemmings family. Surprisingly, Vassar allowed her to graduate and today touts her as Vassar's first black graduate. In both examples, white physical appearance mattered little; black ancestry simply defined them as black.

5. Like most people defined as black in the United States, Vanessa Williams and Beyoncé Knowles also have non-black ancestry. Williams has African American, white (Welsh), and Native American ancestry. Beyoncé Knowles' maternal grandparents are Louisiana Creoles and her father is African American.

6. The fact that the majority of respondents publicly identified as biracial (or some related term) may be explained in several ways. First, it is plausible that respondents publicly identified as biracial because they knew the interviewer was biracial and may have felt that was the appropriate or "right" answer in the context of the interview. Second, respondents may have been primed to identify as biracial given the topic of the interview and the focus of the study. Finally, with the increased visibility of celebrities and public figures who publicly identify as biracial or multiracial (e.g., Tiger Woods), it may be more popular and accepted to identify as multiracial today than in previous decades. Recent empirical studies showing similar trends suggest that publicly identifying as multiracial is becoming increasingly popular (Brunsma and Rockquemore 2001; Korgen 1998; Roth 2005).

7. For example, Barack Obama has a white mother and black father, and can be considered biracial or multiracial. Less well known, however, is that his wife, Michelle Obama (who is considered black), also has white ancestry—her great-great-great grandfather was a white man who impregnated a teen slave (her great-great-great grandmother). According to a 2009 *New York Times* article, Michelle Obama's ancestry "highlights the complicated history of racial intermingling . . . that lingers in the bloodlines of many African Americans" (Swarns and Kantor 2009). Thus, like biracial Barack Obama, Michelle Obama and many other black Americans could be considered multiracial. For this reason, biracial people and many black Americans share a commonality—some degree of white ancestry.

8. These respondents describe a range of responses from whites once their ancestry is revealed, including prejudice and discrimination (racial slurs, exclusion) as well as "special treatment" (they describe how whites "tiptoe" around them as not to offend them or appear prejudiced). For these respondents, it must also be noted that there may be situations in which they do not share their ancestry (e.g., they do not have the opportunity or they actively choose not to share the information). In cases where others see them as white based on their racial appearance, they will likely interact with these individuals as if they are white. Hence, *in these situations,* they may be less restricted in the ways they can identify themselves if they so choose (e.g., they may have the option of identifying as white).

4

"Blacks Accept Me More Easily Than Whites"

The Push and Pull of Day-to-Day Interactions

As described in the last chapter, racial identities are not formed in a "social vacuum" (Felson 1981); rather, they are constructed through social interactions with others.[1] Identity for biracial individuals, for instance, is a *process* by which they come to understand themselves, at least in part, through day-to-day social interactions with family, friends, peers, coworkers, and others. In 2002, Kerry Ann Rockquemore and David Brunsma argued in their own study of black-white biracial people, that the "types" of interactions that biracial people have with others in their social networks can affect their racial identities (Rockquemore and Brunsma 2002a: 58). Conceptualizing types of interactions as "push" and "pull" factors, they describe "pull" factors as those that pull an individual towards a racial identity because of positive experiences in their social networks (e.g., a sense of closeness with a group), and "push" factors as those that push individuals away from an identity because of negative experiences (e.g., discrimination, negative treatment).

In this chapter, I take a closer look at and further extend Rockquemore and Brunsma's (2002a) concepts of "push" and "pull" factors shaping racial identity. Like Rockquemore and Brunsma, I explore how discriminatory experiences shape identity. While they argue that discrimination by whites pushes individuals away from identifying as white, I find that these negative experiences can also function to pull individuals towards black identities. Moreover, I add to Rockquemore and Brunsma's (2002a) work by examining additional types of "push" and "pull" factors that appear to be important in identity formation. Specifically, I look at how perceived acceptance by a racial group (i.e., a positive experience) acts as a "pull" factor, while perceived rejection by a group (i.e., a negative experience) functions as a "push" factor. I examine these "push" and "pull" factors (acceptance, discrimination, and rejection) within the context of social interactions between these biracial respondents and (1) whites and (2) blacks. Respondents in this study tend to describe experiences of discrimination and rejection by whites, yet they often describe feeling accepted by blacks as black (at least for the most part). In looking at biracials' experiences with both whites and blacks, I also examine the role that gender plays in influencing experiences of rejection and acceptance, and its subsequent impact on racial identity.

SOCIAL INTERACTIONS WITH WHITES

In many cases, respondents described experiences of discrimination and rejection by white peers, friends, extended family members, and whites more generally—often to explain why they more strongly identified as black than white. These negative experiences repeatedly functioned to remind them that they were different from whites, and as a consequence often pushed them away from white (and sometimes even biracial) identities. At times, these negative experiences even worked to pull them towards black identities, either because they recognized the commonalities they shared with their black counterparts (shared experiences of discrimination, for example) or because discriminatory experiences put them in "defense mode" and made them feel protective of their black backgrounds. Further, rejection by whites appears even more pronounced for biracial women as compared to biracial men, especially in the arena of heterosexual dating relationships in adolescence and young adulthood.

Perceptions of Discrimination and Rejection

Ursula Brown (2001) finds that being biracial often "invited negative attention" for those growing up in white communities and, indeed, a few respondents in this study report being called names such as "half-breed," "mutt," or "oreo" (i.e., black on the outside and white on the inside) that targeted their biraciality (84). The majority of respondents in this study, however, describe few negative experiences as a result of being biracial. Instead, they more often describe experiences of discrimination targeting their black rather than biracial selves, especially from whites. Because these biracial respondents are frequently raced as black by whites (see chapter 3), they often face many of the same discriminatory experiences as their black peers—62.5 percent of respondents describe personal experiences of discrimination directed at their black, not biracial, backgrounds. According to Miri Song (2003), "The different physical features between mixed and monoracial black people . . . does not prevent White people from stereotyping and lumping together all Black people of various shades" (79), and indeed sociologist Melissa Herman (2004), in a study of multiracial and monoracial youth, finds that part-black biracials perceive just as much discrimination as their black counterparts (see also Campbell and Herman 2010). Respondents in the present study describe a range of discriminatory experiences stemming from interactions with whites who perceive them as black, including racial slurs, racial jokes that negatively stereotype blacks, racial profiling, physical intimidation, and social exclusion.

Julie, for example, labels herself as mixed but internally identifies more strongly as black than white. She reflects on an experience in high school. She says, "My friends and I went out to lunch in high school. In high school, I pretty much had all black or Hispanic friends, and high school kids went out for lunch. We're rowdy, and I guess we were talking kind of loud and this [white] woman on the corner was like, 'Oh, you niggers always talk loud, I can't believe this.' And we just all stopped and looked at her." Because she had few experiences with whites (outside of her family), this racial slur stands out in her mind as the first instance in which she realized how she was perceived by whites—as black.

Similarly, Angie, who labels herself as black and who also has a strong internalized black identity, has spent considerable time working in Germany. Reflecting on her experiences in Germany, she says:

Overseas, even when I go back [to Germany] now, people just look at me like they've never seen a black person in their life. That bothers me . . . [white Germans] just stare like they've never seen anything other than white. Like on the bus, I remember in Germany, this old white man screamed out throughout the whole bus, "Go back to where you came from, you nigger child." I took heavy offense to that . . . even when I go back [to Germany] now, I get frustrated. I get extremely frustrated.

Angie's experiences of being singled out frustrate her. Being called a racial slur further reinforces how whites perceive her—as black. Other respondents also describe instances in which they were direct targets of racial epithets. These negative interactions highlight the fact that they are different from their white counterparts, which functions to push them away from identifying as white. Even more important, however, these experiences underscore how whites perceive them—as black. Not as white. Not as biracial.

Like Angie, Blake has a strong internalized black identity. When asked whether he has ever experienced any hostility or negative treatment from whites for being biracial, he responds:

I've been followed around in stores, stopped by police. It makes me so mad because they assume I'm black and that I'm going to steal something. . . . I've been called not the nicest names in the world. [*NK: By whom?*] When I was in high school, by other white kids. I feel like it's constantly pointed out to me that I'm black. . . . At the end of the day, they see my skin and they see a black person walking through the door. I've been called nigger before, or they make assumptions about me. It makes me so mad. . . . [NK: *What sort of effect do you think these experiences have had on your racial identity?*] I obviously don't feel very white when they're calling me a nigger. [NK: *What about being biracial?*] I don't really feel that biracial either.

Blake experiences racial profiling and racial slurs—not for being biracial, but rather because people (white people in his case) perceive him as black. In fact, he feels as if it is "constantly pointed out" that he is black, which pushes him away from identifying as white (or even biracial).

Perceptions of rejection by whites, in addition to experiences of discrimination, also work to push some respondents from white identities. Because many of these respondents are perceived as black by whites, they describe feeling socially excluded and rejected by their white peers. Stephanie, who labels herself as biracial and internally identifies strongly as black, describes feeling distanced from her white peers and says, "I've never been accepted [by white people]. Like my white friends never accepted me as a white friend. I was always the black person. I wasn't the biracial person. I was the black person who acted white." Other respondents similarly describe how they were labeled as the "black girl," the "black kid," or the "black person" by their white peers, which ultimately made them feel different and distanced from their white peers.

Carrie, who grew up in a predominantly white community, discusses her experiences with white peers growing up:

When I was in kindergarten, a little [white] girl told me I had a big nose. . . . I guess that was the first time my differences were pointed out in my physical appearance. . . . Later, in middle school, I was always referred to as the "black girl," "the little black girl." I guess that's the first time I really noticed other people pointing out the differences. When I was growing up, I felt different in terms of race.

When asked how this influenced her racial identity, she says, "I feel white, but I think that white people look at me and see the darker skin and say, 'Well, she's not white.' So it's kind of hard. Sometimes the connection isn't there from the other end."

As Rockquemore and Brunsma (2002a) argue, these negative discriminatory experiences and perceptions of rejection from whites push biracial people away from identifying as white; I find, however, that these negative experiences can also function to pull individuals towards black identities. Leslie labels herself as mixed and more strongly identifies as black than white. She describes how her experiences of being targeted for racial slurs have pulled her towards a black identity because they highlighted for her the commonalities she shares with blacks:

> I can identify with black people because I have been discriminated against. I have been called names and things like that. [*NK: Can you give me an example?*] Actually, I remember the first time somebody called me a nigger. I was in the fourth grade. We had just learned that word . . . and this boy, he realized that I was different and so that's why he said it. Because I went to a primarily white middle school. You could count the black kids on one hand with fingers left over.

Being called a "nigger" reinforces the common experiences Leslie shares with blacks in terms of discrimination, which pulls her towards identifying as black.

Likewise, Kristen's negative experiences with white peers in school allowed her to see the commonalities she shared with black peers, which strengthened her own black identity. Although she outwardly appears white, she talked about experiencing racial slurs on a frequent basis:

> I've been called nigger lots of times. . . . [*NK: You have? Can you give me a specific example?*] I've been called a nigger by a white guy actually recently. . . . His girlfriend went to a store and bought a little dress. Very cute. He goes, "She bought it from a nigger store.". . . I was in the [dressing] room and I heard him and I was just like, "I'm not going to say anything if no one else says anything, because I don't really feel like dealing with that right now." And one of my friends . . . goes, "Dude, you know Kristen is mixed, right?" And he goes, "What? . . . You're a nigger?" And I was like, "What?" And he goes, "You're a nigger, aren't you?" I said, "No." I said, "What's that supposed to mean, anyways?" He goes, "You're black. . . . You're a nigger now." . . . Like I said, I've been called nigger plenty of times by white people.

In spite of her white racial appearance, Kristen internally identifies more strongly with being black than white. Negative interactions with white peers (i.e., racial slurs) push her away from a white identity as her racial differences are highlighted. To further explain why she strongly identifies as black even though she is often "mistaken" for white, she notes the commonalities she shares with her black counterparts:

> I guess growing up it seemed harder to be black to me, and I could identify more with being black than I could with being white because it was like, I guess at the [predominantly white] school I went to, it was like if you're black, you're also an outcast. So it was easier for me to say, "Well, yeah, I'm different too" . . . because of my experiences, I would probably put myself much more black.

For some biracial respondents, negative interactions with whites also led to defensive feelings and put them in "protection-mode" regarding their black ancestries. Angie, who both publicly and internally identifies as black, explains her identity by saying, "I guess I'm kind of rooting for the underdog type of thing. It makes me more passionate about certain issues and things and being black . . . you know, I can be a positive on that black name. It just makes me cling to my black side even more . . . I'm black, and yes, I can still do all these things."

Certainly interactions with whites may influence identity more broadly, but they may also impact identity more situationally or contextually. Kate outwardly appears white and is often perceived as white by those who are not aware of her racial background. She labels herself as white and identifies strongly as such, but she notes an experience in which she internally identifies more strongly as black: when white peers tell racial jokes about blacks. Describing her momentary reaction, she says, "I would be like, 'Wow. Hey, I am black' . . . it bothered me. I would think, 'I have black in me. You shouldn't make fun of them and say those things because I am black.'" Although Kate generally identifies as white (both publicly and internally), her black identity becomes more salient in the context of hearing anti-black jokes (even though they are not directed at her). When her white peers make jokes about black people, Kate describes feeling protective of her black background, and is momentarily pulled towards a black identity.

Gendered Rejection

The push and pull of perceived discrimination and rejection by whites often shape black identities—especially for those with frequent contact with whites. Moreover, perceptions of rejection by whites are also fundamentally gendered, in that these biracial men and women in predominantly white environments face noticeably different experiences during adolescence. Specifically, biracial women in this study were much more likely than biracial men to report feeling rejected by their white peers (by those of the opposite sex, in particular) in the arena of dating. While biracial men generally describe being desired by white females, these biracial women often describe rejection from white males. Several studies have looked at how one's racial identity affects one's choice of partners (for examples, see Kilson 2001; Twine 1996a); however, few known studies have examined how experiences regarding dating in adolescence and young adulthood may also influence one's racial identity (for an exception, see Twine 1996b).

Kendra, for example, describes having felt rejected by white males in adolescence. At a young age, she more strongly identified as white than black, but as she got older she began to more strongly embrace her black identity (today she labels herself as black and internally identifies as such). During her interview, she describes how she moved from a white to black internalized identity as she began to feel rejected by her white peers, white males in particular, in adolescence. She says, "Sixth grade was the end of elementary school for me. There was only one black guy in the whole grade, but I had a crush on a whole bunch of white guys. I kind of realized at that point that I didn't feel like any of the white guys would see me as beautiful . . . that wasn't their ideal of what they wanted their girlfriend to look like."

Like Kendra, other biracial women also discuss feeling excluded by white males in the area of dating, particularly in middle school and high school. Natasha, who grew up in a predominantly white environment, says, "I did not date like all through high school based on my [racial] looks. I've got to tell people here [at this HBCU] I had my first boyfriend in college. Nobody believes me. I felt left out in high school. I mean all my friends were dating, and I was sitting at home watching TV." In this context, Natasha felt "left out"—white male peers overlooked her, which made her feel socially isolated from her white peers in school. These feelings of perceived exclusion explain, at least in part, why she both publicly and internally identifies as black today.

Caroline, who grew up in a predominantly white environment, discussed similar experiences of exclusion from dating in high school:

[I went to] a very small private school and I never had a boyfriend in high school. Nobody ever asked me out. My [white] friends got asked out and my [white] friends had boyfriends, but nobody ever asked me out. And you know, I'd go home and I'm like, "Mom, am I ugly?" and she's like, "No, you're pretty." And I'm like, "You're my mom, you have to say that" [laughing] . . . and then when I graduated, the very next year I was out at a party and I saw a bunch of people that I went to high school with. And I saw all those guys that I went to high school with, and a couple of them told me, "Oh my gosh. You are so pretty." And I was like, "Thanks. Did I just suddenly turn pretty overnight, or was I pretty in high school?" And they were like, oh, their parents didn't agree with them dating anybody that was outside their race. Or they didn't feel comfortable. They thought their friends were going to say something to them . . . it wasn't generally acceptable. . . . And then sometimes, just assuming that a guy, a white male, would find me attractive and that's not always the case. It's hard. It's hard.

Kristen also describes feeling excluded in the arena of dating in her predominantly white high school:

As far as dating and stuff like that, it was harder because people . . . they would be my friend, but they didn't want to date me. Probably because of maybe what their parents would think, what people might think when we go out. . . . I dated a white guy and his father cared a lot. His dad didn't really like me. His dad never came out and said anything, but it was like if I came over, he didn't talk to me . . . growing up in a predominantly white school, yeah, it was kind of difficult. . . . It was just like, "Well, we don't want to hang out with her or we don't want to date her because—she's a cool friend, but that's it." . . . I think a part of me felt a little bit left out.

Kristen, like other biracial women in this study, felt "left out." For some biracial women, dating in the context of a white environment can prove difficult. Beverly Tatum (1997) notes this difficulty and argues that in white environments biracial girls, like black girls, often become socially isolated in adolescence. I further argue that rejection by their white peers during these formative years often pushes them away from identifying as white as their physical differences are highlighted and isolation from white peers increases. They notice their white girlfriends being asked out on dates, while they are often ignored and perceived as unacceptable dating partners by white males or those males' parents and friends. Whereas biracial women in this study often described this rejection in adolescence, only one biracial man described rejection by a white female peer.[2]

SOCIAL INTERACTIONS WITH BLACKS

Unlike their experiences with whites, in which they often felt discriminated against or outright rejected based on their non-white physical appearance and black ancestry, these biracial respondents generally describe feeling accepted and embraced by blacks, which may partly explain why more respondents internally identify as black rather than white. Historically, the black community has embraced biracial people as black, and respondents in this study frequently invoked the one drop rule (or found it cited by blacks) to explain why. Rarely did they find their black identities challenged; although this perception differed to some extent for biracial women versus biracial men. Biracial women were more likely than biracial men to describe feeling rejected, and they more often reported experiences in which they found their black identities challenged.

Perceptions of Acceptance

Beth publicly identifies as black and internally identifies strongly as such. When asked to explain her strong black identity, she replies:

It's the culture I feel most accepted in. I always just felt that I was considered black. It's never really been a question for me within the black community. It's been more, "We know you're mixed. What you're mixed with, we don't know that. But just come over here. We'll accept you." Whereas I don't feel that with white people. And I think that there's some conditioning that, in general, the makeup within the black community, that is more accepted. . . . But I think that what I've learned the most was that . . . being mixed was okay with being black, if that makes sense.

Beth feels more accepted by blacks than by whites, a sentiment shared by the majority of respondents. Even though black people recognize her mixed racial background, she feels they nonetheless accept her as black. These positive interactional experiences with black people pull her towards a black identity.

Likewise, Monique talks about her perception of acceptance by black people despite her biracial background, ambiguous racial appearance, and light skin:

> I definitely look biracial, not black, but there have been black people that have wondered why other people asked me what my race is, because it's obvious. It would be obvious to them. And so maybe because there are so many different ends of the spectrum in the black culture too as far as how people look on the outside, that it's not hard for other black people to accept me as black.

According to Monique, because of the phenotypic diversity in the black community, she is accepted as black. The black community varies widely in skin color, eye color, hair texture, and facial features, so having light skin, straight hair, blue/green eyes, or facial features commonly associated with whites does not necessarily preclude acceptance by other blacks as black (as explained in the last chapter). The one drop rule, so ingrained in American society and the black community, has led to the acceptance of black-white biracial people by blacks despite their physical differences, and these respondents often referenced the one drop rule, both directly and indirectly, to explain why they believe they are so readily accepted by blacks.

Michelle, for instance, who outwardly appears white, publicly identifies as biracial but internally identifies strongly as black. To explain, she indirectly references the one drop rule:

> I think that during my college years was when I really started to get into the whole identity thing. I think I wound up being accepted more by black people. There's a whole thing that if you're just a little bit black, then you're considered black. So, I think that's just what I've identified with. . . . I think it's because of that acceptance, you know, who I've been accepted by.

Despite her white physical appearance, she feels more accepted by blacks than whites and implicitly draws on the one drop rule. The one drop rule was created and historically enforced by whites, yet blacks have also embraced it for the purposes of inclusion and racial unity. Other biracial respondents describe their perception of acceptance by blacks and similarly reference the one drop rule—albeit in subtle ways. Monique says:

> It's suggested [by black people] that I should embrace the black part of my culture more than the white side of the culture because to [black people], I will always be treated like I am black. . . . I think that has to do with historically, because I am half black, I'm just black. And I have to learn how to deal with that and how, you know, that's the way of the world.

Other biracial interviewees in this study more directly reference the one drop rule to explain why they think they are readily accepted by blacks as black. Angie, who labels herself and strongly identifies as black, says, "[Black people] accept me. The one thing that I've always felt is that black people tend to accept me more easily than white people . . . basically, it's like that one drop rule. If you have one drop of black blood, you're black. You're one of us. . . . Black people have always been much more easy to accept me." Blacks give her a sense of belonging, and these positive interactional experiences pull her towards a black identity.

While the one drop rule is used for inclusion by blacks, Stephanie, who labels herself as biracial and internally identifies strongly as black, argues that it is also used as a tool of exclusion by whites even today:

> I can take away the black part of being biracial, and I can be black on its own. So there were times when I'd say "I'm black," but there was never a time in my life when I'd say "I'm white." I don't think that white culture allows us to do that. If your great-great-great-grandmother was black, you're not white. I hear that all the time. If you're $1/8$ a black woman back in the day, you were black. So I don't think I can detach white from being biracial to say I'm white.

Monique also describes, at least from her own perspective, how whites use the one drop rule for exclusion and says:

> I am more accepted by the black community than by the white community . . . so I guess in relationship to other blacks, I feel different, but not necessarily apart . . . and I definitely feel that if somebody who was white didn't know my background and didn't question it, didn't think I looked different, then it wouldn't be a question. But if they knew my background, I don't think they would consider me to be white at all. I think part of it is because just historically in the U.S., if you are not totally white, then you are not white. So whatever percentage black you are, for a long time that automatically made you black.

Monique, like other respondents, feels accepted and embraced by black people, and cites the one drop rule to explain her perception of belonging. Feelings of acceptance afforded by the one drop rule work to pull individuals towards black identities, while at the same time the one drop rule simultaneously operates to push individuals away from white identities. An important caveat, however, must be addressed: while the majority of biracial respondents in this study describe feeling *generally* accepted by black people, not everyone feels universally included and accepted by *all* black people. In particular, biracial women face unique pressures from black women, who at times reject them as black and openly challenge their black identities.

Gendered Rejection

Interactional experiences with black people may differ significantly for biracial men versus women (see also Rockquemore 2002; Rockquemore and Brunsma 2002a). While biracial men in this study generally feel accepted by black people, biracial women describe a markedly different experience: they feel accepted by black men, but often describe feeling rejected by black women. In fact, the majority of biracial women in this sample describe negative interactions with black women, whom they perceive as resentful and jealous of their biracial backgrounds and, most importantly, their white physical characteristics (e.g., light skin, light eyes, or long hair). When asked whether they ever faced hostility or negative treatment from black people, 61.3 percent of women said yes, while only one biracial male agreed. When probed further, all these women discussed a distinction in their treatment by black men versus black women. Alicia, for instance, says, "[Black] girls don't tend to like me because a lot of girls don't like light-skinned girls. And especially when they find out that I'm mixed. Like, for some reason it's the girls. [Black] boys don't really ever have a problem. They probably think it's cool that I'm mixed."

Others draw similar distinctions. Noting the "resentment" and "jealousy" on the part of black women, Olivia says:

> With African American women, [my racial background] comes up as a primary thing. It always comes up. So I've always had to explain my hair or whatever . . . when [black women] first meet me, it's like, "What are you? You're not black. So what are you?" It's always like that. Black men are always nice. There's never, never been a problem for me with men, period . . . but with black women there was a lot of resentment when I was growing up. . . . I think it's a jealousy thing.

According to Olivia, who labels herself as multiracial and internally identifies as both black and white, black women challenge her blackness when they say, "You're not black"; this functions to push her away from a black identity. Black men, on the other hand, do not question her blackness, a distinction she explains as follows:

> There was a lot of resentment when I was growing up from [black] women because then it's like all these black men want these light-skinned women with long hair. That's their ideal woman. So, since I fit that ideal, there was a lot of resentment from women. As a matter of fact, me and another black woman had a conversation about that, and she said that "black men want light, damn near white women" . . . and this is her talking to *me*. [She said], "You get all the best men, and that's not fair" . . . so there's a lot of resentment now because of that. I mean, I get that all the time. . . . I think that in our society, in the black culture, that the lighter-skinned women with longer hair are seen as more

valuable, whether you are or not. People see you as better looking. Also, with
women, because there's such a competition for men in this society . . . and then
with black men, you have a problem with a lot of them being in prison or out
of work, so the cream-of-the-crop black men are the men that women want.
But then you have the thing where, if they're considering the woman with the
lighter skin, the finer features, and longer hair is the woman they want, then,
yeah, there's going to be a lot of hostility.

Because of the value placed on white beauty in American society (Hall
1995; Hunter 1998; Lakoff and Scherr 1984; Wolf 1991) and the shortage
of marriageable black men, "interpersonal tension between Black and biracial women currently runs high" (Rockquemore 2002: 498). Three times
in the preceding quotation, Olivia describes the "resentment" that black
women feel towards her because of her white physical characteristics (e.g.,
her light skin and long hair), and because (in her opinion) these characteristics fit the "ideal" of what black men want. Indeed, studies show that even
black women perceive that black men have a preference for light-skinned
women (Bond and Cash 1992).

Like Alicia and Olivia, Kim also points out a distinction between interacting with black women and black men:

I don't ever have any trouble talking to a black guy. It's never been a problem
for me. I feel like a lot of black women just don't like me. I'm the light-skinned
white girl, and they just don't want to have anything to do with me. . . . There
are some black women that I can immediately tell whether they dislike me or
not, whether I should not say a word to them, or whether I can befriend them.
I think that's definitely more likely to happen with black women more often.
They say, "She thinks she's light skinned." . . . [NK: Can you give me a specific
example of an experience with another black woman?] I was on the train one time,
and I was with my [biracial] friend and this [black] girl was talking out loud,
these black girls were saying, "They think they're so great," that kind of thing.
That kind of stuff you can chalk up to jealousy and bitterness.

Because of her light skin and long hair, Kim claims that black women are
jealous, bitter, and "just don't want to have anything to do with me"; feeling rejected by black women pushes her away from a strong black identity.
On the other hand, she feels accepted by black men, who are often interested in pursuing her romantically and sexually.

Moreover, when black men show interest in biracial women, this often
further fuels the conflict between black and biracial women. Stephanie
describes how attention from black men has further heightened tensions
with black women:

I remember a lot of the darker-complexioned girls around our high school
didn't really like me because my hair was longer [and because] I was light

skinned. I don't know why. . . . There were some guys that might have thought I was more attractive because my hair was longer or whatever. And a lot of guys liked girls who were mixed. . . . I did feel stress actually from the girls, not the guys. . . . [*NK: Can you give me an example?*] I remember early in high school, one of my friends didn't want to go hang out with me because she didn't like the fact that when we went out more guys would talk to me because I was light skinned and my hair is longer. And I had to be like, "Look, I'm sorry. I don't know what to do. Do you want me to wear a hat?" [Laughing.] You know, I wasn't trying to be rude or diss her, but I really didn't know what to do.

Like Stephanie, who experiences "stress" from black women, Caroline describes feeling tension from black women because they perceive her as a threat. Reflecting on an experience in high school, she says:

When I was in the ninth grade and I first got to high school, there were maybe, like, four other black kids in the school, and there was one black girl and she was a grade older than I was. Immediately, she took me as a threat and I heard through the grapevine that she wanted to beat me up . . . because her boyfriend thought I was pretty. I had no interest in her boyfriend at all. I thought he was ugly, frankly. And she took me as a threat because I was lighter skinned . . . she didn't like me because I was a threat and I was seen as competition.

Later in her interview, she describes more recent interactions with black women. Describing the "tension," she says:

I think sometimes when I walk into a place, if there's a group of black women, I feel like I get looks. Like sometimes they may think I think I'm better because my skin is lighter than the rest of the black people. . . . I've felt some of that tension in a bar or when there are men and women around who are black. And the black men look at me or respond, I'm like, "Oh, please don't, because I know these women are gonna get pissed." I *know.*

Rockquemore and Brunsma (2002a) similarly find that biracial women often encounter negative experiences with black women because of their biracial backgrounds and physical characteristics (described by these respondents as "tension" and "stress" with black women; see also Rockquemore 2002; Rockquemore and Brunsma 2004), and I argue that it is the perceived exclusion and challenges to their black identities from black women that are most detrimental to forming black identities; exclusion and challenges to their blackness push some biracial women away from identifying as black. Kendra points out the distinction between black men and women, claiming that, "Black men are attracted to me and black women are jealous of me. I've experienced exclusion. Definitely exclusion [from black women]." Thus, black women (at least from the perspective of these respondents) may be resentful and jealous of the biracial women's looks, but they can also be exclusionary and actively shut them out of their social circles.

Nicole, who grew up in a racially mixed community in a large northern city, labels herself as multiracial but more strongly identifies as white rather than black. Throughout her interview, she talks about feeling excluded by blacks because of her biracial background, specifically pointing to black women. To explain why she does not identify with being black, she says:

> I have had to deal with misperceptions that black people have of mixed-race black-white people . . . that we think we're better than they are because, you know, we have good hair, so we are better. Being light skinned—we get things they don't get, you know, socially, economically. . . . I guess I just more identify as white. I think there may be more of an acceptance for me [among whites]. But given my history of being around all sorts of different groups of black people, this is not true for all of them; but just some of the negative experiences I've had, I get kind of uncomfortable, and I think it's just because of how I've been treated. And so I tend to not like to be in all-black settings because of my past experiences.

When further probed about her experiences with black people, Nicole cites examples centering on black women (e.g., female coworkers, female peers at school) who alienate and ignore her when they learn of her biracial background. Because of these negative experiences with black women, Nicole feels pushed away from a black identity and as a consequence more strongly identifies as white. Moreover, her perceived acceptance by whites (especially in comparison to blacks) has pulled her towards a white internalized identity.

Others similarly feel that their black identities are challenged by black women. As described earlier, Olivia described how black women challenged her identity by asking her, "What are you? You're not black. So what are you?" Further noting challenges to her black identity by black women, she later adds:

> I think when I was growing up, [black girls] just did not accept me as being a black girl. When [black] men ask me the question, "What are you?" it's just curiosity. But with [black] women, I still think there are some instances where they don't see me as an authentic black woman, because they'll make a comment about how something was so hard for them, like getting a job or whatever. And I'll say, "Oh, yeah, it's not that way" and they'll say, "Oh, it's different for you."

Black women question Olivia's experiences with discrimination because of her white phenotypic characteristics, and in doing so question her authenticity as a black woman. Margaret Hunter (2005), in her study of skin color stratification among both African American and Mexican American women, finds that while lighter-skinned women benefit in the dating and marriage markets because they are perceived as beautiful (by both women and men alike), their light skin has its costs—namely, their authenticity as a legitimate member of the ethnic/racial community is frequently called into question. For black women in her study, "authenticity was the vehicle through which darker-skinned women took back their power from lighter-skinned women . . . one of the most common ways they regained their power, and felt better about themselves, was to accuse light-skinned black women of not being black enough. This tactic has particular power against those lighter-skinned women who are from racially mixed backgrounds" (95). Hunter (2005) argues that it is a "serious insult" to multiracial women, but I argue that the cost is much heavier: challenges to their authenticity as black women, for some, come at the cost of their black identities. Even today, Olivia perceives that her authenticity as a black woman is continually challenged, and she argues that as a result she identifies less strongly as black today than she did when she was younger. These cumulative experiences with black girls and black women have pushed her from her once-strong black identity.

Allison, who labels herself as mixed and internally identifies strongly as white, describes how her interactions with black women have similarly pushed her away from a black identity. When asked whether she has experienced any negative treatment from black people, she says:

Yeah. Especially—mainly the girls. I mean, I don't want to sound conceited or anything, but I almost feel like they're jealous of me because I don't have to deal with the full-on [phenotypic] stereotype of a black person. And so in that sense I feel like they're almost just hostile towards me because I have more white features than I do black features. . . . You know, like sometimes they'll just look at you, like this evil look like I just murdered somebody, and I'm just minding my business shopping in a store. Like today, I went to [this store] to look around, and there was a bunch of black women there. As soon as I walked in, they stopped talking and they just stared me down like I just killed somebody . . . like just looking at me in a negative way and it's, like, I didn't even do anything. I'm like, "I just walked into this store to look around."

When further asked how these "hostile" experiences have influenced her racial identity, she responds:

It keeps me from wanting to identify with being black because all the black encounters that I've had—they've all been negative. So, I'm like, "Well, why would I want to identify myself with that?" You know? Like, everybody's just going to treat me negatively when I'm trying to be nice or just minding my own business. . . . And, like, the white women, they always stop me and they're like, "Oh, you're so beautiful" and things like that. . . . The white people are always like, "You're really pretty and you have a really pretty name" and the black people, they just stare at me and give me these nasty looks. [*NK: Black women and black men?*] Just the black women.

Though respondents in this study often describe feeling rejected by whites, Allison describes mostly positive experiences with whites (this likely has something to do with her near-white phenotypic appearance). In her case, positive interactions with white women pull her towards a white internalized identity, while negative interactions with black women push her away from identifying as black.

While negative experiences with black women push some biracial women away from identifying as black, others actively work to negotiate their black identities in the face of blatant identity challenges. Natasha, who labels herself as black and who internally identifies strongly as black, notes that her black identity is frequently questioned by black women. When describing her current experiences with black women at the HBCU she attends, she says:

> For some [black] people, [a biracial background] is a strike against you. Actually, just the other day, I overheard some girls talking about a girl who was biracial, and they were not saying the nicest things. . . . I guess with girls, I can't escape [my white] side. It's constantly being brought up . . . they always seem to make sure to tell me I'm not really black. If I would tell someone I'm black, they would say, "No, you're mixed." . . . I would prefer to be black. I don't like being mixed. . . . I would say from junior year of high school, I woke up every single morning thinking, "I'm black," living my life like I'm black and everything, but when people are always reminding you you're mixed. . . . trying to discredit you, it's hard.

Although she is repeatedly reminded by black women that she is "not really black," Natasha works to negotiate her black identity in those situations where she finds it challenged. She performs *identity work* (see Snow and Anderson 1987, 1993) to emphasize her black identity to others. *Identity work* refers to the strategies these respondents use to highlight, downplay, or conceal particular racial identities with others. In Natasha's case, she highlights black cultural symbols as a way to counter challenges to her black identity (e.g., she wears her hair in cornrows or an Afro, she listens only to "black music," and she wears "urban" clothing).

Additionally, Michelle, who describes herself as looking white, discusses how black women have called attention to her physical appearance to question her blackness and authenticity as a black woman. When asked to give an example, she reflects on an experience in college:

> I remember going to a freshman dance given by the Black Affairs Council. I went with a couple of my friends, and we went in and had a good ol' time, but I remember the president of the Council . . . who is a dark-skinned [black] woman . . . I remember her saying, "You're not black. You're Hispanic. There's

no way that you're black. You can't be black because your hair is not nappy" or whatever. And I was like, "A lot of black people don't have nappy hair 'cause they put chemicals on them." And she was like, "Well, you have the good hair. You're not black." She kept telling me I wasn't black. I cussed her out. And it made me question a lot. It made me feel alienated. Really, actually, it just made me feel bad because I can't help the way my hair looks.

Being repeatedly told "You're not black" directly challenges Michelle's black internalized identity. Black women point out and draw attention to her physical differences (e.g., her straight hair, light skin), often in negative and hostile ways, which often makes her feel "alienated." Michelle admits that these comments often make her question herself (and her black identity). However, unlike those who are pushed away from their black identities (to identify as biracial or white), she holds strong to her black identity. Instead of shaping a non-black identity, these challenges become sites of negotiation and opportunities to perform identity work. To signal her black identity to others, Michelle dated only black men in college, wore her hair in cornrows, and altered her speech (i.e., used slang). (Strategies of identity work and the ways in which individuals negotiate their racial identities will be further explored in chapter 6).

Olivia, too, describes how black girls did not accept her as a "black girl" when she was growing up. Reflecting on her childhood and adolescent years, she talks about the frustration she felt when black girls called her "white" or "white girl":

They said stuff like, "I thought you were a white girl standing there," stuff like that. They didn't think I was a white girl standing there, they're just saying that. They used to call me "white girl" because my hair was very long, and it would blow in the wind and all that kind of stuff. And they'd say, "She has white-girl hair" or, "She thinks she's white," you know, that kind of stuff.

Instead of being pushed away from a black identity, Olivia worked to counter these challenges to her blackness. Like other interviewees, she performed identity work to present her black identity to others: like Michelle, she used slang when around her black peers, and she managed her hair so as to "blend in" better with black girls (in particular, she tied her long hair back so as not to draw attention to it). Over the years, however, she admits that these cumulative experiences have nonetheless weakened her black identity.

DISCUSSION AND CONCLUSION

Day-to-day interactions with others, and the perceptions of those experiences, can have a profound influence on one's racial identification. Building on Rockquemore and Brunsma's (2002a) concepts of "push" and "pull" factors, I find that the positive and negative interactions respondents had with blacks and whites pushed and pulled them towards various racial identities. For the most part, biracial respondents in this sample describe feeling rejected by whites and embraced by blacks. This is not to say that *all* whites rejected them or that *all* blacks embraced them: often their experiences of rejection or acceptance depended upon their phenotypes and how closely they physically resembled stereotypical black or white appearances. In terms of broad trends within this sample, however, most respondents perceived a general acceptance by blacks and a general rejection by whites, which I argue can be traced back to the one drop rule, to their physical appearances, and to the fact that they were frequently raced as black.

In interactions with whites, biracial people were frequently perceived as black, and they often faced the same discriminatory treatment and social exclusion that their black counterparts arguably experience in similar circumstances. Interestingly, social exclusion appeared more pronounced for women than men in this study within the context of dating in adolescence and young adulthood. While biracial men in this study described feeling desired by white female peers in dating relationships, biracial women told a markedly different story. White males, they argued, ignored and overlooked them as potential romantic partners, leaving those who grew up in predominantly white communities feeling unattractive and socially isolated. This parallels findings by Beverly Tatum (1997), who argues, "Biracial girls are often considered beautiful objects of curiosity because of their 'exotic' looks, but this attention does not necessarily translate into dating partners. Like monoracial Black girls in White communities, biracial girls in White communities often become more socially isolated in adolescence" (183–84). As a consequence, for some biracial women, rejection from white males only further reinforced their differences—both physical and racial—and pushed them, especially those who grew up in predominantly white communities, away from white identities.

In contrast, biracial people in this study described feeling generally accepted by black people despite their biracial backgrounds and white phenotypic characteristics. They frequently referenced the one drop rule (or found it cited by others) to explain this acceptance, and as it does with reflected appraisals, I find that the one drop rule still persists in shaping black identities even today. Respondents commented, "If you're just a little black, then you're considered black" (Michelle, this chapter) and "If you've got a little (black) in you, it's all you" (Monique, chapter 3), illustrating the ways in which blacks sent the message, "Hey, you're one of us." Further, some respondents noted that they were easily accepted by blacks largely because the black community itself varied widely in physical appearance; thus, despite their white phenotypic characteristics, they did not differ significantly from many of those classified as black, and it was not hard for blacks to accept them as such.

While they feel accepted by black people *on the whole*, however, this acceptance appears to be largely gendered: biracial women more often describe feeling rejected than their male peers do. Specifically, biracial women report that whereas black men seem to accept them as black, black women often directly challenge their black identities; this suggests that the source of rejection is fundamentally gendered as well. It is interesting to note that while biracial women in this study frequently felt rejected by white men as desirable partners because of their black phenotypic features, they felt desired by black men who (in their opinion) perceived them as attractive and pursued them for their white characteristics (light skin or long hair, for example). Black women, in contrast, frequently appeared resentful and jealous of the attention biracial women received from black males, and this frequently fueled tensions between the two groups.

Margaret Hunter (2005) looks at skin color stratification (otherwise known as colorism) and identifies what she calls a "beauty queue" among African Americans—"a rank ordering of women from lightest to darkest where the lightest get the most perks and rewards, dates for example, and the darkest women get the least" (69). Women with light skin and more anglicized features are racially privileged because they are considered more beautiful (based on the cultural construction of beauty in the United States) (Hunter 1998). Because beauty has become a form of social capital, especially for women, biracial women are more likely to marry the high-status husband. For women competing for the relatively small pool of marriageable black men (those who are not incarcerated, underemployed, or unemployed), this inevitably creates resentment and jealousy on the part of women who are disadvantaged in this market (i.e., those with darker skin). Biracial women in the study describe feeling resentment from black women, and indeed, Margaret Hunter (2005) finds in interviews with dark-skinned black women that they too describe feeling "hostile" and "resentful" towards light-skinned black and biracial/multiracial women for the privileges they receive (72).

Some women in Hunter's (2005) study dealt with their jealousy and resentment by ostracizing lighter-skinned women from their social circles, and I found a similar dynamic here. These biracial women often felt that black women ostracized them by directly and openly challenging their black identities, saying, "You're not really black." These challenges functioned to push some biracial women away from identifying as black. However, it must be noted that most respondents in this study (both men and women) more strongly identified as black than white due to the more general acceptance they found among blacks as compared to whites. Jon Michael Spencer (1997), in his book *The New Colored People*, helps explain this trend by focusing on children and argues, "Despite the fact that black children are sometimes cruel to mixed-race black children and the black community is sometimes tentative about mixed-race adults and interracial marriages, there is a measure of acceptance in the black community that is rarely matched by the whites" (55). Thus, while some biracial women are pushed away from identifying as black by black women who challenge their blackness, most biracials (men and women) more strongly identify as black because, for the most part, they feel more accepted by the black community than anywhere else.

Thus far, I have examined reflected appraisals and how biracials' day-to-day interactional experiences with whites and blacks shape their racial identities. The next chapter further explores identity processes, looking at an underlying social psychological process that has previously gone unexplored with regard to racial identity—namely, social comparisons. Put simply, biracial respondents in this study frequently compare themselves to others (black, white, and biracial others, both real and imagined) on several dimensions to form their identities and to gauge where they "belong" racially. I look at how their social comparisons with others shape their internalized racial identities, and the role that the racial composition of their social networks plays in this process.

NOTES

1. Some excerpts from this chapter appeared in 2010 in *Sociological Spectrum* 30: 639–670 ("Black Is, Black Ain't: Biracials, Middle-Class Blacks, and the Social Construction of Blackness").

2. This is not to say, however, that biracial men did not face problems dating white peers. Indeed, two biracial male respondents claim that while they had little difficulty obtaining dates with white female peers, they sometimes faced resistance and rejection from the girls' parents.

5

"I'm Not Like Them at All"

Social Comparisons and Social Networks

According to social psychologist Leon Festinger (1954), "There exists, in the human organism, a drive to evaluate his opinions and his abilities" (117), in order to satisfy a basic motive for self-evaluation. To satisfy this desire, people draw on *social comparisons* with others. Joanne Wood (1996) defines social comparisons as "the process of thinking about information about one or more other people in relation to the self" (520–21), and according to social comparison theory, people learn about and assess themselves through comparisons with other people. While Festinger's (1954) original theory focuses on comparisons regarding one's opinions and abilities, Jerry Suls and Ladd Wheeler (2000) broaden the theory's realm to include opinions, abilities, emotions, personality traits, and self-concept, and they argue that "anything that can be compared is in the theory's realm" (7).

In this chapter, I draw on social comparison theory to better understand racial identity formation among biracial people. How they identify themselves is, in part, related to the social comparisons they make with monoracial and biracial/multiracial others on a variety of dimensions. The social comparison tradition and symbolic interactionism (from which the concept of reflected appraisals is derived) come from different roots: social comparisons are rooted in psychology, while symbolic interactionism is rooted in sociology. They do not, however, contradict each other. In fact, both are important in the development of the self, and they can be viewed as complementary. While much of the research on biracial people draws on the symbolic interactionist frame (as explained in chapter 3), none draws on social comparisons. Yet social comparison with others is arguably another fundamental process underlying identity development.

I begin the chapter by discussing the role of social comparisons in shaping racial identity. Fundamental questions facing black-white biracial people such as "Who am I racially?" may be answered by comparing themselves to black, white, and other black-white biracial people on several dimensions, including (1) phenotype (i.e., how they look); (2) culture (e.g., how they dress, what they eat, how they speak); and (3) experiences of privilege, prejudice, and discrimination. While social comparisons influence racial identity in general, I also illustrate the contextual nature of social comparisons and their impact on situational identities. Certain racial identities may become more salient in a given context due to the immediate comparisons biracial people make with others in that situation.

After describing the different dimensions of social comparisons and their influence on racial identity, I then examine how social networks—namely, the *racial composition* of one's networks—shape social comparison processes (and hence, identity). Little work on social comparisons takes social networks into account, yet sociologist C. David Gartrell (2002) suggests that comparisons are "embedded" in social networks as people compare themselves to peers, friends, parents, siblings, extended family members, coworkers, and others *in their networks*. Specifically, Gartrell (1987) theorizes that networks impose limits on social comparisons in that they constrain one's choice of referents (i.e., those people readily available for social comparison).

Moreover, scholars working in the areas of biracial and multiracial identity note the importance of the racial composition of an individual's social networks in shaping identity (for examples, see Hall 1980; Harris and Sim 2002; Herman 2004; Holloway et al. 2009; Masuoka 2011; Rockquemore 1999; Rockquemore and Brunsma 2002a, 2002b; Root 1990; Saenz, Hwang, and Anderson 1995; Twine 1996b; Xie and Goyette 1997). In particular, studies show that white-minority multiracial people in minority contexts (e.g., friendship networks, schools, neighborhoods) are more likely to identify with their minority race, whereas those in whiter contexts are more likely to identify as multiracial, biracial, or white (see Brunsma's 2005 discussion). These studies reveal patterns regarding how network composition affects racial identities, yet few studies examine the underlying processes by which this occurs. Those that do find that networks influence identity in at least two ways. First, social networks partly determine what opportunities are available for cultural exposure, which in turn, affects racial identity (see Stephan 1992). Second, interactional experiences within one's networks also influence identity. Rockquemore and Brunsma (2002a), as described in the previous chapter, described the push and pull of positive and negative experiences that occur in one's network, and the consequences for one's racial identity.

Drawing on social comparison theory and the work of Gartrell (1987, 2002), this chapter further extends what we know about networks and identity. The racial composition of their social networks (whether predominantly white, black, or racially mixed) provides both *opportunities for and limitations to* the types of social comparisons that these biracial individuals make with others. In turn, the types of comparisons that respondents employ influence their racial identities.

SOCIAL COMPARISONS AND RACIAL IDENTITY

Throughout their interviews, biracial respondents frequently made spontaneous comparisons with others to explain their racial identities. Specifically, they drew on three types of social comparisons: (1) phenotypic comparisons (they compared their looks with those of black, white, and biracial others); (2) cultural comparisons (they compared themselves to black, white, and biracial others based on perceived cultural similarities and differences); and (3) experiential comparisons (they compared their experiences of privilege, prejudice, and discrimination with those of other black, white, and biracial others).

Comparing Phenotype

The majority of respondents (31 of 40) compare themselves to black, white, and biracial people in terms of physical appearance, most often noting their differences and similarities with others with regard to their skin color and hair texture, and to a lesser extent, hair color/length, body type, and facial features (e.g., lips, nose shape, eye color). Respondents draw on comparisons with a range of people, including extended family members, siblings, and parents, to explain their internalized racial identities. Alicia, for example, who internally identifies more strongly as black than white, says:

> My [white] mom's family made me realize that I was black. Like, it's really weird going out to lunch with my extended all-white relatives and being the only black person at the table. . . . It's weird to look at people I'm related to and not see any familial connection. . . . When I'm hanging out with them I feel black, I don't feel biracial. I feel like the black person hanging out with the white family. . . . I look so different from all the people sitting with me. I mean, if we all took a picture, I would stand out. It's just the fact that I look different.

Alicia repeatedly emphasizes the differences between herself and her white extended family members in terms of physical appearance. Because of these differences, she says it made her "realize" that she was black, directly linking these physical comparisons with her black identity.

Like Alicia, Lauren, who internally identifies very strongly as black, similarly draws on social comparisons with extended family and says, "I mean, if you see me at family reunions on that [white] side of my family, I definitely stick out in the group. So I've just never really identified [as white]. I mean, I know that's part of my family, but as far as me racially, I've never identified myself that way." While she knows that she is related to her white family, she claims that she does not identify as white because physically she looks so different from them. Later in her interview, she describes herself as the "odd man out" at family reunions:

> I think in some I instances when I was younger [being with my white family members] made me acutely aware that I was different. . . . You know, because when I'd go in these situations with my [white] mom and . . . her family, I mean there was me and then there was everybody else with their blonde-haired and blue-eyed kids. And then there's me . . . it was just kind of filtered into my brain that I was different. It makes it easier for me to identify with being black. I look at [black] people [and] I'm like, "Okay, you look like me. So obviously I'm one of you if I look like you and you look like me."

She specifically points out how her eye color and hair color differ from white family members, while at the same time noting the physical similarities between herself and black people to explain her black identity.

Chris, too, draws on physical comparisons with family members, but in this case notes the distinctions between himself and his black cousins, aunt, and uncle. Chris, who more strongly identifies as white than black, says, "I remember I'd get around my [black] cousins, and my cousins were a lot darker than me. . . . I didn't really know what I was because I would look at my aunt and uncle, and they were both black . . . and I was very young when I realized that I'm not like everybody else." Recognizing the differences in their skin color, Chris realizes that he is not like his black family—at least not in terms of physical appearance.

In addition, respondents draw on physical comparisons with their siblings and parents. Lauren notes the physical differences between herself and her white family members (see above), but she also draws direct physical comparisons with her white mother to further explain her black racial identity. When asked why she identifies very little as white, she highlights the physical distinctions between herself and her mother regarding skin color, eye color, and hair texture. She says, "Probably just because of the coloration of my skin. I mean, if you see me next to my [white] mother, my mother is very pale, with blue eyes and wispy, straight hair, and I'm nothing like that at all."

Kate, who internally identifies very strongly as white, notes the physical similarities and differences she sees between herself and her (biracial) sister and (white) mother. Comparing her phenotype and hair texture, she says:

> I don't really feel like I look really black compared to black people that I know. Or even like biracial people. I don't even look anything like my [biracial] sister. She has, like, the black person hair and I have the white person hair and I look really different. . . . I would say I look more white based on some of my features, I guess. I look more like my [white] mom.

Kate draws on physical comparisons with black, white, and biracial people. She compares herself to black and biracial people in general, but also compares herself to her biracial sister and white mother more specifically to note her physical similarities and differences. Likewise, Caroline internally identifies very strongly as white, and when asked to explain her identity, she compares herself to her white mother: "Because my mom and I look so much alike. It's almost scary sometimes how similar we are. . . . We just look so much alike. It's mentioned all the time when we're together, 'Oh, my gosh, you guys look just alike.' We're very similar in the way we look." According to K. Jill Kiecolt and Anna LoMascolo (2003), physical resemblances to parents may influence ethnic/racial identity among transracial adoptees and biracial people, and Jewelle Taylor Gibbs (1987) suggests that biracial adolescents may identify more with the parent they most resemble.

Monique, who internally identifies with both racial groups (i.e., as biracial), notes similarities in her facial features with *both* parents to explain why she does not identify more strongly as black or white. She says, "I don't think I fit into one [race] or the other. I think it's mostly because of the hair. And I look so much like both my parents, too. Like, from the nose up, I look like my dad, and my nose down, my mom. It's weird . . . so I don't identify myself as one or the other."

Respondents also often draw on comparisons with friends and peers in their networks. Natasha, who internally identifies very strongly as black, discusses how comparisons with her white peers in high school influenced her racial identity:

> Physically, I was very different than [white girls]. . . . I didn't share the same clothes and, also, getting ready for the prom, I didn't go to the same hair place . . . so there was always that difference. I guess from the time I was little until about when puberty started, I thought I was white . . . and then, I guess, when my body began to change, I started developing . . . I really thought there were differences between me and my [white] friends. Like me and my friends were not going to use the same cover-up, you know? And I remember one time my friend tried to flatten my hair, and it wouldn't flatten. So that's when I started to realize that I was both black and white.

Natasha draws on physical comparisons with her high school friends, who because she grew up in a predominantly white area, were mostly white. Interestingly, she describes how her identity changed from "white" to "both black and white" as she grew up in this social setting. As she went through puberty and her body changed and developed, she began to notice physical differences between herself and her white peers regarding her body type, skin color, and hair texture, leading to a shift away from the white identity that she held in high school.

Cherise, who also grew up in a predominantly white area, similarly draws on physical comparisons with her white peers to explain her strong internalized black identity. She says, "I remember in high school, I'd be walking down the hall and be, like, 'Oh, nobody sees me as black.' I'll forget what color I am until I look down at my hands. I'm, like, 'I'm not like you or you or you' [pointing around]." Comparing herself to her white peers in her predominantly white high school, she notes the dissimilarity in skin color, which she says influenced the black identity that she holds today.

Shane, too, draws on physical comparisons with his white peers to explain his racial identity. He labels himself as mixed or biracial, and internally identifies as both black and white. When explaining why he does not exclusively identify as white, he says, "I think mainly because of my skin color. . . . I don't look white. I don't. I just don't look white and, I mean, I noticed it in my circle of friends. I have a lot of friends that are white, and I identify with them pretty well, but there's always—I think simply because of the way I look, there's always that separation."

Finally, Natalie also identifies publicly and internally as biracial. When asked why she does not identify more strongly with one race over the other, she explains:

> I could perhaps identify myself as a very light-skinned black. But I don't know, I still don't think my skin tone is quite right for light-skinned black either. But maybe my [facial] features. I think I have a fuller mouth and maybe [a] rounder nose than is directly associated with white people. . . . Looking at pictures of me and my [black] mom, we look exactly alike, so I'd say I ended up with primarily black features. But for the skin color, I think, I don't know, in the winter I don't look quite as pale as some of my other white friends. My skin, otherwise, is pretty light. So I think, you know, somewhere with that contradiction, with more black features and light skin, I think I look somewhere in between.

Her physical comparisons with her black mother and white peers regarding her skin tone and facial features tell her that she is "somewhere in between" black and white. Hence, she does not more strongly identify with one racial group over another.

Comparing Culture

Another frequent type of social comparison are cultural comparisons with white, black, and biracial people (24 of 40 respondents draw upon this social comparison). Cultural comparisons most often hinge on respondents' *perceived* differences between blacks and whites regarding dress and clothing styles, language/way of speaking, and musical styles/tastes. Cultural comparisons, although to a lesser extent, also include perceived differences in food, sports (e.g., basketball versus skiing), hair-care or hair-maintenance norms (for women in particular), and even perceived differences in values between blacks and whites (e.g., family, educational values).

Beth, for example, internally identifies very strongly as black. When asked about her black identity, she reflects on cultural comparisons she made in college with her freshman college roommate, who shared her black-white biracial background. Both biracial women were adopted, but while Beth was adopted by two black parents, her biracial roommate was adopted by two white parents. Describing this college experience as "pivotal" regarding her racial identity, she says:

> My freshman year in college, I had a roommate that was biracial. And she was adopted by a white family. And she looked more black than I did. But she was totally immersed in white culture. And I was immersed into black culture. And it was so interesting. I mean, she had really, really curly hair. And we were trying to say, "Oh, you should just put a perm in your hair. You're not going to get it straight. You don't need to put mousse in it and all that stuff." And it was so interesting. I think it was like an epiphany for me that I was really black . . . the things that she was doing were so foreign to me that I couldn't connect. . . . I think it was an eye-opening experience. We couldn't cross over into each other's worlds.

Previous research finds that people use physical cues (e.g., skin color, hair, facial features) and cultural cues (e.g., language, food) to identify others' gender and racial identities (Cahill 1989; Van Ausdale and Feagin 1996), and I find that these biracial respondents use the same types of cues to *form* their own racial identities. While Beth draws on physical comparisons (she points out that her roommate looks more black than she), her cultural comparisons form the foundation of her identity; the comparison gives her an "epiphany" that she is black. Further, she perceives a disconnect between black culture and white culture, describing them as different "worlds."

When explaining their racial identities, other respondents similarly describe a divide between black and white cultures and often describe personal experiences of "culture shock" or feelings of awkwardness with a particular racial group. Explaining why he does not strongly identify as black, Grant says, "A lot of it has to do with today's pop culture. Like when

I go and try to hang out with [black people], I feel a bit of a culture shock. The Ebonics talking, the dialect—I guess a lot of it has to do mainly with that." He describes differences in black and white culture based on ways of speaking to explain why he identifies as he does.

Kate, who labels herself as white and internally identifies strongly as such, also describes what she perceives as differences in "culture" between blacks and whites. Similarly noting differences in ways of speaking, she says:

> When I am with black people, I think I am just like this little white girl. I feel like a white person hanging out with them. . . . Like, my sister's husband is black and so with his family I just kind of sit there, and I am all quiet and I don't really get along. Not that I don't get along, just that I don't fit in, I guess. . . . I think there is some language differences, like in the way [black people] talk to each other. I don't understand it a lot of the time. Or I don't understand some of their interactions. I don't really think I could identify with being black. . . . I am just thinking of social situations . . . it will be like different music all the time, and if it's hip-hop and there's obviously a larger black crowd, I just find myself sitting in a corner, but if it's a rock band and it's mostly white people, I'm out there talking away to people. It's just different. It could be more of the culture between different groups.

Kate notes the dissimilarities between herself and black people, and as a consequence, internally identifies as white. Drawing on cultural comparisons, Kate points to differences in language, interaction patterns, and even musical tastes (hip-hop versus rock). Her essentialized notions of blackness and whiteness prevent a black identity precisely because she perceives herself as culturally different from black people. Further, she draws on a very stereotypical and one-dimensional image of black people, overlooking comparisons with black people who may interact and speak just like her.

Anthony, who internally identifies strongly as black, also remarks on what he perceives as cultural differences between blacks and whites—ways of speaking, differences in dress, and even ways of greeting each other:

> I haven't been around [whites] so much. . . . For a short time, I went to a private middle school, which was mostly white . . . and I didn't associate with them at all, and it was kind of awkward. [NK: *Why awkward?*] Just different things. Different styles of dress. Different manners of talk. For one instance, this is minimal, but when I see friends at black schools, I give them high-fives and, you know, kind of slap hands or something. At [white] schools, they shake hands. It was just kind of weird to me. Like, you know, I went like that [*puts his hand in the air to high-five*] to a white guy that I worked with and he stuck out his hand and it was kind of awkward. It just didn't fit.

Nick similarly draws on cultural comparisons:

> I think I just kind of fit in with being black. That's just like looking at the shell because of the way I dress. I don't wear a lot of the clothes that white people wear. I don't fit into khakis very well, and mostly because of my body type, I have to get oversized clothing in order to fit my legs. . . . I tend to dress with a baggy feel. . . . Also, my music interest is more like the old R&B, like Motown. . . . I think not very many white people like that kind of music. I don't listen to a whole lot of rock and roll. I don't have a truck. That kind of rules out that I'm white.

He highlights his similarities with blacks and differences with whites to explain his internalized black identity, pointing to his style of dress, musical interests, and even the car he drives. The cultural similarities he shares with black people and his cultural differences with whites, according to Nick, "rule out" a white identity.

Like Nick, who draws on various aspects of white and black cultures to differentiate himself from whites, Kate points to perceived cultural differences between blacks and whites to differentiate herself from blacks. To further explain her strong internalized white identity, she points out cultural differences in food:

> I definitely don't feel that I identify with being black at all. I mean, even the food we ate. When I go to my brother-in-law's house—and he is black and his whole family—they eat an entirely different menu than we do. I mean, they just have, like, the collard greens and, like, fried chicken, and all of these vegetables, like okra and things like that. I grew up eating stir-fry and grilled chicken. . . . My parents are very healthy people, so we ate all that organic stuff. . . . I would say we were very white, I guess.

While respondents draw on a variety of cultural aspects of race, Kate draws on food for social comparison to explain why she does not "identify with being black at all." Interestingly, she perceives a link between food and race, highlighting the cultural differences in food and eating between blacks and whites. Kate contrasts her family's diet to that of her black in-laws in order to differentiate her family from black families. While she comes from a multiracial family with a black father, she perceives her family as white in comparison with other black families, and hence, perceives herself as white.

Furthermore, the cultural characteristics that Kate attributes to race are arguably linked to social class (e.g., black families eat fried chicken, while white families eat stir-fry and organic food).[1] Cultural differences may indeed exist between blacks and whites regarding food preferences and preparation, yet some of the differences Kate describes likely also reveal the underlying influence of social class. Studies show that income directly affects food consumption (Cockerham 2007); put simply, foods that are expensive (e.g., organic food) are more available to wealthier families. While consumption of organic food is racialized here as "white," eating organic food may have more to do with social class than race. For instance, lower-class and working-class people of all races may be less likely to eat organic food than their middle-class counterparts because of cost.

Respondents also draw upon cultural comparisons regarding values of family and education (e.g., black people care more about family; white people value education), and often social class also seeps into the contrasts they draw. Nicole, who internally identifies more strongly as white than black, points to differences she perceives in upbringing to explain her identity:

> I think as I look at how I was brought up, I was brought up with more white American values. . . . I wasn't brought up doing things that [black] children or teenagers normally did, like join the Jack and Jill Club or whatever it is. I mean, I wasn't brought up like that. [*NK: When you say white values, what are you referring to?*] Probably education. You know, wanting to go as far as I can academically. You know, going to museums. I don't know if that's white, but I don't think it's very typical [of black people]. I may be wrong, but I don't associate that with black people.

Here Nicole draws on several cultural comparisons based on her perceptions of blacks and whites: black people join the Jack and Jill Club[2] (while whites do not), white people go to museums (while blacks do not), and most relevant here, white people value education (while blacks do not). Like Kate's linking of race and class with regard to food, there is some confounding of race and class in Nicole's perception of cultural differences between blacks and whites. Nicole links museum-going with whiteness, yet social class may be a better predictor of museum-going than race. The middle and upper classes arguably have more leisure time and disposable income to enjoy what others might perceive as a luxury. Lower-class blacks (and lower-class whites) may, in fact, be less likely to go to a museum (or ballet, opera, or play, for that matter), but these activities may be more available to middle-class black Americans who have comparatively more money and time. Nicole, however, overlooks that her experiences growing up may look similar, not only to middle-class whites, but also to middle-class blacks.

Finally, Kim draws on cultural comparisons between blacks and whites to explain her internalized biracial identity. Pointing to differences in terms of dress, sports, and academics, she says:

> I wish I had been able to identify more with the black people at my school and been better friends [with them], but I wasn't going to force it, force myself to be somebody I wasn't. [*NK: Why do you think you couldn't identify with them?*] Just dressing, like I liked to dress like my white friends, like the GAP and Abercrombie and things like that. My parents were really involved in the school, and most of the black kids' parents weren't. Academics were important to me,

and that wasn't necessarily true of all the black kids . . . but [it was for] all my white girlfriends. . . . I swam group swimming and played tennis. Those are not sports typically that black people participate in and I had a lot of [white] friends do swimming and tennis.

Kim links whiteness with academic achievement and parental involvement in their children's education. Framing these differences as cultural, Kim also overlooks how social class may play into them. Parents of lower-class students, for instance, may work multiple jobs and hence have less time to become involved in their child's school activities (e.g., attending PTA meetings or other school events). While lower-class black parents may be limited in their involvement in their children's schools and academics, studies show that black middle-class parents tend to be very involved (Harris 2004; Lareau 2003).

Kim also races tennis and swimming as "white," yet research suggests that different rates of participation in certain sports are class-based. Some sports require more money and leisure time, and the upper classes have more of both (Coakley 1998; Nixon and Frey 1996). Sociologist Jay Coakley (1998) argues that "historical circumstances combined with economic inequality have given rise to connections between certain sports and the lifestyles of people with differing amounts of wealth and power. . . . Sports sponsored by private clubs and sports that require expensive equipment and facilities gradually become parts of the lifestyles of the well-to-do" (277). In contrast, sports that do not require expensive equipment or facilities often become part of the lifestyles of the lower classes. Michael Collins (2003) notes that one issue often studied with regard to sport in the United States is the overrepresentation of black Americans in some sports (e.g., football, basketball), and their underrepresentation in others (e.g., tennis, swimming). Arguably, tennis and swimming require expensive facilities and are as a consequence more accessible to the middle and upper classes. Kim, for instance, describes tennis courts and a swimming pool as being part of the neighborhood where she grew up. These neighborhood amenities are, no doubt, less available to children from poorer classes.

Comparing Experiences

A third type of social comparison is experiential. In particular, respondents compare their experiences of privilege, prejudice, and discrimination with black, white, and biracial others. This type of comparison was less frequent (made by 8 of 40 respondents), yet was integral for some in terms of their identity formation. Biracial respondents compare themselves to whites with regard to their experiences of privilege, or compare themselves to blacks with regard to their experiences of prejudice and discrimination.

When explaining his strong black internalized identity, Michael draws on experiential comparisons with black people. Describing a critical experience in college regarding the formation of his black identity, he says:

> My sophomore year, I was arrested on campus and I had to go through the legal system, and I think it jumped out at me about what it meant to be an African American man and be going through the legal system. . . . And when I was in jail, all I saw was people who looked like me, who were black. I don't know, I think I'm a good person with good moral character and good moral standing, but when you go to jail, you become like everyone else. There's nothing really differentiating you. . . . Like, no matter where you came from, what you look like, or what your background is, you're all the same, [the officials] treat you the same, very minimal respect.

Michael realizes that despite his biracial background and arguably light skin, in the eyes of others, he is black and merits the same treatment as other black men in the same situation: "very minimal respect."

Kendra, who internally identifies more strongly as black than white, notes a similar experience of realization:

> Once I was getting pulled over by a white police officer. And I was with a bunch of my [black] class friends and I realized like, "Oh shit, I'm, like, no different to this police officer than the other black kids." I can't be like, "Excuse me, officer, I'm half-white so let's be cool okay?" . . . I felt very black. I felt like in that powerless sense was something that the white person side of me wouldn't experience. But it's a reality of being black.

This experience shows Kendra that she is experiencing the world (and in this example, treatment by police) like her black peers—at least from her own perspective.

Likewise, Michelle's social comparisons with black people convey her similar experiences of prejudice and discrimination. Michelle internally identifies strongly as black and says, "I have a lot of the same issues [as black people] as far as job-wise. . . . Not moving up and not being taken seriously and not being trusted or seem as I don't work as well as my white counterpart. My white counterpart will get the job or get the specific thing, you know . . . that's been my experience." Even though Michelle admits she outwardly appears white, she feels that common experiences of discrimination with black people partially explain her internalized black identity.

Whereas Michael, Kendra, and Michelle describe experiences in common with other black people, John notes the distinctions. Describing himself as looking like a "regular white guy," he says:

> I would feel very uncomfortable identifying solely as a black person. Like, I have friends who are the same mix as me, they identify as black people. They

look a lot more black than they do white. They look very light skinned. I don't think it's wrong for them [to identify as black], because that's how the world sees them, and when a person passes them on the street, they don't see a white person or a biracial person. They think of them as a black person. It seems like they've had different experiences. They have the same blood as I do, but a different set of experiences. People on the street look at them in a different way than me.

Here, John draws on phenotypic comparisons with his biracial friends (he believes they look more black than he does), but more importantly, he notes differences in their experiences based on how they are perceived by others (they are perceived as black, while he is perceived as white). When comparing himself to his wife, who is black, he later adds, "My experiences have been lacking a huge piece of the normal black experience, which is having the outside world treat me as black. The outside world has always treated me as white." Thus, he points out that he has more experiences in common with whites than blacks to explain why he would feel "uncomfortable" identifying as black (at least publicly).

Having described the different dimensions of social comparison for racial identity, I now turn to examining the contextual nature of social comparisons and implications for situational identity.

Comparisons in Context

While social comparisons with black, white, and biracial others influence one's overall racial identity, I also find that social comparisons can shape situational identities. In other words, one may internally identify as black, white, or biracial, but immediate comparisons in a given context may also influence one's internalized racial identity in a particular situation. Occasionally, respondents described how they felt "more black" or "more white," depending upon the situation and the social comparisons they made in that particular context.

Natasha, for example, labels herself as black and internally identifies very strongly as such, but notes that she occasionally feels "more white" when she is around black people because her physical differences are highlighted in these contexts. In particular, differences in her hair, facial, and bodily features become more salient in the context of her predominantly black college:

When I'm around other black people, it's obvious that I'm not 100 percent Jamaican or Haitian or anything like that. I know I don't look completely black. And also because I have . . . red hair and I have freckles . . . I don't know many black people with freckles. There's non-stereotypical black characteristics that I have. And I don't fill out a pair of jeans. Not that *every* black girl does, but you know. I'm kind of like the white girl here [at this HBCU].

When she is around her black peers, her physical distinctions become more obvious, which lend to a situational shift in her racial identity. For the most part, she strongly identifies as black, but in this context, she feels like a "white girl."

Later in her interview, Natasha again points out that while she generally identifies as black (both publicly and internally), she has not *always* felt black. When asked to give an example, she describes her first contact with other black students her age. She was raised by two white parents, grew up in a predominantly white community, attended predominantly white schools, and had mostly white friends and peers. Reflecting on one of her first experiences interacting with black peers, she says:

> In junior year of high school, I went to . . . a leadership development conference, and I'd been to leadership conferences and other conferences before, however, this one was only for youths of color, and the majority of youths were black. So this was the first time I ever interacted with black people my age. And I remember I walked in and I had on dark maroon sandals. I had this little pink-and-white flowered sundress, a jean jacket, and I wore my hair natural. But I didn't know how to properly comb it or take care of it or anything. So I had like a distorted 'fro. And I walked in and I got scared. I felt like a white person walking into a room with all black people. . . . I mean, I looked like I just walked out of the GAP.

While social comparisons may influence identity in broad terms, Natasha's experience illustrates that social comparisons may also influence identity in situational, fleeting, and momentary ways. Despite the fact that Natasha strongly identifies as black, she "felt like a white person" based on the immediate cultural comparisons (e.g., hairstyle and clothing) with black peers in this situational context.

A final example is Monique, who both publicly and internally identifies as biracial. She describes a situation in which she felt her black identity became more intensified because of experiential comparisons:

> I've never been in a situation where I've been with a group of white people who have been talking about black people, except for one time. And I totally called this person out on that because he didn't know [my racial background]. It was a bunch of friends, and we were hanging out, having a little house party, and this guy—he started talking about the n-word this and the n-word that and I turned around and was like, "You really need to be careful about what you say and who you say it in front of because you just don't know." And he was shocked. . . . At that moment, I suddenly had an experience that people in my family who are black have experienced for most their lives. In that situation, I felt black.

Drawing on social comparisons with black family members regarding experiences of prejudice, Monique more strongly identifies as black in this context. Like other biracial respondents who outwardly appear white, Monique experiences a situation in which a stranger unaware of her black ancestry openly expresses racial prejudice towards black people. While her white outward appearance often prevents her from identifying with black people, the effect of prejudice *in this situation*, momentarily intensifies her black identity.

SOCIAL NETWORKS, SOCIAL COMPARISONS, AND RACIAL IDENTITY

Now that I have described the various dimensions of social comparison (phenotypic, cultural, and experiential) and their impact on racial identity, both broadly and situationally, I now turn to describing the link between social networks, social comparisons, and racial identity. As described earlier, few scholars have examined the link between social networks and social comparisons, with the exception of C. David Gartrell (1987), who suggests that our social networks limit our referents (i.e., who we have to compare ourselves to). Indeed, I find that these biracial individuals' choices of referents are limited by the racial composition of their social networks. Biracial individuals embedded in racially diverse networks with significant representation of both blacks and whites tend to have numerous references (both black and white) readily available for social comparison (e.g., peers, friends, coworkers, neighbors). In contrast, those embedded in one-sided networks, either in predominantly white networks or predominantly black networks, are comparatively more limited in their choice of referents. For instance, those in predominantly white networks have many readily available white referents, but often have limited black referents with which to compare themselves.

Further, social comparisons often involve comparisons with real people in one's networks, yet a relatively recent development in social comparison theory has been the differentiation between two types of comparisons: *realistic* and *constructive*. Social comparison theorists claim that self-evaluation through social comparisons "can actually take place without any real social comparison information. Rather than dealing with actual comparison data, people might simply imagine or make up information about what others are like" (Goethals and Klein 2000: 31). Thus, in addition to drawing on real comparison information, they may also construct information about others.

Goethals, Messick, and Allison (1991) define realistic social comparisons as self-evaluations based on "actual information about social reality" (154). Here, people compare themselves to real others (e.g., family members, friends, peers, coworkers). In contrast, constructive social comparisons are self-evaluations based on "'in-the-head" social comparisons regarding social reality (154). People may ignore social reality and instead fabricate, make up, manufacture, and construct persons for comparison. Although *both* realistic and constructive comparisons are socially constructed, the key distinction between the two types is that realistic comparisons involve comparisons with actual others, whereas constructive comparisons arise from imagined others. When do people rely on constructive rather than realistic comparisons? According to Goethals and Klein (2000), people may rely on constructive comparisons for many reasons, but most notable here, they may do so when they do not have the comparison data that they need—in other words, when a direct social comparison is unavailable. In the case of black-white biracial people, they may rely on constructed comparisons when real (black or white) referents are underrepresented in their social networks, and hence, when real referents are unavailable for direct comparison.

Upon analyzing the interview data, I discover an interesting relationship between network type (mixed or one-sided) and comparison type (realistic or constructive). Individuals in mixed and one-sided networks draw on realistic comparisons about equally, yet those in one-sided networks are much more likely also to draw on constructive comparisons. This is likely because some racial groups are underrepresented in their social networks. Hence, rather than compare themselves to real others of a particular racial group, they instead compare themselves to a constructed image of the group. The differential use of constructive comparisons between those in one-sided versus racially mixed social networks has implications for how biracial people identify racially.

Realistic Comparisons

Regardless of the type of network in which they are embedded, the majority of biracial respondents, at some point in their interviews, draw on realistic comparisons with black, white, and biracial others in their networks (parents, siblings, extended family members, friends, peers, and coworkers). Most often, these realistic comparisons are phenotypic (e.g., they compare their skin color and hair type with those of real others in their networks), and to a lesser extent, cultural or experiential. I find that even those in one-sided networks, who arguably have limited contact with a racial group, have opportunities for "realistic" social comparisons with members of both racial groups. Because of their multiracial family backgrounds, most respondents have at least *some* contact with members of the other racial group. For instance, a biracial woman embedded in a predominantly black social network may have limited contact with whites, yet compares herself with her white mother or white extended family members. For examples of realistic comparisons, see earlier comments by Alicia, Lauren,

Monique, Natasha, Cherise, Beth, and John (respondents in mixed-race networks) and comments by Kate, Caroline, and Anthony (respondents in one-sided networks).

Constructive Comparisons

In contrast, I find striking differences between network types regarding constructive comparisons. Those in one-sided racial networks are much more likely than those in racially mixed networks to draw on constructive comparisons. They often construct referents of the racial group less represented in their social networks, whether white or black, because they have little direct contact with members of that group and, hence, limited information about them.

Further, I find that these constructions tend to be stereotypical and, for some racial groups more than others, negative and unflattering. In particular, I find that the stereotypes frequently reflect *cultural stereotypes* regarding blacks and whites in American society (e.g., how members of a racial group speak, dress, act). Thus, realistic comparisons, which are found in both racially mixed and one-sided social networks, tend to be phenotypic (and less commonly cultural or experiential), but constructive comparisons, which are more often found in one-sided networks, are most often cultural and reflective of negative racial stereotypes.

Moreover, while stereotypes may be applied to both whites and blacks, *negative* stereotypes may especially pertain to minority groups. Indeed, I find that respondents in this study more frequently invoke negative stereotypes of blacks than whites. The greater prevalence of black stereotypes is likely due to the fact that black Americans have been historically oppressed and negatively stereotyped by the dominant white group. In a white-dominated society, negative stereotypes are arguably more abundant for minorities. Thus, while some respondents in predominantly black networks identify as black to distance themselves from negative white stereotypes, more frequently those in white networks identify as white or biracial[3] to distinguish themselves from negative black stereotypes commonly found in white-dominated American society.[4]

As described earlier, those in mixed-racial networks tend to make realistic comparisons with others, while those in one-sided black or white networks use *both* realistic and constructive comparisons. Interestingly, I find that respondents in one-sided networks regularly draw on their real referents when constructing comparisons, albeit in different ways. In particular, I find two patterns regarding the use of real referents in one-sided social networks: (1) respondents either generalize information from their few real referents to *all* black people or *all* white people to construct a stereotype for comparison; or (2) they construct an image of a group (based on negative racial stereotypes) and discount their few real referents as "exceptions to the rule." In both scenarios, respondents contrast and differentiate themselves from the stereotypical (and often negative) image they construct of the racial group. Hence, they identify in the "opposite" direction.

First, if only a few real referents of a racial group are available in one's social networks, these few referents can become representatives of the entire racial group. Biracial respondents in predominantly white networks, for example, may have a black friend or black parent who is readily available for social comparison, and they generalize information from this real referent to *all* black people. Thus, they use their few real referents to construct comparisons with black people in general.

Caroline, who internally identifies very strongly as white, describes growing up in a predominantly white neighborhood and attending a predominantly white church and schools. Her contact with black people is limited to her black father and his black children from a previous marriage. When explaining her strong white internalized identity, she draws on social comparisons with the few real black referents she has: her black half-sisters. She generalizes the information she has about her black half-sisters to *all* black people:

> My [black] half-sisters, they are older. . . . One of them used to call my sister and I awful names like "mixed bitches" . . . they irritate me. I think that's where I get a lot of my stereotypes from. I didn't want to be like them at all. *At all.* I didn't think their personal hygiene was up to our standards, because there's a big difference between personal hygiene in most black people and most white people. A lot of black people, in general, just think, "Oh, I don't have to shower every day. I don't have to wash my hair every day." . . . I always grew up very hygienic and that sort of thing. Like, "Yes, you do wash your hair every day. You do need to take a shower every day." You know, there are basic things. I'm not like them at all.

Admitting that her half-sisters provide her with many of the stereotypes she holds about black people, Caroline contrasts herself with black people based on her self-created stereotypes of black people (e.g., black people are unhygienic). Caroline, who has had limited contact with black people, differentiates herself from this negative black image, and as a consequence, she identifies as white.

Another example is Isabel who, like Caroline, grew up in a predominantly white community. She describes her contact with other black people as limited, with the exception of black relatives in another state. Because of the geographic distance and an ongoing family rift, however, this contact is limited. Isabel internally identifies more strongly as white than black and when explaining this identity, she contrasts herself with her extended black family:

Just sometimes when I go down to Florida, I just don't really fit in. . . . My [black] family is so different. My family down there is crazy. I have so many cousins. There are so many children that don't know who their kids' parents are. It's just crazy down there. . . . I would say that a lot of black people are raised like my cousins—tons of kids, not too high of an educational level. . . . I started to identify myself more as white just because I'm so different.

Isabel generalizes information about her few real black referents (her extended family members) to *all* black people. Thus, both Caroline and Isabel use their realistic comparisons with family members to construct their stereotypes of black people, then differentiate themselves from these images to explain their white identities.

Allison also grew up in a predominantly white environment. She was raised in a predominantly white community, attended predominantly white schools, and was raised solely by her white mother. She describes her middle school as mostly white, and her high school as having only a "handful" of black kids, with whom she had limited contact. While she labels herself as mixed, she internally identifies very strongly as white. To explain her strong white identity, she says:

When I've had conversations with [black] people because, like, you know, I don't want to sound racist towards a group because I'm not. I'm not racist. But I've found that when I talk to black people . . . they just look at me like I'm stupid because I'm not talking in like slang or anything like that . . . I just think they sound ridiculous because I just feel like, "How are you supposed to become a respected intellectual when you can't talk to somebody or always using the F-word and things like that?"

To further explain her white identity, she later adds ". . . the way, I guess, black people talk, because they do talk differently. They talk slang . . . what I've noticed in my experience is they don't use proper English. They don't do it." Thus, while she admits that she has had little contact with black people, she draws on her limited experiences with black peers and contrasts herself to a stereotype created from those interactions. Drawing on these cultural comparisons (regarding negative stereotypes of language and way of speaking), she then differentiates herself from black people.

A second (and more common) trend in the data among those who grew up in one-sided racial networks is to draw on negative racial stereotypes but discount the few real referents they know (people who may defy these stereotypes) as "exceptions to the rule." Psychologists Susan Fiske and Shelley Taylor (1991) argue that stereotypes are difficult to change, and people are often resistant to information that may disconfirm their stereotypes. Rather than generalize their stereotype-disconfirming experiences from one person to the entire racial group, they may instead ignore what they perceive as an exception. Because they discount real referents who defy the stereotype, their negative stereotype (of blacks or of whites) remains intact. Thus, respondents compare themselves not to the real people they know in their networks, but rather to a constructed (and negative) image of the group.

Kate, who internally identifies very strongly as white (and the only respondent to publicly identify as such), grew up in a predominantly white small town and community. She describes having attended predominantly white schools with few black students, and having limited contact with black people even as an adult. When explaining why she does not identify as black, she invokes cultural comparisons with black people based on racial stereotypes:

> If I'm not being politically correct and I'm just like, "Hey, this is what I think"—honestly, I think of my [white] boyfriend's neighborhood, of where he lives . . . it's just, I don't know, I think of that African American English and very hip-hop culture. Usually, like, lower class, but then again I know black people who aren't any of those stereotypes . . . one of my favorite professors. She is black and her [black] husband is a physician, but I wouldn't think of that first. I really don't identify with being black because I'm not into the, like, hip-hop culture and the bling-bling with the jerseys.

Kate draws on several cultural stereotypes regarding black people (e.g., they speak Ebonics, they like hip-hop, they are lower class). Even more interesting, she discounts her few real referents (e.g., her black professor and her professor's black husband) as exceptions to the stereotype, and instead draws on her constructed stereotype for comparison with black people to explain her white identity. Later in her interview, she adds: "I guess I don't know any black people that grew up in the same environment and culture that I did. . . . So I think that might be why I don't feel like I associate with being black—besides, like, my [black] dad in my family, but he's different." Instead of drawing on her black father as a real referent for social comparison, she excludes him (like her professor and the professor's husband) as an exception.

Similarly, other respondents describe how their black or white parents are "different" from (their stereotypical image of) black or white people. Michael describes differences between his white father and other white people, saying:

> So, a lot of my friends say my father's not white. He's not. He's not a white guy because he's been around African American culture so much. He doesn't look at us, I guess, as a typical white person because we are his children . . . he kind of feels one with [black] culture. You know, even though he's not black . . . I definitely feel he's more open-minded than other white people . . . he's not a typical white person, you know.

Often, biracial respondents differentiate themselves from monoracial people by pointing out their "open-mindedness" and broad worldview, which parallels findings in other studies of biracial people (see Korgen 1998). In contrast, monoracial blacks and whites (especially other whites) were sometimes described as closed-minded. Michael, too, views whites as generally narrow-minded, but perceives his white father as an exception to that stereotype.

Another example is Jack, who internally identifies very strongly as white. He grew up in a predominantly white community and was raised by his white mother and white stepfather. When asked how strongly (if at all) he identifies as black, he responds:

> As far as, I don't want to use the word "stereotypical," but as far as the popular image, not at all. [*NK: Not at all? Why is that?*] Because a lot of it is, and not that it's bad, but a lot of it is hip-hop dancing, you know, the hats with the price tag still attached, the bad English. . . . I don't really speak that way. I don't dress the way they do. I don't listen to the same music. So I don't identify with it. Again I'm going to repeat, I don't think it's bad. I just plain don't identify with it.

Jack draws on black cultural stereotypes and differentiates himself from those images (e.g., dancing, dress, way of speaking, music). Later in his interview, Jack describes being pushed away from identifying as black. When asked to explain, he continues:

> Well, I guess being exposed to a more ignorant culture where being thuggish is celebrated and killing people for a dollar—and I saw a magazine cover the other day . . . it looked so ridiculous because it had this guy on there who was black . . . and he was decked out in thug gear, had this big, sixty-pound golden thing on his neck, and he had the most sour expression on his face. He looked like a fish . . . he was supposed to look all hard and tough. . . . And that's why—I don't want to say it's driven me away [from identifying as black] . . . I really hate to say this, but I just see what I see, you know? I just notice that so many black people are accepting that culture, not all but a lot of them are. But the greater number of the white population seems to be more on par with getting an education, speaking properly when occasion calls for it, wanting to succeed, wanting to be classy."

Jack draws on what he describes as stereotypical images of black people based on what he sees in the media (magazine covers, for example). While he recognizes them as stereotypes, he nonetheless draws on those negative stereotypes to explain why he feels pushed away from a black identity. Later he adds:

> You know, don't get me wrong. . . . I mean, I've had lots of wonderful experiences with black people. You know, they're not all about killing, and they're not all about being rude and mean . . . I guess I should have prefaced the whole thing with, "This doesn't apply to everyone."

Jack acknowledges, but simultaneously discounts, comparisons with the few real black referents with whom he's had "wonderful experiences" as exceptions to his (stereotypical) rule.

What Does This Have to Do with Racial Identity?

Individuals in both one-sided and racially mixed social networks make realistic comparisons with others in their networks, yet those in one-sided networks also draw on constructive and stereotypical comparisons, especially regarding the group with which they have limited contact. I find that whether their stereotypes are created from information gleaned from their few real referents or from racial stereotypes found in larger society, those in one-sided racial networks contrast themselves to these constructed images to form their racial identities.

Because constructive comparisons are "based on people's thoughts about others" (Goethals and Klein 2000: 32), they *may or may not* resemble actual members of the racial group. George Goethals and William Klein (2000) argue that constructed comparisons "may have anywhere from an imperfect relation to social reality to no relation at all" (32). Biracial people who have limited information about a racial group may construct comparisons based on what information is available to them; this information may come from real others, but because real others are limited in their networks, the information more likely comes from third-party sources (e.g., media, peers' and friends' descriptions of what another race is like). Because the information is more indirect, I argue that the constructed referent is more likely to be distorted and reflective of racial stereotypes than are real referents in their social networks (e.g., parents, friends). Indeed, I find that the constructive comparisons made by biracial people in one-sided networks tend to be distorted and stereotypical. For those in predominantly white networks, I find that not only are the constructive comparisons with other blacks stereotypical, but they are also frequently negative. As a consequence, I find that biracial respondents in predominantly white networks are less likely to identify as black as compared to those in predominantly black or racially mixed networks; they contrast and differentiate themselves from these negative images.

All respondents who describe their networks as predominantly black identify as black (4 of 4 respondents; 100 percent); however, only one respondent draws on a negative white stereotype to differentiate himself from whites. More notable, however, are the respondents who describe their networks as predominantly white and who identify as white or biracial (9 of 12 respondents; see table 5.1). Eight of nine respondents explicitly draw on negative black stereotypes to differentiate themselves from blacks. Because they negatively stereotype black people (the group with which they have

Table 5.1.   Social Networks and Racial Identities

	Racial Composition of Social Networks		
Internalized Racial Identity	*White*	*Black*	*Mixed*
White	7	0	2
Black	3	4	17
Biracial	2	0	5
Totals	*12*	*4*	*24*

had limited contact), they differentiate themselves from that group and identify as white or biracial.

In contrast, those in racially mixed networks who have numerous real referents (e.g., both black and white family, friends, peers) more often rely on realistic comparisons with others. Likely because they have contact with both racial groups and more opportunities for real comparisons than those in one-sided networks, their identities are shaped more by the realistic comparisons that they make with others in their networks (which are most often phenotypic), and less by constructive comparisons (which are often culturally based, highly stereotypical, and frequently negative for minority groups). As a consequence, the physical similarities and differences that individuals perceive between themselves and others (black, white, biracial) affect their racial identities.

Thus, for those in mixed networks, physical, realistic comparisons with real others are likely more important than comparisons based on negative cultural stereotypes. This may partially explain why so many biracial respondents in mixed networks identify more strongly as black (17 of the 24 respondents): because most believe that they outwardly appear black (see chapter 3), they perceive physical similarities between themselves and blacks (and physical differences from whites), and at the same time, they feel comparatively less pressure to differentiate themselves from a negatively stereotyped black image than do those in predominantly white racial networks (see figure 5.1 for an illustration of the relationship between network type and comparison type).

DISCUSSION AND CONCLUSION

This chapter reveals that social comparisons are yet another process shaping racial identity for biracial people. How they identify themselves is, in part, related to the social comparisons they make with black, white, and biracial others on several dimensions, including (but not necessarily limited to) phenotype, culture, and experiences of privilege, prejudice, and discrimination. At times, they compare themselves to real others (e.g., friends, peers,

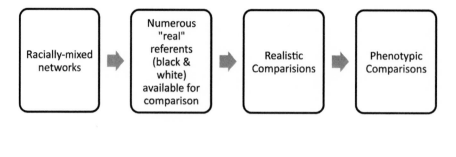

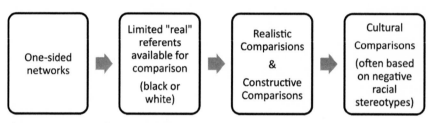

Figure 5.1.   Network-Type and Comparison-Type

parents, siblings, extended family members), and other times they draw on comparisons with their imagined or constructed images of black or white others.

Regarding cultural comparisons in particular, respondents frequently draw on racial stereotypes to explain why they identify one way or another. Black people are described as speaking Ebonics or "bad English," listening to hip-hop and R&B, and dressing in baggy clothes; white people are described as speaking "proper English," listening to rock music, and dressing in GAP or Abercrombie and Fitch clothing (to name a few stereotypes described in this chapter). Respondents in this study often reduce "black culture" and "white culture" to oversimplified, one-dimensional images. Notably, while respondents often acknowledge that not *all* black people or white people fit their stereotypical images, they nonetheless compare themselves to blacks and whites based on these rigid and essentialistic stereotypes.

Furthermore, I find that for some biracial respondents, their perceptions of "white culture" and "black culture" reflect social class disparities between blacks and whites in American society at large. For example, respondents connected "white culture" with going to museums, playing tennis, swimming competitively, and eating organic foods; and "black culture" with a "thuggish" mindset, lack of parental involvement in schooling, and lack of value given to educational achievement.

Arguably, such "cultural" differences between blacks and whites may in fact reflect differences in social class, not race alone. For instance, people of lower classes may be less likely to frequent museums (they do not have the leisure time), less likely to play tennis or swim (these sports are linked to the middle and upper classes), and less likely to buy and eat organic foods (which are relatively more expensive than conventional food). This conflation of culture and class is not surprising given the wide disparity in average social class status between blacks and whites in American society. Black and white Americans fall at opposing ends of the American racial hierarchy, a hierarchy based in part on social class and economic power. Using income and education as indicators of social class, it is easy to see the dramatic difference between the racial groups (see tables 5.2 and 5.3). Wealth is an even more powerful indicator of social class, and the difference in wealth between blacks and whites is even more staggering—the median net worth of whites, for instance, is approximately ten times that of blacks (Hao 2007). Historical and present-day discrimination have contributed to this race-class correlation (Albelda, Drago, and Shulman 2001; Oliver and Shapiro 2006; Shapiro 2004), and I find that this race-class correlation finds its way into respondents' perceptions of black and white "cultures." Given that social class and racial culture are intertwined in the minds of these respondents, their social class position affects their racial identities. Indeed, France Winddance Twine (1996b), in her study of multiracial women, similarly finds a link between social class and identity; in short, her respondents frequently "equated being middle class with having a white identity" (213).

These findings also reveal the negative racial stereotypes that several biracial respondents in this study hold about blacks (and to some degree whites), which challenge the notion that biracial people, by virtue of having two racial ancestries, are racially unbiased. One of the most famous concepts attributed to biracial people is the notion of the "marginal man," described by sociologist Robert Park as "one whom fate has condemned to live in two societies and in two, not merely different, but antagonistic cultures" (Stonequist [1937] 1961: xiiii; see also Park 1928, 1931). While

Table 5.2. Educational Attainment of the Population 25 Years and Over by Race, 2007

	High school or more	Some college or more	Bachelor's degree or more	Advanced degree
Non-Hispanic White	87	56.6	29.1	10.7
Black or African American	80.1	45.8	17.5	5.9

Source: U.S. Census Bureau.

Table 5.3. Median Household Income by Race, 2007

	Median Household Income (in 2007 dollars)
White	$54,920
Black or African American	$33,916

Source: U.S. Census Bureau.

described as marginal to both cultures, biracial people live their lives strad-dling two worlds, and in doing so, Park argues that they gain a "wider hori-zon, keener intelligence, [and] more detached and rational viewpoint" than others (Stonequist [1937] 1961: x). In fact, he argues that they have a more objective and "cosmopolitan" view of society than monoracial Americans, and research on biracial people has, until now, provided support for this view.

Kathleen Korgen (1998), for instance, found that the biracial respon-dents in her sample frequently described themselves as open-minded, color-blind (e.g., they don't notice the race of people they interact with), and non-prejudiced (e.g., they argue it would be "impossible for them to be prejudiced against any racial group because they themselves are the product of two feuding races" (Korgen 1998: 78; see also Roberts-Clarke, Roberts, and Morokoff 2004; Tizard and Phoenix 2002). Like a participant in Korgen's (1998) study who described herself as being "freed from the racial blinders most monoracial persons wear" (78), participants in the present study similarly described themselves as "more open," "more toler-ant," "color-blind," and "more relaxed about race" as compared to their monoracial counterparts.

I find, however, that their self-purported unbiased and color-blind views of race were often in direct contrast to statements they made throughout their interviews in which they at times reduced blacks and whites (or "black culture" and "white culture") to oversimplified and sometimes quite negative stereotypes. This was especially true for respondents who grew up in predominantly white networks (and as adults were still embedded in this type of network). These respondents drew on negative stereotypes about blacks (e.g., they are unhygienic, they do not care about education or success, they have children out of wedlock, they cannot speak "proper English"), and they sometimes explained the few black people they knew, who defied these stereotypes (e.g., their black parent, a black professor), as "exceptions to the (stereotypical) rule." These findings suggest that al-though biracial people may potentially be less prejudiced and more open-minded than their monoracial counterparts by virtue of having varied racial backgrounds, they are certainly not immune to racial bias and stereotyping. They, too, live in a racialized society and are not impervious to the insidi-ous effects of race and racism in the United States.

In addition to describing the various dimensions of social comparisons and their effect on racial identity, this chapter also examined the influence of social networks on social comparison processes. These findings extend work on social comparison theory, but also add to the growing body of research on multiracial identity by further unpacking the relationship between the racial composition of social networks and racial identity. Previous work has shown a link between networks and identity, yet little is known about the process by which this occurs. This chapter shows that social networks influence racial identity, in part, through the social comparisons that individuals make within these networks (see figure 5.2). Social networks provide both *opportunities for and limitations to* the types of social comparisons that individuals can make with others (realistic or constructive), and as a consequence, the types of comparisons they make influence their racial identities. While respondents embedded in both racially mixed networks and one-sided networks drew on realistic comparisons, those in one-sided networks more often drew on constructed comparisons. Constructed comparisons, in general, tended to be stereotypical, and when biracial respondents drew on constructed comparisons because of their limited contact with a particular racial group, those stereotypical comparisons were often negative and unflattering. Wanting to differentiate themselves from these negative stereotypes, biracial respondents identified in the "opposite" direction (e.g., "black people are unhygienic and I'm not like that, so I more strongly identify as white").

These findings may have important practical implications for parents deciding where to raise their biracial children—in areas that are predominantly white, black, or racially mixed. If parents choose to raise their children in predominantly white communities and send them to predominantly white schools, they may need to offset the racial imbalance by making sure that their children also have significant contact with blacks. Parents may need to balance those racial networks with black peers, rather than relying on black extended family members as their child's only contact with black people. As shown here, biracial people in predominantly white networks may view black family members as "different" from other blacks—in other words, as exceptions to the stereotype. Some respondents in this study report that,

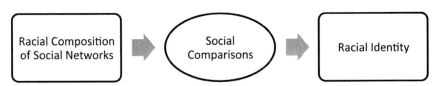

Figure 5.2. The Relationship between Social Networks, Social Comparisons, and Racial Identity

although they were raised in predominantly white communities, their parents made conscious efforts to involve them in after-school programs, extracurricular activities, and church groups that were predominantly black. Parents who raise their children in one-sided networks, such as white communities, without balancing the racial composition of those networks through other outlets, risk having their biracial children develop negative stereotypes of blacks. This may, in turn, lead them to dis-identify with black people and with being black.

Now that I have described several processes that shape one's racial identity (i.e., reflected appraisals, day-to-day interactional experiences, and social comparisons), I now turn to examining the considerable amount of agency that biracial individuals expend in asserting their preferred racial identities to others. Larger society certainly has an influence on racial identity, but I find that biracial people are also quite active and creative in presenting their (public) identities to larger society. The next chapter explores the ways in which these respondents "do race," and their motivations for doing so.

NOTES

1. Discussion of the links between race, culture, and social class also appear in 2010 in "Country Clubs and Hip-Hop Thugs: Examining the Role of Social Class and Culture in Shaping Racial Identity" (Khanna 2010b).

2. Jack and Jill is one of the oldest black social organizations in the United States.

3. Those in white networks stereotype blacks, and as a consequence, work to differentiate themselves from black people. For some, this means identifying as white, for others, identifying as biracial. Some scholars have been critical of the biracial label, arguing that identifying as biracial is a way for some individuals to separate themselves from black people (Daniel 2002; Spencer 2006a). I find that respondents in white networks who internally identify as biracial (like others who identify as white) often do so as a way of differentiating themselves from negative black stereotypes.

4. Although those in predominantly black networks rarely brought up white stereotypes, caution must be taken in interpreting this finding. While negative black stereotypes *may* be more abundant than white stereotypes in larger American society, my white racial appearance (see discussion of my positionality in chapter 1) may have hindered respondents from openly expressing negative white stereotypes.

6

"I Was Like Superman and Clark Kent"

Strategies and Motivations of Identity Work

According to symbolic interactionists, humans are not merely passive objects subject to society, but they are also active agents who have a hand in shaping their self and identity (Cooley 1902; Gecas and Schwalbe 1983).[1] In their work on homeless men, for example, David Snow and Leon Anderson (1987) find that individuals do *identity work* and "engage in a range of activities to create, present, or sustain identities that are congruent with or supportive of their self-concept" (1348; see also Snow and Anderson 1993). They argue that to present particular identities, individuals employ several strategies, such as (1) procuring or arranging physical settings or props; (2) doing cosmetic face work or arranging their personal appearance; (3) selectively associating with other individuals or groups; and (4) asserting personal identity through verbal construction or identity talk (Snow and Anderson 1987).

Regarding ethnic identity, in particular, scholars find considerable flexibility and choice in identity (for examples, see Espiritu 1992; Kibria 2000, 2002; Lieberson and Waters 1986; Nagel 1994, 1995; Song 2003; Tuan 1998; Waters 1990), as well as conscious identity work. For instance, Nazli Kibria (2002) explores identity strategies used by Korean and Chinese Americans, finding that they employ tactics such as verbal dis-identification ("I'm not Korean, I'm Chinese!") and use external identity markers of ethnicity (e.g., clothes, mannerisms, language) to assert their preferred ethnic identities.

Although there is a growing body of literature on ethnic identity work, scholars have been more cautious about the notion of racial identity work—especially for multiracial Americans with black ancestry. Roth (2005) argues that "it has often been assumed that few identity options exist for multiracial individuals who have Black heritage" (36), because they are often constrained by larger society to identify exclusively as black (Gibbs and Hines 1992; Waters 1990, 1996, 1999). Mary Waters (1990), for instance, claims that multiracial Americans with black ancestry are "highly constrained to identify as blacks, without other options available to them" (18). Hence, little serious attention has been given to their racial flexibility, and the ways in which they actively assert and manage their racial identities in day-to-day situations. In fact, drawing on an example of a hypothetical multiracial person, Waters (1999) argues that "a person with black skin who had some Irish ancestry would have to work very hard to present himself as Irish—and in many ways he/she would be denied that option" (203). There is no doubt that these individuals are frequently raced as black by society at large (sometimes because of the one drop rule, and other times because of their physical appearance), yet as we have already seen in chapter 3, individuals sometimes resist this classification. Indeed, Teresa Kay Williams (1996) suggests that multiracial individuals are "not mere receivers of social messages or conformists to prescriptive social categories. They are also active participants in shaping their identities" (208).

Debbie Storrs (1999), in her study of multiracial women, provides support to Williams' claims. She finds that these women employ several techniques to manage their preferred non-white identities and, echoing Williams (1996), she argues that "racial identities are not simply imposed on individuals, but achieved through interaction, presentation, and manipulation" (200). In order to manage and present their chosen identities, women in her sample did two things. First, they highlighted cultural and physical symbolic signs of belonging, such as wearing ethnic clothes, jewelry, and hairstyles. Second, they used selective disclosure to maintain their desired identity by failing to reveal their white ancestry unless directly asked or challenged. Her sample, however, varied in terms of racial background, and only nine of twenty-seven respondents had a black-white background (see also Storrs 2006). Brunsma and Rockquemore (2001) maintain that racial identities are subject to more constraint than ethnic identities, *especially* for those with black ancestry. They do admit, however, that "it remains to be seen how much negotiation and strategy [of race] is involved" (244).

Extending this work, this chapter examines the racial identity work of black-white biracial people who, as shown in previous chapters, are frequently raced as black by larger society. I begin by describing the range of strategies these biracial individuals used to assert their chosen racial identities—sometimes they identify as biracial or even white; in some cases, they also used strategies to present themselves as black. Next, I further extend what we know about racial identity work by examining the underlying motivations for presenting and managing biracial, white, and black identities. In other words, I ask: *Why* do people present biracial, white, or black identities?

STRATEGIES

Biracial individuals in this study describe a range of strategies and tactics they use to express or to downplay particular aspects of their racial ancestries. To manage their racial identities, whether as monoracial (black or white) or as multiracial/biracial, the strategies they employ include (1) verbally claiming or disclaiming identities, (2) manipulating their physical appearance, (3) highlighting cultural symbols of belonging, (4) selectively disclosing aspects of their racial identities, and (5) selectively associating with certain racial groups.

Verbal Identification/Dis-identification

First, respondents do identity work via verbal constructions. In short, they claim or disclaim an identity by verbally asserting, "I'm this" or "I'm not that." According to George McCall (2003), identity processes must be studied in terms of the "Me," or self-identifications, but also the "Not-Me," or self-dis-identifications. Anthony works to present a black identity through verbal identification, saying, "I guess I just always make sure people know I'm black. Like, even when I went to an all-white school, I used to say, 'I'm black'—call myself black. Even though they knew I had a white father, if they ask, 'I'm black.' That's it. By saying "I'm black," Anthony invokes a "Me" identity (McCall 2003).

Dis-identification, according to McCall (2003), is a form of reactive identity work in social interaction—often people invoke the "Not-Me" identity in response to being labeled by others. Caroline, for example, who is often told she is black by her black peers, resists being classified as black by verbally disclaiming a black identity. Reflecting on two experiences at school, she says:

In my [graduate] program, I think we maybe have, like, four black people, not including myself. And the other day, one of the [black] guys said to me, "Oh, in our class, there are only three of us." And I said, "Three of who?" And I didn't know what he was talking about, and he just looked at me. And I was, like, "Don't do that. Don't lump me in [with black students] because I don't see myself that way, and I don't like it when you just assume that." And then, one time, I was taking an African cultural studies class, and our teacher was black and she made reference to the black students in the class and lumped me in there with them. And I raised my hand and I was, like, "I'm not black." And she almost wanted to argue with me, like, "Yes, you are." And no, no I'm not. And it pissed me off. She wasn't privy to my background. The only thing she knew about me was what she saw.

Even though she is often raced as black by her black peers, Caroline resists this classification by verbally saying, "Don't lump me in" (with blacks) and "I'm not black." By refusing an identity imposed by others, Caroline creates a "Not-Me" identity—an identity based on self-dis-identification (McCall 2003).

Others, too, verbally claim or disclaim particular racial identities. Many individuals in this study want to claim a biracial (or multiracial) identity. To do so, they often work to resist being monoracially classified by others who want to label them as black *or* white. Nick, who publicly identifies himself as mixed, says:

> I don't feel like people accept [the "mixed" category]. Let's just say you have two options on the table. You have either option one or option two. You can't pick both. And I know that has nothing to do with race or anything like that, but I feel that sort of mentality ties into race also, because people don't want to have more than one option. They want them to be one or the other, and that's something I don't agree with personally. But going through life and having people decide to categorize me, classify me, and constantly ask why do I consider myself this or that, or why do you dress like this, or why do you blah, blah, blah . . . I'm trying to be myself. I'm not trying to fall into any sort of category. I'm not trying to play into what people expect me to be. There was always people who would question [my mixed identity]. . . . They would say, "Why?" I said, "I don't pick," and they left it at that.

Nick negotiates a mixed identity by simply saying, "I don't pick."

While respondents talk about verbally asserting identities by saying, "I'm this" or "I'm not that," many times that declaration is not enough to claim or disclaim an identity. Racial appearance is an essential factor in determining how others respond to the claim. For instance, verbally claiming to be black when one outwardly appears to be white, or vice versa, will likely pose a dilemma. An individual may identify as white, for instance, only to have others invalidate that identity based on his or her black physical characteristics (e.g., dark skin), and according to Kerry Ann Rockquemore and David Brunsma (2002a), validation of one's identity by others is important to racial identity development. Hence, biracial individuals may employ additional strategies to manage their racial identities.

Manipulating Physical Appearance

Another strategy respondents described is manipulation of their phenotype, or physical appearance. Because race is so closely tied to physical appearance in American society, how people outwardly look often determines how they are perceived racially by others. These respondents recognize that others' perceptions of their race influence their identity; however, rather than simply allow others to classify them based on their looks, they often work to modify their phenotypes in order to influence how they are perceived by others. According to Gregory Stone (1962), "appearance" can serve as the source of one's identity (e.g., looking black may lead to a black identity), but it can also be used to present one's identity to others. Respondents in this study describe altering their physical characteristics in several ways to present biracial, white, or black identities to others or to draw attention to particular aspects of their racial ancestry.

For instance, Caroline describes how she plays around with her looks:

> I feel that, a lot of times, my looks can go either way, and it really depends on how I play it. And lots of times, I mean, I do. [*NK: What do you mean?*] Just little things. Like manipulating how I look. Like my hairstyle or my makeup or the clothes I wear. And there are lots of very random things sometimes . . . it really depends on what sort of mood I'm in. I mean, I always identify myself as biracial, but I definitely have the ability to play around with my looks, and I do.

Noting her ability to "play around" with her looks, she often manipulates her hair, makeup, and clothes to that end. Other respondents similarly talk about how they modify their outward appearance, and Rockquemore and Laszloffy (2003) similarly claim that "negotiations over racial identity for Black-White mixed-race people frequently center on issues of hair, skin color, and eye color (121; see also Rockquemore 2002; Root 1998). Hair and skin color are the most common areas of manipulation in this study. Approximately a third of respondents (13 of 40) describe altering their hair, and six respondents describe altering their skin color in ways to express particular racial identities.

Hair

Respondents describe altering their hair or hairstyles to manage their racial appearance (and consequently racial identity) by straightening their hair, leaving their hair natural, and coloring their hair. Stephanie changes her hair to appear more white, black, or biracial, depending upon the context. Although she strongly identifies as black (internally), she describes a phase in high school when she wanted to "be a little more white." She says, "I went through a period where I was still black, but I tried to be a little more white. . . . I don't know if I was thinking I was being more white, but I went to dye my hair blonde." Later in the interview, she talks about her hair within the context of her predominantly black college:

> You know the funny thing: I haven't been blonde since I've been at [this HBCU]. And I dye my hair all the time, and every time I dye my hair, I think it's red . . . a part of me, when I got down here, shifted to try and assimilate into the HBCU, I think. Like, I wanted to [dye my hair blonde], but for some

reason I didn't . . . maybe subconsciously I didn't do it because I didn't want people to put me in that box. Like, "Stephanie, what are you doing? Are you trying to be white?"

Trying to "assimilate," or fit in with her black peers, Stephanie refrains from dying her hair blonde so as *not* to appear as if she is trying to be white.

She does, however, admit that at times she asserts her biracial identity to feel unique in this predominantly black context. Again, she talks about how she manages her hair to highlight her biracial identity:

Here [at this HBCU] I'll get up, and if I feel like wearing my hair straight, I'll wear it straight. If I want to wear it curly, I'll wear it curly. And when it's curly, of course, I get all kinds of questions about what my ethnicity is. And I enjoy that. I enjoy people asking me what I am. I love that. It just makes me feel different and unique, so I enjoy playing [my biracial background] up.

Knowing that wearing her hair curly prompts questions about her background from black peers, she uses her hair to "play up" her biracial identity. When asked, "What are you?" she has the opportunity to claim a biracial background. Thus, Stephanie consciously uses her hair to play up her white ancestry, to downplay her white ancestry, or to draw attention to her biracial background. Furthermore, how and when she manages her hair is contextual, reflecting the contextual nature of her racial identity.

Georgia similarly describes arranging her hair to appear white, black, biracial, or another race/ethnicity altogether. Describing the malleability of her hair, she says:

I can go to the mirror and straighten my hair, make it really light . . . and I can definitely look white. I can go to the mirror and do my hair in a different way and look completely different. I can make my hair really wavy because I'm mixed, so my hair can wave and people think I'm Puerto Rican. Or I can go in there and get some braids and now all of a sudden, I'm black. It's just that I can really play around with my appearance.

Others describe altering their hair to "prove" a particular identity. Anthony, for instance, who labels himself as mixed and who internally identifies very strongly as black, describes manipulating his hair and hairstyle to appear more black than white, especially to his black peers in middle school. Even though he describes himself as having "white hair," he says, "I used to have really long hair and sometimes I would pick it up into a 'fro. And people would be like, "I didn't know you could do that. I didn't know you could have a 'fro." I was, like, "Yeah, I can. I am proving to you that, yeah, I can do it. I can do whatever you can do."

Likewise, Jack labels himself as biracial, but internally identifies very strongly as white. He talks about occasionally wishing for more white racial features:

> When I started getting towards the end of my high school years, the beginning of college, I started kind of wishing I had more Caucasian traits. I have very few, obviously. . . . But it really wasn't until the end of high school, like, I said. That's when I kind of wished, if I'm going to identify with [white] people, I kind of wish I looked a little more like them.

To highlight his white identity, he manages his hair: "I try to keep very short hair. I mean, well, one, I hate afros anyway. But I try to keep very short hair because I can't have the long fine, thin hair that white people do." To conceal his hair's different texture from his white peers, he consciously keeps it cut short in order to downplay his black ancestry.

Kristen identifies as biracial and internally identifies strongly as black. She talks about the ways in which she alters her hair to appear more biracial and to counter perceptions that she is white:

> I just recently dyed my hair darker. I did go darker because I wanted to fit in with my family—with my brother and my sister who have darker skin, darker hair, darker eyes, and I look totally different. I love being who I am, but when I say I'm biracial, people look at me like, "No, you're not." And that's kind of always offended me. Because this is who I am, and you're telling me that I'm not. It didn't necessarily upset me, it just kind of offended me. [*NK: Why is that?*] Because they think I'm white. And not that I hate white people, I just don't want to be white. And so I think my hair's been the only thing that I can maybe go both ways with, because if it's straight and it is lighter, people just assume I'm a white girl . . . when it's frizzy, curly, darker, people can see that I'm maybe white and something else, not necessarily black.

Thus, respondents style their hair not only to claim an identity, but also to *avoid* association with a particular race. Jack refrains from growing his hair out to avoid an afro that might identify him as black. Kristen darkens her hair to avoid being classified as white. Managing their hair to avoid association with a particular race is a way that they assert a "Not-Me" identity (McCall 2003): "I'm not black" or "I'm not white."

Similarly Olivia, who growing up faced challenges from black girls regarding her black identity (as described in chapter 4), explains the ways in which she consciously altered her hairstyle to avoid being raced as white:

> When I was younger, it was embarrassing because I had very long hair and I identified more with African Americans. So during that period, if you had long

hair and were lighter skinned, there was a lot of conflict. So I usually kept my hair pulled back or kept it up or tried to do different things to blend in more. . . . [Black girls] used to call me "white girl" because my hair was very long, and it would blow in the wind and all that kind of stuff. And they'd say, "She has white girl hair" or "She thinks she's white," you know, that kind of stuff. Back then, I used to get up in the morning for school and leave my hair down and run out. And then when they started saying I was a white girl and I had white girl hair, then I would never wear my hair down. And it's funny because I have another girlfriend in New Orleans who's Creole and she went through the same thing. . . . So we always pull it back and keep it braided or keep it where it's not showing. And so it was a big deal for me to start wearing my hair down. [*NK: When did you start wearing it down?*] Oh, wow, probably my mid-thirties.

To counter challenges from other black girls that she was a "white girl," Olivia spent her childhood and young adulthood tying her long hair back so as not to draw attention to her white phenotypic features. Of the respondents who describe altering their hair, eleven are women and only two are men, which suggests that this option is gendered, given the multitude of hairstyles available to women (as compared to men).

This may also point to gendered differences regarding the importance of hair more generally, and the politics of hair for women within the black community more specifically. As described in chapter 4, colorism within the black community may be especially salient for women because of the competition for black men. Biracial women with so-called good features (e.g., straight hair) may experience more antagonism from their black female counterparts and comparatively more pressure to downplay those features than biracial males do.

Skin Color

In addition to hair, skin color is another physical aspect of the body that can be *somewhat* manipulated by lightening or darkening. Whereas skin-lightening creams were popular among African American women in the 1950s (Hunter 1998), no respondents admitted trying to lighten their skin tone. Those who did manipulate their skin color were light-skinned people working to darken their skin tone.[2] Beth, who both publicly and internally identifies as black, cites ways in which she tried to alter her skin color when she was younger to appear more black. Wanting to fit in and thinking she would be perceived as black if she was darker, she says:

If I could just be a shade darker. So even in the summertime, that was cool because I could get a tan. And I'm *in* now . . . [black] guys were like, "Oh, you're so pale." Like them knowing that I was black, but like, "God, you're so pale, Beth." So, yeah, I went to the tanning booth. I think it was more the outward appearances. I think the talk, the lingo, all of that was proven as black, but it was just the outward things that are still questionable. You know? I think for me, if I had a tan, if I didn't look as pale, wore things that accentuated me in a certain way, I think those were all of my focuses.

Beth tanned, believing that darker skin would make her "in" with her black peers. Marion Kilson (2001), in her study of biracial people, also finds that some of her respondents desired darker skin so that other people of color would not challenge their racial loyalty. Similarly, I find that respondents darken their skin in order to "prove" their blackness and fit in with black peers and friends. Also, as described earlier, I find that biracial women more often than biracial men describe challenges to their black identities (mostly from black women), and in this sample, it is the women who describe tanning for darker skin. No men in this study openly admitted wanting darker skin.

Natasha's comments further illuminate the motivation behind tanning. She labels herself as black and internally identifies strongly as such, and she tans to make herself darker to "blend in" with her black friends and peers. She says, "I do tan. I don't go to a tanning spa, but at the beach I do like to get a bit more color. I'm too pasty. I'm still not comfortable with my shade. [*NK: You want to be darker?*] I would like to be darker, yes. My whole life I stuck out, and now I want to blend in. I just want to blend in. And I thought just being around black people I would, but I don't."

Michelle also describes tanning to appear darker. Michelle, who outwardly appears white but internally identifies strongly as black, describes being frustrated when others perceive her as white because of her light skin, "white" facial features, and straight hair. To work against being raced as white, she admits, "I'm hooked into the sun. But part of that is I have a skin disease and the sun helps it. . . . But then the other part of it is I want to be darker. Because I don't want to be seen as a white person."

Georgia, who more strongly identifies as black than white, has also worked to appear more black to her black friends and peers by trying to darken her skin. When asked how she has worked to highlight her black identity, she responds:

I definitely have tried to darken my skin just because I'm so pale and I don't like being this pale. . . . I've seen white girls with darker tans than I have. I definitely want to be darker, I do. So I've tried to tan. It'll come and go like that [*snaps her fingers*]. . . . My [black] friends are, like, "Why are you so pale?" I'm not going to put on tanning lotion. That's too much. But I went out and got my hair highlighted just to make it lighter because the lighter [color] contrasts with my skin. I don't look as pale and people are, like, "Oh, you look so much darker now." Because I colored my hair! [Laughing]

Because the effects of tanning are fleeting, Georgia lightens her hair to make her skin color appear darker by contrast.

In addition, respondents also describe strategies such as drawing on cultural symbols (of blackness and whiteness) as forms of identity work. This strategy may be particularly useful for individuals for whom altering how they look is difficult, if not impossible.

Highlighting Cultural Symbols

Herbert Gans (1979) argues that multiethnic Americans practice "symbolic ethnicity" by drawing on ethnic symbols (e.g., food, clothes, holidays, involvement in political issues) to express an ethnic identity. For instance, those wanting to express an Irish ancestry might cook and eat Irish food, openly celebrate St. Patrick's Day, and occasionally wear traditional Irish clothing. While Gans focuses his discussion on multiethnic whites, "symbolic ethnicity" or "symbolic race" may also be practiced by biracial people wanting to express a particular racial or ethnic identity to others. I find that more than half of the respondents draw on what they perceive as cultural differences between U.S. blacks and whites to highlight symbols of blackness or whiteness (e.g., dress/clothing, food, language, dialect, music, television shows, political viewpoints, etc.).

For example, Michael, who labels himself as mixed and biracial and prides himself on his unique heritage, talks about how he likes to "express" his Italian ancestry to draw attention to his biracial background. He says, "You can't really tell by looking at me, but I'm very proud of my Italian culture, and I like to express it a lot. I feel like it's a unique quality about myself that people don't know when they see me." When asked how he expresses his Italian ancestry, he responds:

> I love Italian food, and so I like to cook a lot of Italian food and I follow soccer in Europe. You know, Italian soccer's very big. . . . I have an Italian flag in my room and I have lot of Italian sports clothing. . . . I have this shirt that says 'Italian Stallion,' and it has a[n Italian] flag on it. And my [black] girlfriend always kind of jokes about it and says, "I feel like sometimes you'd like to be seen as more Italian than black." I think I do because people don't really treat me like an Italian person. So I like it to be known. I like to express it more. . . . Like I said, I have a lot of clothing that highlights it. I have a lot of Italian sportswear, Italian shirts that say "Italy" on them. My room has a poster of Italian architecture, and so it's certain things like that. . . . [Other people] may ask me where I got it, and then when I say "Italy," they're like, "Oh, what do you mean?" you know? [I respond] "I'm Italian. My father got it from Italy."

Because others do not see or treat him as an Italian or biracial person, he seeks to "express it more" through various cultural symbols, including food (cooking and eating Italian dishes), sports (following Italian and German soccer), ethnic/national symbols (hanging an Italian flag in his room), clothing (wearing Italian sportswear and shirts that say "Italy" on them), and various other symbols (hanging an Italian architecture poster in his room). The ways he expresses his Italian identity mirror Snow and Anderson's (1987) strategies of identity work: he arranges physical settings and props (e.g., Italian flag and Italian architecture poster) and arranges his personal appearance (e.g., wearing Italian sportswear and clothing). Michael uses these cultural symbols to prompt questions about where he got them, which gives him the opportunity to talk about his background and the chance to express a biracial identity. According to Michael, he wants to express his biracial identity because it makes him feel unique in the predominantly black context of the HBCU he attends.

Similarly, John draws on cultural symbols to express his preferred racial identity. John internally identifies more strongly as black than white, but to his disappointment is typically perceived as white because of his white physical appearance. When asked whether he has ever tried to highlight any aspect of his racial background to others, he says:

I would never try to play up my white side. My skin does that all by itself, and I don't want to go in that direction. I wouldn't feel good about it. I mean, I've had a certain kind of guilt, I guess, because I know that there are many advantages because of it, and I wouldn't have gotten them if my skin was much darker. And at different points in my life, I've felt guilty about that. I can't say I'm totally at ease with it, because it's like I can't really show any black parts. But sometimes I feel guilty about it.

Three times in this statement, John refers to the "guilt" he feels because of the advantages afforded by his white skin. Clinical psychologist Carla Bradshaw (1992) explains this guilt and how those feelings may influence racial identity:

Racial consciousness and experiences of oppression compel some degree of identification with people of color. Though the biracial person may not be individually responsible for perpetuating racial oppression, access to social privileges and power implies identification with the oppressor and may evoke feelings of guilt and betrayal by association. (87)

Thus, John feels guilty about his white phenotype and may compensate for those feelings by identifying as black. Because he cannot, in his own words, "show any black parts," he consciously works to express his black identity. When asked how he does this, he describes several strategies:

I do all kinds of things that don't fit into boxes. Like, for example, when I say "playing up the black side," that might mean just revealing my politics, the way I look at things. To others it doesn't necessarily mean anything, but to me, I know it has something to do with my [light] color, but it's also just how I look at the world. To make a concrete example, talking about Hurricane Katrina. I was with a group of all black friends, and I say that I think the government's slow, and the response has a lot to do with the fact that people were mostly black and mostly poor. Now does that mean I'm framing my black side? Or I'm kind of adhering to that side? I know it doesn't have to be that way. Anyone could say that [about the government response to Hurricane Katrina]. It doesn't necessarily frame my identity, but to me it feels that way. It has something to do with it.

John admits that he has certain political viewpoints and views of the world, and his strategy is to reveal those viewpoints as a way of "framing [his] black side," which cannot be readily observed based on physical appearance.

Others also draw on cultural symbols to express their racial identities. Denise, who both publicly and internally identifies as black, describes ways in which she works to fit in with her black peers. She explains how she consciously thinks about her clothing and style of dress when she is in an all-black context:

Like, if I were trying to get into a step team or I were trying to get into a choir where there was a black person auditioning me, or I'm trying to become something where people in the organization are black, like a fraternity or sorority, I strive more to prove that I am black. [*NK: How do you do that?*] Probably the way I style my clothes and my hair . . . looking like I dress like I'm a black person. . . . I'm in an African American dance class . . . so it's mostly black students. I have to change how I appear. Not that how I dress affects my grade, but how the people in the class view me: "Oh, she's black. She can be in this class."

Chris, who labels himself as biracial but internally identifies more strongly as white than black, talks about the ways in which he worked to highlight his white identity to his white friends and peers at his predominantly white high school:

In high school I would overly dress white. I would have to wear GAP [clothing], because GAP was more identified with white. So everything I had was GAP, so that I could be like, "Yeah, it's GAP. I'm white. See, it's GAP" [*Gesturing to his clothes and laughing*]. . . . You'd better believe that I would have my GAP stuff on, so that everybody knew that I shopped at a white store.

Here, GAP, a national clothing chain, is raced as white. By wearing GAP clothing, Chris works to express his white (and biracial) identity.

Similarly, Anthony talks about how he alters his clothes, in addition to using a number of other strategies, to express his black identity with his black friends. Reminiscing about himself in high school, he says:

I remember wanting to prove myself black. . . . I felt like my [black] friends in my neighborhood were kind of almost cooler than me because they were black. So, like, whatever they did, I wanted to do too. Because I had to prove myself. [*NK: In what ways?*] Aw man, this is embarrassing. I had a friend named Lamar . . . and so I used to try to imitate him. Even though now I realize that was stupid, but I kind of associated all that stuff with being black. [*NK: Like what types of things?*] Kind of how he was free to do whatever he wanted to do. He was cursing before I was. He smoked weed, so I wanted to smoke weed. It was stuff like that. I wasn't really into weed, but then I wanted to do it because they were doing it. I mean, just all the stereotypical stuff. Like, you know, pants sagging. . . . I used to kind of slur my speech a little bit because I used to talk very properly and I used to force myself to sound different. Sound like I was more black.

Like Denise and Chris, Anthony consciously considers how his clothes code him racially. He lets his pants sag, which he perceives as black. He does (or used to do) additional things he perceives as black: he curses, smokes marijuana, and alters (slurs) his speech to "sound . . . more black." These acts are significant, not only because Anthony does them in response to peer pressure, but also because he equates them with being black—he describes them as "all the stereotypical stuff" associated with being black.

Other respondents, like Anthony, also modify their speech to appear more black or white, often admitting that they work to "talk white" or "talk black." Stephanie, who internally identifies very strongly as black, remembers trying to appear black to her black peers in middle school. Because her black friends told her she was "acting white" and "talking white," she worked hard to alter her speech to fit in with them. Describing this as literal identity work, Stephanie says:

I just remember my [black] friends . . . always telling me that I'm acting white. I need to act more black. . . . But, like, my mom's very businesslike, so it's very proper. So I got it from her. Like I wasn't very slangish or whatever. And I went through a period where if someone heard me, they'd say, "Why do you talk like that?" [So my friends] taught me how to talk. I remember I'd take the school bus to and from school, and they would have sessions on teaching me how to talk. All of my friends would teach me how [to talk]. Like, "Stephanie, say it this way. You're not saying it right." So stuff like that. Like just kind of having to go through a whole identity switch. . . . I had to change my identity so I could fit in.

To fit in with her black peers and appear black, Stephanie literally worked to change her identity by having learning "sessions" with her black friends, who taught her how to "talk black."

Jack also modifies his speech to appear more white, especially with his white friends: "I tailor my speech at times. Like, I mean, I'll use the word *dude*. I'll probably use that word twice a day, but if I'm around white guys,

I'll probably increase how much I use that or the stereotypical [white] words like *sweet, awesome*. But, the thing is that I say it around black people, too, but I'm more conscious about it when I'm around white people." Georgia is also conscious of the language she uses and the way in which it codes her racially: "Trying to fit in with [black friends], you try to pick up the lingo they say. I will say 'crunk this,' you know, 'that's the bomb.' Like, you're trying to pick up that kind of language which, of course, identifies you with being black." Both Jack and Georgia draw on what they perceive as white and black slang to draw attention to their white or black backgrounds.

In addition to modifying her speech (as described above), Stephanie has used other strategies to assert her black identity. In middle school, she faced identity invalidation: she perceived herself as black, but black peers told her she was white. To "prove" her blackness, she drew on a number of cultural symbols:

> When I was in middle school, like I said, they used to tease me a lot. And it was an all-black school, so all my friends were black then. Like, it was weird, I remember [the white band] *NSYNC being out when were in, like, the seventh or eighth grade and my friends listened to them and I hated that. I hated any music that wasn't black. I hated any clothes that black people didn't wear. Like, I hated all of that. . . . I felt like I had to stress to people that I was black. It wasn't a gray area. Biracial didn't exist then. It was either you're white or you're black. So, I felt like, okay, "I hate *NSYNC. I hate this white music." They would realize that I'm down, you know? . . . I was trying to prove I'm not white. And since I can't be biracial, then the only thing I can be is black. So let me just be black.

Because being biracial was not an option (at least not in the eyes of her black peers growing up), Stephanie worked to express her black identity. In doing so, she distanced herself from anything she perceived as symbols of whiteness (e.g., pop music, clothing styles).

Selective Disclosure

Another strategy respondents in this sample describe is selectively disclosing an identity or identities to others. Storrs (1999) finds that multiracial women use selective disclosure to maintain a minority identity by failing to reveal their white ancestry unless directly asked or challenged. These respondents also use selective disclosure at some time or another (1) to reveal or conceal particular racial identities, but also (2) to resist racial classification altogether.

Revealing and Concealing Racial Identities

To begin, when asked whether they ever highlight one racial identity over another or whether they ever downplay their multiracial background, many biracial respondents talk about being selective in revealing or concealing particular racial backgrounds to others. They selectively disclose particular identities both in face-to-face social interactions with others and on "What is your race?" questions found on faceless forms and applications.

With regard to face-to-face social interactions, Beth, who publicly and internally identifies as black, notes situations in which she has downplayed her black background. When describing how she once presented herself at work with her white coworkers, she says:

> I used to be a caseworker. Some of [my white coworkers] assumed I was white and I just rolled with it . . . yeah, you're just sitting there like, "You really don't have a clue. I'll just continue to be white, if that's what you're going to insist on." So people didn't know who I am. You know, they really didn't know who or what I was identifying as. I just left it as "I'm going to let you assume [I'm white], and I'll go along with it."

When white coworkers assumed she was white, Beth went along with the assumption never correcting them. Later in the interview she describes this as a protective strategy: in short, she never reveals her black ancestry at work as part of a conscious effort to avoid racism or discrimination. By concealing her black identity and biracial background, she manages a white identity in the work context.

Similarly, Kim sometimes disclosed only her white identity when she was younger:

> I definitely tried to downplay [my biracial background] when I was younger. Like, if I'm going to pass for white, I would, like, in a situation where I think people might be racist. I wouldn't bring it up. If they asked me, I wouldn't mind telling them, but I definitely wasn't going to yell it out loud just because I didn't want to deal with it. I didn't want to deal with any racism.

Both Beth and Kim conceal their black ancestry to avoid the potential for racism and discrimination from whites, and others selectively reveal only their black ancestries in order to fit in with black peers. Samantha, who internally identifies strongly as black, talks about wanting to fit in with black friends and peers in middle school. Like in Beth's case, others make assumptions about her racial background:

> There was a time in middle school [that] I never told anyone what I was. A lot of times they never asked. They just kind of assumed, "Well, she's black." They just assumed. [*NK: Was there a reason you didn't tell people?*] I didn't think it was important. No one ever asked. I'm like, "Okay, what's the reason for bringing it up?

Likewise, Kendra also wanted to fit in with her black peers growing up. When talking about her experiences in high school, she says, "In high school, I was trying to fit in. Like, I didn't want people to know that I was half white. That I was mixed. I just wanted to be black because there was a majority of black kids there. I would be more hesitant to tell them my background. Like, if [black peers] asked, I would just say I was black." Natasha employs the same strategy at the HBCU she attends, where she is surrounded primarily by black students and wants to fit in. Natasha, who internally identifies strongly as black and who describes wanting to be "just black," says:

> I would prefer to be black. I don't like being mixed. . . . Since I've been at college, I don't even mention [that I'm biracial]. I don't bring it up unless it's brought up to me. [*NK: And why is that?*] Because I don't want any attitudes about it. I don't want to deal with that . . . I don't want that. I would just rather say I'm black and that be the end of it. It's definitely not something that I advertise.

Natasha conceals her white background as a way to avoid others' "attitudes"—in particular, from black women who may be resentful of her biracial background. While some individuals, such as Michael and Stephanie, "advertise" their biracial backgrounds, Beth, Kim, Samantha, Kendra, Natasha, and Kim downplay their biracial backgrounds by choosing not to reveal them to others.

In addition to selectively disclosing particular identities in face-to-face social interactions, several respondents selectively disclose particular identities when filling out "What are you?" race questions commonly found on school, job, and scholarship applications. These respondents describe ways in which they strategically reveal or conceal particular racial identities, depending upon what they perceive they might gain or lose from the situation. Natasha, who earlier describes revealing only her black background to black friends and peers in order to fit in, also explains how she discloses particular identities depending upon what advantage it may afford her. When asked how she identifies herself to others, she says:

> I guess it would depend. I mean, when I fill out the little question things, I used to always check "other." Now I just check "black." But if you were asking me what's my background, I would say biologically I'm black and Irish. If it's coming down to something that has to be the truth, like doing an interview, I would say, "Yes, I'm biracial." But I've also learned to manipulate the situation that I'm in. I know that if I say I'm biracial I will get certain things, and if I say I'm black I will get certain things. So I know I probably play with that a little bit.

Caroline, who also appears non-white, cannot claim an exclusively white identity in day-to-day encounters because her outward racial appearance prevents her from doing so. If she claims a white identity, others (especially other whites) are quick to remind her that she is not white. However, she claims an exclusively white identity when filling out forms:

> There have been times where I've marked "Caucasian" on things, and I definitely feel that I'm within my right to do that. . . . Because my mom is white and my dad is black, and I've told some people that [I mark "white" on forms] and they think it's wrong. They think it's wrong for me to mark "white" on a form, but it's okay to mark "black." . . . I didn't really care. I was, like, "I can mark whatever I want." Because I can. And I don't feel like I'm lying about anything.

Caroline internally identifies very strongly as white, and while she cannot claim a white identity in her face-to-face encounters with others without being challenged, she exercises that option on forms and applications. Here, she selectively discloses her white identity because she identifies strongly as such, and she has more freedom to negotiate her racial identity on these forms.

Similarly Michael, who internally identifies strongly as black, describes a situation where he selectively disclosed only his white background. When asked whether he has ever tried to highlight or downplay any aspect of his background to others, he says, "Yeah, only when it's to my advantage. For instance, there was an Italian heritage scholarship given, and in the essay I didn't even comment about my African American background. I just spoke solely about my Italian heritage." Because he outwardly appears black, Michael cannot claim an exclusively Italian or white background in face-to-face encounters, but often he can do so on written forms and applications because of their faceless quality. In other words, his selective disclosure of his identity likely will not be challenged unless someone sees his physical appearance.

Resisting Racial Classification Altogether

In addition to disclosing only certain aspects of their racial background in face-to-face interactions or on forms and applications, biracial individuals also use selective disclosure and, at times, avoid disclosing *any* aspect of their racial backgrounds to others in order to resist racial classification altogether. When asked "What are you?" respondents occasionally avoid giving a racial answer as a strategy to prevent being racially categorized or "boxed in" by onlookers. These respondents challenge others' inquiries about their race with non-racial responses. Michelle reports that when asked "What are you?" or some related question, she answers with "I'm American." When asked how others respond to her answer, she says:

> They're really put off because I always tell them that I'm American. And they say, "Well, what are you? Are you African American? Are you Hispanic

American?" [I say] "I'm American. What does it matter to you what I am?" You know, like, if I'm at the job or something, and a customer comes up to me, "Oh you're pretty. What are you?" [I say] "I'm American." I mean, if I say, "Yes, I'm African American" or "Yes, I'm Caucasian," are you going to look at me differently? Chances are you are.

When biracial and multiracial people appear racially ambiguous and are not easily racially pigeonholed by others, some onlookers experience a "state of discomfort and momentary crisis" (Williams 1996: 193). This discomfort frequently prompts questions such as "What are you?" giving biracial individuals the opportunity to disclose whatever information they choose about their ancestry. Instead of disclosing her biracial background, or any racial background for that matter, however, Michelle answers with her nationality ("I'm American"). While she recognizes that some people are "put off" by this answer because it does not end the racial mystery for them, this identity strategy provides her with a means of resistance and of avoiding racial classification altogether.

Similarly, Kate occasionally tries to avoid being raced by others by evading "What are you?" questions. When asked about her background, she facetiously replies, "I'm a girl." Likewise, Angie says, "I love that question. [I respond] What are you? What does that mean, What are you? [I say] I'm human. We're all human. . . . What am I? What are you?" To resist racial labeling and categorization, Michelle, Kate, and Angie avoid answering frequent "What are you?" questions by giving non-racial answers: "I'm American," "I'm a girl," and "I'm human." Whereas other respondents use selective disclosure to reveal or conceal particular components of their racial backgrounds, these respondents decide not to disclose *any* aspects of their racial backgrounds.[3]

Selective Association

Finally, biracial individuals also use selective association with others as a strategy to signal their preferred racial identities to others. In particular, respondents talk about selectively associating with a particular race in terms of their friends, romantic partners, and even various organizations and institutions (e.g., clubs, groups, schools, churches).

Friends

While the majority of respondents maintain that they choose friends based on common interests and values, some respondents (11 of 40) talk about consciously selecting friends based on race for identity-related reasons (at least at some point in their lives). John, who internally identifies more strongly as black than white, describes selectively seeking out black friends to "reinforce" his black identity. When reflecting on his experience in college, he says:

In college I think I sought out minority friends of all kinds, but especially black people. And that was maybe because I had gone through some growth in my head, and I thought "I need to be having black friends." . . . And it's important to me . . . for example, at the college I went to there was a multicultural theme night, and I went to [it], and I had great experiences there and made great friends. They're still my close friends today. . . . I never made an effort to surround myself with white people. If anything, I tried to seek out other minorities, and black people in particular. . . . I've been very conscious about having black friends as a way to kind of reinforce that part of my identity.

Similarly, Nicole selectively associated with a particular racial group while in college; namely, other whites. She says, "I went to a predominantly white college, and my two closest friends were white. I didn't really associate with the black group. . . . I was more with whites. [*NK: Do you think that was a conscious decision on your part?*] I think at that time it was. I didn't feel good about that part of me." Because at that time she felt some degree of shame about what she perceived as a stigmatized identity, she tried to highlight her white identity by surrounding herself with white friends. She continues, "I think I was going through a phase. I don't think I felt good about being black—about being part black. So I don't think I wanted much to do with other blacks. I didn't want to associate with my black side. I was kind of ashamed of it."

At a young age, Stephanie was often told she was white by her black female peers. To counter being raced as white and to "prove" her blackness, she rejected anything white including white friends. She says:

When I got to high school, all the white people were so nice. . . . And I hated them. I didn't want to be friends with them. I didn't want to sit with them. I didn't want them to talk to me. I wanted to sit at the black table. I felt like I had to stress to people that I was black, because in middle school, I had to prove myself to them. That I wasn't white. That I was black.

Olivia also selectively associated with particular friends to signal her racial identity to others. She attended a predominantly white grade school, and initially she perceived herself as white. However, this changed when black students began being bused to her school. Wanting to identify as black, she deliberately adjusted her peer networks:

After I started meeting the black girls when they came to our grade school, I would seek out black girls to be friends with because I just wanted to be black. I was like, "Okay, well I need to be black. And I need to have black friends only." And it was kind of sad because I had some white girlfriends back then who had been with me since kindergarten, and I kind of stopped playing with them because I needed to be black and that meant I can't have white friends.

With the shift in her racial identity, Olivia deliberately altered the racial composition of her network of friends (from white to black) to reflect her new black identity.

Romantic Partners

Respondents also describe choosing romantic partners based on race. According to Lise Funderburg (1994), "A biracial person's choice of lover and spouse serves for many observers as yet another racial litmus test" and "an affirmation of the biracial person's own racial affiliation" (197). Indeed, France Winndance Twine (1996a) finds, in her study of multiracial black college students, that they perceived their choice of partner as a way to manage and negotiate their racial identity by signaling to others their "allegiance" to a particular racial group (Twine 1996a: 304; see also Kilson 2001). While the majority of respondents in my study describe choosing partners based on common interests and interpersonal attraction, I find that a minority of respondents (8 of 40) describe consciously selecting dating partners based on race, as a way to outwardly reveal to others their racial identity.

Olivia not only chose black friends "to be black," she also described consciously dating dark-skinned black men when she was younger as a way to signal her black identity to others:

> I used to only date very dark-skinned black men because I didn't want people to think I was trying to be white. . . . I didn't want people to think I was trying to be white or pass [as white]. . . . So I stayed with dark-skinned men because it's like I want[ed] to prove that I was black. Yeah, that I'm this black woman. "See, I've got this very dark man." It sounds stupid now, but back then it was important.

Like Olivia, Michelle, who is currently married to a black man, admits to dating black men in her younger years as a way of signaling her black identity to others. Because of her white racial appearance she has struggled to assert a black identity and says, "I think that if you're biracial and you decide to date and marry somebody of one race, then it's almost like—I don't want to say you're being forced to choose—but I guess you're kind of saying, 'All right, well, this is really what I've decided to identify with.'"

Similarly Beth, who internally identifies strongly as black but faced challenges to her black identity from black women, gravitated towards black men in high school as a way to "prove" her blackness to her black peers. Finding her black identity challenged, she says:

> I felt [dating black men] was my entryway to say that I'm more black . . . . Like, would I have done that if there wasn't such a need to kind of prove myself to

be part of being black?. . . And that really fit for me at that time. I think everything was so focused on "Oh, you're not black" or "You're different." [They would say], "Do you think that you're black, Beth? You're not black. You're not black." So I think that was why there was such an urgency to have that relationship with black guys at school.

Organizations and Institutions

Finally, seven respondents also discuss joining or attending organizations, clubs, schools, and churches that reflect their preferred racial identities. Alicia, who internally identifies very strongly as black, reports being drawn to black organizations:

I'm pretty black. Like, now. I didn't used to be, but probably over the last year, year and a half, I'm pretty black. . . . It's just like something has changed. And my mom sees it too. Maybe I'm just more concerned about being black right now. And maybe it's just a phase. I don't know. I just have this whole idea of life that has to be black. And I want to have kids that are part of Jack and Jill and I'm infatuated with my [black] boyfriend. I want to marry him and have children with him. I can't imagine a life where I wasn't part of Jack and Jill and I wasn't in AKA, I wasn't doing black things. Things that are exclusively black . . . maybe when I get out of college, I'll go back to being a little more integrated than I am now. But, right now, I feel like I'm pretty segregated. I kind of segregate myself, and I pretty much just hang out with black people.

Alicia, like others quoted previously, admits gravitating towards black men as one aspect of what she describes as her black "phase." She also describes "segregate[ing]" herself and consciously controlling the racial makeup of her circle of friends. She says she is concerned about being black and wants to be involved in organizations she perceives as "exclusively black"—Jack and Jill (one of the oldest black social organizations in the United States) and Alpha Kappa Alpha (the first sorority established by black women).

Other respondents talk about why they decided to attend an HBCU, and some explain that their choice is linked to how they want to identify themselves racially. Natasha, who grew up in a predominantly white community, talks about wanting to learn about her black background. Reflecting on the leadership development conference where she was, for the first time, exposed to other black peers her age, she says:

After that [conference], that's when everything started to change for me. [*NK: What do you mean?*] It was sad. I wanted to learn more about my black side and . . . spend more time in the black community and everything. And it was really frustrating because I couldn't even do that. I went back home to a little bubble and I couldn't do anything . . . I wanted to go to a small liberal arts school. It's in Wisconsin and it was like the perfect school for me, but I knew I needed the black experience, and so that's why I came to Spelman. This was like the only place I would go . . . I needed to get this identity experience. You know what I mean? Being one race—it has become important to me.

Because she had little opportunity to associate with black people while growing up in a predominantly white community, she made the decision to attend a predominantly black college to get "identity experience."

Thus far, I have outlined various strategies and tactics that biracial individuals use to negotiate and manage their racial identities. While some scholars argue that multiracial black Americans are constrained by one drop rules to identify exclusively as black (Davis 1991; Waters 1990, 1996), I find that there is some flexibility for identity negotiation. Some individuals negotiate exclusively black identities, but others work to negotiate biracial or white identities, often depending upon the situation or context. They highlight and downplay particular racial identities (as black, white, or biracial), as well as resist racial classification altogether, to gain some measure of agency in influencing how others perceive them. While I have discussed some of the reasons why people negotiate particular identities, I now turn to exploring in more depth the motivations underlying their identity work.

MOTIVATIONS

I find that biracial individuals do identity work for a range of reasons, and I focus here on four broad (and sometimes overlapping) motivations. Individuals work to claim or disclaim particular racial identities (1) to fit in, (2) to feel different or unique, (3) to avoid a stigmatized identity, and (4) to gain some perceived advantage or benefit.

To Fit In

First, respondents often describe wanting to "fit in" with their black or white peers. Not wanting to stand out as different, they work to blend in and feel accepted. Some respondents want to fit in with both black and white peers, and to do this, they alter how they present themselves in various situations. Kristen, who grew up going to a predominantly white school, also participated in a predominantly black gymnastics program. She talks about "switching" how she presented herself to her white peers and black peers: "Going to school and going to the gym were just two totally different things for me. So it's like I had to switch. I was like Superman. I was kind of like Clark Kent—take off my glasses going to the gym, and then put them back on when I was in school. . . . I would just kind of change. I would just do little things that I very well knew what I was doing." When asked why she did these "little things," she responds, "To fit in, probably. Because I wanted friends in both areas." To fit in, Kristen performs identity work in two contexts (with black peers, with white peers), revealing the contextual and situational nature of this type of work. In general, respondents in this study describe highlighting their black identities to fit in with black peers, and their biracial or white identities to fit in with their white peers.

Fitting In with Black Peers

When explaining how they work to fit in with their black peers, respondents often talk about trying to "blend in" so as not to stand out. Stephanie worked to express her black identity to fit in with her black peers growing up:

> First grade through eighth grade I was in the same school, and it was an all-black private school. So everybody there was black. I mean no Caucasians, no Asians, no whites. So there is where I suffered through [questions] like, "What are you?" And all the kids—you know how kids are if you're not the same complexion, then you're something else. So they basically told me I was white. . . . And I got so frustrated because I wanted to fit in, and they kind of made me feel like I wasn't going to fit in if I didn't go along with being totally black.

In the context of an all-black private school, Stephanie felt like she stood out because of her light skin color. Questions such as "What are you?" constantly highlighted her physical differences, but Stephanie wanted to "fit in" with her black peers. The only way she felt she could do so was to identify as black. As described earlier, she uses several strategies to manage her black identity—by *not* dyeing her hair blonde, by working to "talk black," by distancing herself from white music and clothes, and by selectively associating only with black peers.

John, too, highlights his black identity to fit in with black peers and feel accepted when in all-black situations:

> I'm very conscious in those situations. When everyone's talking about some TV show or some musician or whatever, I kind of make a point sometimes of saying I listen to that music too or I watch that show also. I don't, like, bend over backwards to do it or blurt it out and stuff like that. But I will be conscious of that, and I think the reason why I do it is to maybe just kind of ease everyone's comfort level. If I feel I fit in, they feel like I fit in, and we're all kind of comfortable. It's as much for me as it is for them. If they would see me as an outsider, it would be less comfortable for all of us, and I want to feel comfortable. I want to feel accepted.

John's strategy is to highlight cultural symbols of belonging, such as saying that he listens to particular music and watches certain television shows.

He wants to "fit in" and "feel accepted," while not feeling like the racial "outsider."

Biracial women also talk about how their black identities are frequently challenged by black women (see chapter 4). To fit in, they frequently describe working to "prove" their blackness in various ways. When asked whether she has ever tried to highlight her black identity to others, Beth says:

> Oh yeah. Oh yeah . . . I remember on the street where we had a gang called the Fly Girls. "I want to be a Fly Girl, too." I think we used to wear those iridescent colors, the neon pink, and [I would say] "Oh, I can buy that, too. See, I'm really cool and I can be part of the clique." So I think [I was] definitely trying to prove that I am black. I am black like you.

Other women similarly work to "prove" their black identity to black girls and women in order to fit in, and this appears to be a more common theme for biracial women than biracial men. As described earlier, Olivia tied her long hair back so as not to draw attention to her "white features." Beth, Natasha, and Michelle tanned for darker skin to blend in with their black peers. Kendra, Samantha, and Natasha at times concealed their white and biracial backgrounds to fit in with black peers.

That in this study women more often than men report doing identity work to prove their blackness further underscores the notion that biracial women may face more frequent challenges to their black identities. As described in chapter 4, colorism and competition for black men breeds jealousy and resentment from black women (at least from the respondents' perspectives), and these biracial women oftentimes find their authenticity as black women in question. While biracial people with black ancestry have historically been raced as black by the one drop rule, I find that some women in this study describe having to work to prove their blackness in order to fit in with their black counterparts. That these individuals must do identity work to strengthen their black identities (at least in the eyes of blacks) suggests that the "black by default" mentality may be to some degree waning.

Fitting In with White Peers

In addition to trying to identify as black to fit in with black peers, respondents also at times present biracial or white identities to fit in with their white peers. Alicia, Kendra, and Natasha all strongly internally identify as black; however, they describe situations in which they work to express their biracial or white identities to fit in with their white peers. When around whites, Alicia says:

> I highlighted my white side. I wore a little Jewish star [on a necklace]. I mean, I make sure that the way I speak is, like, more proper when I'm with white peo-

ple. Because I mean, like, I can talk ghetto, but I don't tend to do that around white people . . . it was this way of saying to people "I'm not just black." Just because . . . it makes things a lot easier. It really does. It does make things easier when I'm in primarily white situations. Like, "I can do this. I'm half like you." And it doesn't make me completely foreign when people meet me. To know that I'm mixed, I think the little bit of racism in everyone, makes white people a little more comfortable. Like, "Oh, she's not just a black girl."

Alicia modifies her speech to fit in and to show white people that she is "not just a black girl." She believes that highlighting her biracial, rather than black, identity will make other whites be more at ease with her. Because Alicia outwardly appears black, she cannot claim a white identity; instead, she chooses to highlight her biracial identity to say, "I'm half like you."

Likewise, Kendra expresses her biracial identity to other whites to make them feel more "comfortable" and "safe" with her. She says, "I feel like sometimes [when] white people know you're mixed . . . they feel a little bit more safe with you. . . . They'll find out that I'm mixed, and they'll be kind of relieved and feel like they can relate more. . . . [In school] I wanted them to know I was partly white because I wanted to feel like I was kind of like them and have them more comfortable with me." Both Alicia and Kendra highlight their biracial identities with white peers to "fit in," but they also manage these identities to negotiate racism and the very real possibility of being marginalized by their white peers for being black. If they identify as "mixed," both argue that whites will be more "comfortable" since, after all, they are not black.

Finally, Natasha, who strongly identifies as black, also expresses her biracial and white identity to whites to fit in with them. Talking about growing up in her predominantly white community, she says:

> When I was growing up, when I was younger . . . I would always say, I made sure to say, "I'm biracial. I'm white." I got it out there. [I would say] "I'm half of what you are." . . . With white people, they can't tell that I'm from the same area they are. They automatically assume [that I'm not]. So I would make it clear that I was from the same community they were. That I was into the same things, you know? I would push it more than I necessarily should.

Natasha, like Alicia and Kendra, makes sure she expresses her biracial identity to get across the message, "I'm half of what you are," or in the words of Alicia, "I'm half like you."

To Feel Different or Unique

Second, respondents describe expressing particular identities in order to stand out, to feel different, and to draw attention to their racial uniqueness.

Whereas some respondents want only to fit in or blend in with the group, others consciously work to stand out. Earlier Michael described highlighting his Italian background because he feels it makes him "unique" at his predominantly black college. By expressing his biracial background, he may be perceived as "exotic" and "different." Because he outwardly appears black, he works to highlight his Italian background by wearing Italian clothes, eating Italian food, and following Italian soccer. When other black students at his HBCU see his "Italian Stallion" T-shirt, for example, they question him about why he wears it, giving him the opportunity to negotiate and claim a biracial identity. Similarly, Stephanie describes sometimes wearing her hair curly at her predominantly black college so as to prompt questions about her racial background (as described earlier). When asked why she does this, she says, "It just makes me feel different and unique, so I enjoy playing [my biracial background] up."

Anthony also worked to feel different from the group—specifically, he wanted to stand out from his white peers in his predominantly white school:

> Well, when I went to that white school, I remember I used to always try to look extra black and make sure they knew I was black. I always liked feeling different. . . . I would disagree with them all the time on everything. Even if I didn't necessarily believe what I was saying, I would just always take a different point of view on everything to just separate myself purposely.

Anthony highlighted his blackness in the all-white school context to feel "different." Now Anthony attends a predominantly black college, where he works to highlight his white background: "Some days I dress with surfer shorts and skateboarder shoes . . . it makes me feel unique."

To Avoid a Stigmatized Identity

Third, respondents occasionally conceal a particular aspect of their racial ancestry because they perceive it as stigmatized. According to Erving Goffman (1963), the term *stigma* refers to attributes that discredit people, and race is one such attribute in particular contexts. Previous work has focused on blackness as stigmatized. For instance, during the Jim Crow era, some black-white individuals passed as white to avoid the stigma associated with blackness (Daniel 1992; Stonequist [1937] 1961). Storrs (1999), however, finds that multiracial women in her more contemporary sample identify with their non-white race because it is their white identity that is stigmatized. Traditional passing is undesirable for these women, who negatively redefine the meaning of whiteness as empty, bland, oppressive, prejudicial, and discriminatory. In the present study, I find that some biracial individuals perceive their black identity as the stigmatized identity, whereas others perceive the opposite. Biracial identities alone are not stigmatized; only when they signal a black background in a white context or white background in a black context do they become stigmatized.

Blackness as a Stigma

Earlier, Nicole described selectively associating with white peers in college as a way to affirm her white racial identity. Because she felt "ashamed" of her black background at that point in her life, she did not want to associate with anything she perceived as black. In her case, her black identity was her stigmatized identity (at least at that time).

Likewise, blackness is a stigma for Michael, who works to assert a biracial identity. In particular, he describes feeling frustrated when he is "lumped" into a black category:

> I find it really frustrating because I do so much in my education to negate these negative [black] stereotypes. You know what I'm saying? I'm in applied physics with a minor in industrial engineering. So it's, like, I'm not a lazy person. I'm very studious, and I take very seriously my career and what I want to do with my life. And for people to just negate that and just see that I'm black and not even care about the fact that I'm mixed, it kind of hurts me to just kind of lump me into this category like, "You're black. So that means you're ignorant, you're lazy, you steal, this and that." It definitely hurts and it's very upsetting sometimes.

Negative stereotypes associated with his black identity (e.g., ignorance, laziness, criminality) make a biracial identity attractive to Michael.

Caroline also describes wanting to dissociate herself from being black because of negative stereotypes associated with blackness. For a short time in college she wore her hair in braids, and she describes the concern she felt regarding how she appeared to whites:

> I can remember when I was an undergrad, one time I got braids in my hair and my hair was like to here [*points down her back*] and I had longer braids that were down my back. And it wasn't anything dramatic and I thought it looked really nice and I liked it. And as soon as I went back to school in a city, you know, similar to this, I was immediately on guard when I was walking down the street. And I was like, "Oh gosh, I don't want people to think that I'm black because I have these braids in my hair." And I didn't. I was so nervous about it and it was weird. As soon as I started down the street and started walking downtown, that was all that went through my mind, "I don't want people to think that I'm black." I don't want people to think that. I know it sounds awful, but I don't want people to think that I'm stupid or that I'm bitchy or anything like that. So I didn't keep them in for very long.

Caroline was very conscious of how her braids might race her as black. For Caroline, her black identity is stigmatized. To avoid being labeled as black and avoid negative stereotypes that she perceives as accompanying a black label (stupid, bitchy), she does not keep her braids in for very long. Instead she wears her hair long and straight to appear more biracial.

Whiteness as a Stigma

In addition to downplaying their black identities, respondents also talk about downplaying their white identities because of the stigma they perceive associated with whiteness in certain contexts (see also Storrs 1999). Stephanie, who strongly identifies as black, once worked to conceal her white identity because of the stigma associated with it:

> When I was younger, like, when I was in middle school, [my black friends] had never been around white people before. So they only knew what their parents told them. And they were told certain things. Like parents and kids misconstrue things. So their parents might have said something about a white coworker, and [my friends] would have thought all white people were all bad or whatever. And then they'd meet me and it was like, "Oh, I don't like Stephanie." And like I said, I'd changed myself around, and then I was black, so it didn't matter anymore. . . . Obviously, I couldn't be accepted because they thought I was white, so that had to be bad. I didn't want to be associated with it at all.

In this context, white is equated with being "bad," so Stephanie works to distance herself from that identity. To avoid the stigmatized identity, she works to express her black identity. Other respondents also embraced their black identities to resist the stigma of whiteness.

Olivia describes wanting to identify as black at a young age because she perceived whites as "oppressive" and as the "oppressor." Embarrassed about her biracial and white background, she worked to downplay her whiteness by pulling her long, straight hair back to make it less noticeable. Jackie presents herself as black to her black coworkers to avoid the stigma that she associates with whiteness. She says, "Well, at work, I'm black. That's it. No one knows that I'm half white. I don't want to be associated with all that. [NK: What's "all that"?] You know, white people think they're better. They can sometimes be ignorant. And that's not me. You can't trust them either. I don't want anyone to think they can't trust me." By concealing her white ancestry, Olivia distances herself from the associated stigma of superiority, ignorance, and untrustworthiness.

For Goffman (1963), stigma is an attribute that devalues one's identity and, most important here, it is a social construct that varies situationally; it is not an objective reality nor a fixed characteristic of an individual. According to Marvasti (2005), an ascribed status such as race or ethnicity is not inherently stigmatizing, but can become so under certain social conditions. Clearly, in most contexts whiteness is a privileged identity and does not hold the same stigma as blackness, yet *in some contexts* having white ancestry arguably carries at least some degree of stigma (for other examples of stigmatized whiteness, see Killian 1985; Kusow 2004). In these situations, biracial people do identity work (to downplay or hide their white ancestry) to manage what they perceive as a situationally stigmatized identity.

For Perceived Advantage

Finally, respondents also describe asserting white, biracial, and even black identities for some perceived advantage or benefit in a particular context. Generally, they describe a white identity as useful with regard to getting ahead in the workplace, a biracial identity as advantageous for obtaining status within the black community, and a black identity as beneficial for affirmative action.

Advantages of Identifying as White

In some cases, respondents describe identifying as white for a perceived advantage. Individuals who outwardly appear to be white (i.e., can pass as white) or who are racially ambiguous may have more opportunities to claim a white identity than those with identifiable characteristics associated with blackness. Beth and Michelle, who both internally identify strongly as black, describe presenting themselves as white in certain contexts when advantageous—for instance, they both identify as white to white peers at work. As Beth described earlier, her white coworkers assume she is white, and she chooses to "go along with their assumption." When asked why she selectively discloses only her white identity at work, she explains that she sees how her white coworkers talk about other black coworkers (often in very negative and racially charged ways), and she wants to avoid any potential problems of prejudice or discrimination. In short, she believes that by identifying as white, she is making her professional life easier.

Michelle, who also strongly identifies as black, identifies herself as white when at work because of the "convenience" it affords her:

> I [identify as white] more so when it's convenient to me in corporate America. I've witnessed where white people get further than the black people. . . . And I just think in my whole experience, not just with this job but other jobs, I have to kind of, not pretend, but put forth that I'm white. Then they're more likely to trust me. . . . I think I use it to my advantage when I need to. [*NK: In the work setting?*] Yes, 'cause I'm trying to get ahead.

Michelle says she uses her white identity to her "advantage" because she feels other whites will trust her and give her the opportunities she wants to get ahead. She "puts forth" that she is white (i.e., selectively discloses her white identity), which she perceives is an advantage for moving up in the workplace.

Beth and Michelle describe contexts in which they manage their white identities, but identifying exclusively as white (while concealing a black/biracial background) is rare among respondents. That so few respondents passed as white is not surprising given that this option is available only to those with white skin and features, and also because passing as white is arguably "viewed with disdain by other blacks" today (Russell, Wilson, and Hall 1992: 73). Potential charges from other blacks of racial disloyalty, racial shame, and self-hatred arguably prevent some from passing as white. Further, the "great age of passing" occurred in the slave and Jim Crow eras, when blacks had few—if any—rights and opportunities (Daniel 2002). Some individuals, those who could physically do so, passed as white to avoid slavery, institutional discrimination, and blatant racism. Yet in the post–civil rights era, it may be safe to say that the underlying force behind passing has been largely removed. Clearly, however, there remain some contexts (e.g., the workplace) where passing as white may still confer advantages.

Advantages of Identifying as Biracial

Respondents also describe identifying as biracial in particular situations for a perceived advantage or benefit. For instance, Natasha, who strongly identifies as black, recognizes that her biracial background provides her with certain informal benefits with black males in the predominantly black context of the HBCU she attends:

> I know, like here [at this HBCU] especially with black people—okay, probably a lot of [respondents in this study] have said this, but [my friends would] be on the phone and, you know, they'd be going out with [a black guy] and they'd be, like, "Do you have any other friends?" And she's like, "Oh, well, there's Natasha." And they'd be like, "Well, what does she look like?" [My friends would say], "Oh, she's biracial." And I'm *in*. It's, like, with other people, you have to be, like, "Oh, well, she's five-two, da, da, da, has blonde hair." All [my friends] have to say is, "She's biracial" and I'm *in*.

According to Natasha, publicly identifying herself as biracial affords her the advantage of being "in," or automatically included, with some black males. When asked what it is about being biracial that makes her "in," she says, "Honestly, I don't know. Because I myself don't think biracials are more attractive or anything like that. But, I guess, if you're mixed, you're presumed to be a lighter shade. So that's why. . . . So I would throw that out in those types of situations."

Because of our nation's preference for whiteness and our history of privileging white skin over dark skin (Hunter 1998; Russell, Wilson, and Hall 1992), skin-color stratification plagues the black American community. In addition to skin color, two categories have emerged—"good" (white) features (straight hair, long hair, thin lips) and "bad" (black) features (short hair, kinky hair, full lips, wide nose). Expressing a biracial identity is likely equated with having "good" features, and because "good" features are highly valued and perceived as attractive, these individuals may gain some degree of status within the black community. Natasha, for instance, recognizes that her biracial background is equated with having a "lighter shade," which benefits her within the context of the black community. In chapter 4, I discussed how biracial women are often desired by black men and often rejected by black women who are resentful of their "good" features. Expressing her biracial background gives Natasha automatic inclusion and acceptance by black men because of colorism within the American black community.

Additionally, Minkah Makalani (2003) argues that black-white people may employ whiteness to negotiate the racial hierarchy by positioning themselves above African Americans. Rather than passing as white (because they either cannot or choose not to do so), they draw on their white ancestries in order to access some of the privileges that come with being white (e.g., status, job opportunities). In short, identifying as biracial can certainly be attractive in a society that generally privileges white over black.

Advantages of Identifying as Black

Finally, while there have been significant historical disadvantages for those identifying as black (e.g., slavery, lack of rights) and arguably there still are disadvantages today (e.g., prejudice and discrimination), respondents identify several advantages to managing a black identity. Like Kerry Ann Rockquemore and Patricia Arend (2003), who find that biracials sometimes pass as black in order to receive "social, economic, and educational opportunities" (60), I find that a majority of respondents (29 of 40) in this study claim an exclusively black identity in some contexts for perceived advantage—in particular, when filling out applications for college admissions, scholarships, or financial aid. Frequently unaware that being biracial is often sufficient for affirmative action purposes, they present themselves exclusively as black. Stephanie, for instance, who generally labels herself as biracial to others, consciously conceals her biracial identity when filling out applications for college admissions and scholarships and says, "The funny thing is, like, when I applied to [college], like for affirmative action, I checked 'black.' I do not check 'other.' Like if I'm applying for a [United Negro College Fund] scholarship or anything to do with black people, I check 'black.' Yeah, I check 'other' now, but like I say, if I'm applying for scholarships or something, I am 'black.'"

Julie also selectively reveals her black identity in some situations. When asked how she identifies herself on forms and applications, she says, "I put 'other.' Or when you can check both, I put 'African American' and 'Caucasian.' But also, I would have to say that it depends on what I'm trying to do. If I am trying to get more money from the government, I am 'African American.' There is no white aspect to me." While she generally labels herself as biracial to others, she perceives an advantage of identifying exclusively as black, at least in certain contexts. Usually she checks "other" or she checks multiple racial categories to signify her biracial background. At times, however, she consciously omits her white background when she perceives doing so to be advantageous.

Michelle, too, explains why she checks the "black" box on forms: "I thought maybe if I chose black, especially in college, I'd get more financial aid. I'd get more opportunities, and so I kind of thought it was to my best advantage to just say I was black." Michelle, like others, believes it is to her "best advantage" to identify herself as black in these situations, even though she generally labels herself as biracial. Denise identifies herself as black and explains the advantage of doing so in similar terms: "Saying that [I'm black] . . . is important to me. And sometimes there are more opportunities if you're black as well. Some are nicer to you. There are some job opportunities where you have more weight if you're a minority. And there are more scholarships." The choice to identify as black may not be particularly surprising given that (1) most respondents are unaware that being biracial is sufficient for most affirmative action programs, and (2) they may feel less worthy of financial aid or a scholarship because of their biracial/white ancestry. Indeed, studies have shown that people perceive biracials with white ancestry as less qualified for minority scholarships than other racial minorities (Sanchez and Bonam 2009). Mary Campbell and Melissa Herman (2010) also find that most whites and about half of monoracial minorities in their study opposed affirmative action privileges for biracial people. Faced with a mindset that being biracial may somehow make them less deserving, some respondents consciously identify simply as black. In doing so, they arguably pass as black when they believe it to be to their material advantage. This suggests that the phenomenon of racial passing, often believed to be a relic of the past, occurs even today. However, racial passing looks much different today than in decades past: passing during the Jim Crow era involved passing as white, whereas passing in the post–civil rights era of affirmative action sometimes involves passing as black.

DISCUSSION AND CONCLUSION

In this chapter, I have outlined both the strategies and motivations involved in racial identity work. Biracial individuals in this study employ a number of strategies to claim and disclaim particular racial identities, such as verbal identification/dis-identification (e.g., saying "I'm black" or "I'm not black"), manipulation of physical appearance (e.g., altering hair and skin color), highlighting cultural symbols (e.g., clothing, dialect/slang), selectively disclosing particular aspects of their ancestry (e.g., revealing only their white or black ancestry, or no racial ancestry at all), and selectively associating with friends and romantic partners of a particular race, and joining black organizations and institutions. I also explore the underlying motivations of identity work, finding that biracial people do identity work for a number of reasons, including to fit in and feel accepted, to stand out and feel unique, to avoid a stigmatized identity, and to gain some perceived advantage through identifying as white, biracial, or even black.

Because some scholars argue that multiracial black individuals are constrained by the one drop rule to identify exclusively as black (see Davis 1991; Gibbs and Hines 1992; Waters 1990, 1996), little systematic attention has been given to the ways in which these individuals manage and negotiate non-black racial identities (for an exception, see Storrs 1999). I find, however, that black-white biracial individuals *can and do* perform identity work to negotiate non-black identities with others—many individuals negotiate biracial or even white identities, depending upon the situation and, of course, their racial phenotypes. The contextual nature of their identities illustrates their racial fluidity, though this fluidity is not unbounded; biracials cannot *always* identify however they want and, in fact, identifying as white (at least publicly) remains reserved only for those with a particular outward appearance. These findings do show, however, that race is not as rigid and inflexible as it once was under the weight of Jim Crow segregation and the one drop rule.

Mary Waters (1999), for instance, once argued that "a person with black skin who had some Irish ancestry would have to work very hard to present himself as Irish—and in many ways he/she would be denied that option" (203). Raced as black, multiracial people would find other ethnic options (such as Irish) inaccessible to them, whereas white ethnics would arguably have more ethnic options and ethnic fluidity (e.g., white ethnics are easily able to identify with Irish and other white ethnicities in their backgrounds) (see Waters 1990). Indeed, findings from this study suggest that a person with "black skin" will likely be denied the option of identifying as Irish, as Waters (1999) argues; white identities are only accessible for those who physically appear white, and even then, there is no guarantee society at large will allow them to claim that identity if their black ancestry is known.

I argue, however, that black-white biracial Americans sometimes draw attention to their white ethnic or racial ancestry, not to identify as white (or as Irish), but to identify as *biracial* (see also Khanna 2011)—a racial option that has only recently become accessible to the offspring of interracial unions.

This undoubtedly points to some degree of racial flexibility for biracial people today (even for those with black ancestry): they can identify as black *or* biracial. Whether their biracial identities are validated in the public arena remains in question, however. In fact, chapter 3 revealed that many of the biracial respondents in this study feel that they are raced as black by society at large—whites often assume they are black; and blacks, who more often recognize their non-black ancestry, nonetheless label them as black, too (e.g., "Yes, you may be biracial, but *really* you're black"). If their biraciality goes unrecognized and invalidated by others, then this poses a serious challenge to this supposed racial flexibility.

Indeed, more work is needed to examine the extent to which biracial identities are validated by larger society today. However, there is evidence that biraciality is at least beginning to be recognized as a legitimate racial option. First, despite frequently being raced as black in the public arena, many of the respondents in this study do exercise the option of identifying as biracial in their *personal lives*. The majority of respondents in this study identify as biracial (or some related term), which suggests that they do see the biracial category as a valid option today—even if they find it challenged in public. Second, in the last decade, local, state, and federal governments have increasingly recognized biraciality/multiraciality by allowing Americans to choose more than one racial box on government forms and applications (e.g., the 2000 U.S. Census). This growing institutional recognition suggests that biracial and multiracial people are beginning to successfully carve out a space for themselves within the existing racial structure. Once limited to identifying as monoracial (usually as black), black-white biracial Americans today frequently have the option to check multiple boxes to signify their biracial backgrounds. Moreover, while their biracial identities may sometimes be challenged in the public arena, this is one space where they can assert their biraciality with little dispute.

In addition to managing biracial (or even white) identities, many individuals also negotiate and manage exclusively black identities when identifying as biracial or white is undesirable, or when identifying as black is perceived as attractive or advantageous in some way. These findings suggest a shift in the racial landscape, in which blackness has historically stigmatized and disadvantaged people to the point that they (if they could) concealed their black ancestry to the extent possible. Blackness in the post–civil rights era no doubt still comes with considerable prejudice, discrimination, and social disadvantage, yet the legacy of the civil rights movement of the

1960s, black pride of the 1970s, and changes in institutional policies (e.g., affirmative action) have, in some contexts, made blackness something to be proud of and desired (at least among these biracial respondents).

Moreover, these findings draw attention to the fact that some respondents (more often biracial women than biracial men) felt they had to "work" to express their black identities. In some contexts, particularly when among black women, biracial women felt the need to perform identity work to highlight their black ancestry (or in some cases, to downplay or hide their white ancestry) in order to "prove" themselves as black. That these individuals felt it necessary to perform identity work to strengthen their black identities (at least in the eyes of blacks) points to the continued effect of colorism within the black community. Due to the advantages they may receive for having light skin (or other white phenotypic characteristics) and the resentment they may experience from their darker-skinned counterparts, biracial people are sometimes accused by blacks of "not being black enough." This suggests that the "black by default" mentality of the one drop rule may be waning to some degree—at least within the black community. Biracial respondents in this study describe blacks generally accepting them as black, but the repeated efforts of some biracials to "prove" their blackness suggest that this acceptance is not always as straightforward as the one drop rule would suggest. These biracial respondents undoubtedly feel more embraced by the black than the white community, yet their acceptance by blacks is certainly not blind within this post–civil rights era.

NOTES

1. Excerpts from this chapter appeared in 2010 in *Social Psychology Quarterly* 73(4): 380–97 ("Passing as Black: Racial Identity Work among Biracial Americans"; coauthored with Cathryn Johnson) and in 2011 in *Ethnic and Racial Studies* 34(6): 1049–67. ("Ethnicity and Race as 'Symbolic': The Use of Ethnic and Racial Symbols in Asserting a Biracial Identity").

2. The cosmetics industry successfully marketed skin-lightening products to African Americans for decades (particularly in the mid-1900s). This began to change, however, in the 1960s and 1970s when the Black Power movement popularized the beauty of dark skin and other black phenotypic features (e.g., wide noses, thick lips, and kinky hair) (see Rondilla and Spickard 2007).

3. These non-racial responses are similar to what Rockquemore and Brunsma (2002a) call "transcendent" identities—when biracial people refuse to have any racial identity and instead opt to call themselves "human." On the contrary, respondents in this study do have racial identities, but *in some situations* they assert non-racial identities to avoid being raced by onlookers.

7

Concluding Thoughts

This book began with Barack Obama, the son of a white woman and a black man, being elected as the first African American president of the United States. Given the long, harsh history of race relations in this country, it was for many a surprising win. Many Americans celebrated the moment of his election for the barriers it broke for African Americans in this country, while others openly debated his race: Is he *really* black? Is he biracial? Some even asked: If he was raised by his white mother and white grandparents, why doesn't he say he is white (see Sullivan 2008)? At a broader level, his case raises questions about race and the meanings of blackness and whiteness in American society today. It also raises questions about racial identity and how and why people identify the way they do.

The purpose of this book was to identify some of the factors and processes shaping the racial identities of black-white Americans. The goal was not to explain every factor and process, but rather to extend previous research by focusing on the underlying social psychological processes by which their identities are shaped and negotiated with others—a perspective outside the scope of most books on the subject. By drawing on broader social psychological theories and concepts, the aim was to further our general understanding of racial identity among this ever-growing population of Americans.

Chapter 3 revealed the importance of reflected appraisals (how biracial Americans *think* others see them) and the influence of the one drop rule on those appraisals. Clearly, their perception of how others (both black and white) viewed them had a strong influence on how they saw themselves, and even Barack Obama drew on the concept of reflected appraisals when he once remarked about his identity, "I self-identify as African American.

That's how I am treated and that's how I am viewed" (as quoted in Chang 2010). Similarly reflecting on her own black identity, NAACP Vice President of Communications Leila McDowell recently remarked, "Even though my father is white and I have half of his genes, when I apply for a loan, when I walk into the car lot, when I apply for a job, they don't see me as half white, they see me as black. If you have any identifying [black] characteristics, you're black" (Washington 2010). These statements reveal the importance of phenotype, and *others'* perceptions of that phenotype, in influencing racial identity. Because of the one drop rule, which for generations defined anyone with any amount of black ancestry as black, having dark skin, or any features associated with Africa, even today often means one is typically raced as black.

Chapter 4 looked at respondents' day-to-day social interactions with blacks and whites, and the ways in which their perceptions of those interactions pushed and pulled them towards various racial identities. For the most part, biracial respondents in this study describe feeling rejected by whites and embraced by blacks (although clearly there were exceptions), experiences which influenced their racial identities. Although blacks were more likely than whites to embrace these biracial respondents as "one of their own," the acceptance was not universal, at least not from the perspectives of these respondents. Many biracial women in this study felt rejected by black women, suggesting that contemporary intra-racial tensions within the black community affect how some racially identify. For some biracial respondents, this treatment shaped non-black internalized identities (i.e., they identified as biracial or white).

In Chapter 5, I examined the process of social comparisons and the ways in which social networks influenced those processes (and hence, identities). Comparisons with black, white, and biracial others regarding their phenotype; culture; and experiences of privilege, prejudice, or discrimination shaped how respondents viewed themselves racially. Moreover, the comparisons themselves were fundamentally shaped by the racial composition of respondents' social networks—whether predominantly white, predominantly black, or racially mixed. Those in one-sided networks (predominantly white or black) were more likely to invoke negative racial and cultural stereotypes of the group with which they had limited contact than were those embedded in racially mixed networks. As a consequence, they frequently differentiated themselves from these negative images by identifying in the "opposite" direction. Moreover, this chapter furthers our understanding of those who internally identified as white: these respondents felt they could not identify with being black because, culturally speaking, they perceived themselves as having more in common with whites than blacks. This is not surprising considering that these white-identified respondents mostly grew up in middle-class, predominantly white communities.

Further, this chapter revealed some of the stereotypes that these biracial respondents hold about blacks and whites, several of which are closely tied to social class and reflect the social-class disparities that exist between blacks and whites in broader American society. Their stereotypes also suggest that biracial people, at least those in this study, are not without their own racial biases.

While chapters 3, 4, and 5 focused on factors (e.g., phenotype, one drop rule, social networks, social class) and processes (e.g., reflected appraisals, social interactions, social comparisons) that act on individuals to influence their racial identities, chapter 6 revealed that identity is a process: society acts on individuals, but individuals can also play an active role in negotiating their race with others. Unlike previous books, which have tended to focus on external factors shaping identity, this chapter explored the performance of race. Here, I looked at respondents' strategies and motivations for "doing race." Respondents in this study often worked to present themselves as white or biracial—something often assumed impossible given the restrictions of their black ancestry (Waters 1990). Once constrained by the one drop rule to identify as black, they seem to have some measure of racial flexibility today. Further, this chapter revealed that some respondents felt it necessary to work to assert their black identities, which implies that they are not always perceived as "black by default" (at least not by blacks) as the one drop rule would suggest.

THE MULTIDIMENSIONALITY OF RACIAL IDENTITY

In addition to identifying factors and processes shaping identity, and illuminating the ways in which biracials perform race, a key conceptual and methodological contribution of this book was acknowledgment and differentiation of multiple dimensions of racial identity—as public versus internal dimensions—which no doubt added a more nuanced and multifaceted approach to identity. In doing so, three things are evident. First, biracial individuals may identify their race one way publicly and another internally, illustrating a potential for identity mismatches within any given individual. Clearly, identity is a complex and potentially elusive concept to study, although in research it is often treated as something easily ascertained through categories checked on a survey.

Second (and relatedly), tapping one dimension of identity reveals only part of the picture. The majority of individuals in this study identified as multiracial or biracial (or some related term), but this in no way means that their identities are the same. Two individuals may identify publicly as biracial, yet internally identify themselves very differently—one strongly as black, the other strongly as white. This is significant because how they internally identify likely has real implications for their connectedness to their respective black and white racial communities. They may both label themselves as biracial (and indeed identify themselves as such on forms and surveys), yet their divergent internalized identities likely lead to differences regarding their friendship circles, their choice of partners/spouses, the organizations to which they belong, the racial composition of the neighborhoods where they live, their connection to blacks and whites, their views towards blacks and whites, their racial-political attitudes, and so on.

Allison and John are good examples. Although both publicly identify themselves in multiracial terms (Allison as "mixed" and John as "biracial"), they differ in terms of their internalized identities. Internally, Allison strongly identifies as white and John strongly as black, and this has clearly had an impact on their day-to-day lives. Allison's circle of friends are all white, she is married to a white man, she attends a predominantly white university and church, and she describes little interest in seeking out black people for friendships. In contrast, John's circle of friends are mostly black, he is married to a black woman, he attends a predominantly black church, and he sees himself as firmly embedded in the black community, even though phenotypically he appears white. If we focus on the racial labels Allison and John use to describe themselves, we would make the mistake of perceiving their identities as the same (or highly similar), when in reality they are quite different.

Finally, we must not only acknowledge different types of identity, but also engage these different layers in analysis, as I do here. For instance, what are the factors and processes shaping each dimension? Only by studying these different facets of identity was I able to further the debate over the impact of the one drop rule today. Focusing on the public dimension of identity reveals one part of the picture, but taking a deeper look at internalized identity tells yet another story. No doubt, understanding the impact of the one drop rule today lies in understanding these different dimensions.

THE ONE DROP RULE REVISITED

Rooted in slavery and Jim Crow segregation, the one drop rule once rendered biraciality invisible by simply defining black-white biracial Americans as black. Used as a tool to preserve white superiority and maintain the myth of white racial purity, the rule allowed biracial Americans with black ancestry no racial options other than black (unless they outwardly appeared white and actively hid their black ancestry to pass as white). In recent years, scholars have argued that the one drop rule remains a powerful force even today (Bratter 2010; Davis 1991; Song 2003; Waters 1990, 1991; Zack 1996; see also Sweet's 2005 discussion), and several studies have drawn on the one drop rule to explain why black-white Americans often still identify as black—on surveys and census forms, for instance (Brunsma 2005, 2006; Harris and Sim 2002; Qian 2004). Other scholars argue, however, that the rule is waning in influence and black-white Americans have more racial options than in previous decades—no longer must they identify solely as black, but instead can be black, biracial, and sometimes even white (Korgen 1998; see also Rockquemore and Arend 2003; Rockquemore and Brunsma 2002a, 2002b; Roth 2005). In fact, David Brunsma and Kerry Ann Rockquemore (2001) point to the variety of ways in which black-white biracial Americans self-identify to argue that "the one drop rule has *lost the power* to determine racial identity" (101; emphasis added).

The findings of the present study reveal *both* the weakened state and the lingering effect of the one drop rule today. Looking only at public identities, or the ways in which these respondents identified themselves to others, I, too, found that respondents identified in a myriad of ways (as black, African American, biracial, multiracial, interracial, mixed, and white); this clearly indicates that they have more racial options today than the one drop rule once allowed them. Additionally, respondents in this post-civil-rights-era sample were much more likely to identify publicly as biracial or white (85 percent) than black (15 percent), which also suggests that the one drop rule does not have the same influence it once did.

At first glance, these findings, like those of previous studies, indicate that the one drop rule has lost its power (as Brunsma and Rockquemore 2001 suggest). However, taking a multidimensional view of racial identity, something most studies have yet to do, sheds new light on the present-day influence of the one drop rule. The rule has little influence on these respondents' public identities, but a closer look reveals that the one drop rule indeed still has some degree of influence on their internalized identities: 60 percent of respondents more closely identified as black than white, and most of those identified strongly as black. When explaining their black identities, respondents frequently pointed to how they thought they were perceived by others—as black—often because they had some identifying "black" characteristic(s) or because others explicitly or implicitly invoked the one drop rule to tell them that they were black (e.g., other blacks, for instance, said things like, "If you're just a little black, then you're considered black" or "If you've got a little in you, it's all in you"). By taking a more nuanced approach to racial identity, I find that these biracial respondents often publicly identified as biracial, yet societal ascriptions via the one drop rule continue to tell them that they are *really* black (see also Harris and Sim 2002).

Therefore, more and more people may indeed be identifying as biracial today, as scholars have found, but this identity may not necessarily be validated by larger society. This is important because according to Kerry Ann Rockquemore (1999), "an individual cannot have a realized identity without others who validate that identity" (199; see also Rockquemore and Laszloffy 2003). This is particularly interesting given that early results from the 2010 Census reveal that the mixed-race population has grown by about 35 percent in the last decade—and that the number claiming both black and white ancestry grew as well. As they exercise their right to check multiple racial boxes, does this mean these individuals necessarily identify as multiracial? Likely, yes and no. Yes, they are asserting their biracial/multiracial identities in very public ways, but indeed they may not necessarily internally identify as such because, for many, society continues to race them as black.

It is imperative to keep in mind, however, that the sample in this study is not generalizable, and is for the most part southern. The South has "the greatest history of anti-miscegenation legislation as well as cultural adherence to the one-drop rule" (Roth 2005: 45); thus, the legacy of the one drop rule may be strongest in this region. Whether this trend is taking place outside the South remains to be seen, but there is reason to believe that other regions of the United States may also be seeing a lingering effect of the one drop rule. For instance, in studies that force biracials with black ancestry to make a monoracial choice about their race, "black" remains the most common option, even for respondents living *outside* the South (for examples, see Harris and Sim 2002; Herman 2004; Qian 2004; Roth 2005). Melissa Herman (2004), for instance, in her study of multiracial high-school students in California and Wisconsin found that nearly 70 percent of those with black-white ancestry reported being black when forced to choose a monoracial category. Further, the fact that Obama was labeled as the first African American president of the United States, despite his well-known biracial background, also shows that the trend towards black identities (and external black ascriptions) may not simply be a southern phenomenon. No doubt, the one drop rule remains strongest in this region (for evidence, see Brunsma 2005, 2006; Harris and Sim 2002), but arguably black-white biracial Americans are frequently raced as black outside the South as well.

These findings raise questions about the future of the one drop rule and racial identity for black-white biracial Americans. The future influence of the one drop rule remains to be seen, but likely it will depend on the support for a biracial category and whether or not this category is legitimated by society at large. The "check all that apply" format of the 2000 and 2010 U.S. Census suggests some degree of institutional legitimation of biraciality; no longer forced to "choose one box," Americans can check multiple boxes to signify their biracial (and multiracial) identities. Day-to-day societal recognition of their biracial identities, however, appears to lag behind federal acknowledgment of biracial people and their biracial identities—again, as evidenced by the fact that the majority of respondents in this study feel others see them simply as black.

Editorial columnist Leonard Pitts (2007) further highlights this fact when he writes, "If Obama asked to be identified as biracial, I would accommodate him because I believe that . . . people should be allowed to define themselves as they please. But with that said, I must confess I've always found that term rather meaningless insofar as the African American experience goes." Likely Pitts is not alone. Multiraciality is nothing new in the African American community, and for many black Americans it may seem senseless to begin now differentiating biracial people from blacks (since many so-called blacks are actually multiracial). As more and more people claim biracial identities, however, these individuals may eventually carve out a space for themselves within the existing racial structure. If biraciality does become increasingly recognized as a legitimate racial category, the one drop rule will eventually meet its bitter end. How long this will take remains to be seen.

LOOKING AHEAD: AVENUES FOR FUTURE RESEARCH

What I have presented here are several pieces of a larger (identity) puzzle, but in no way is the puzzle solved. Identity is complex and shaped by a multitude of overlapping and interconnected processes, and more research is needed to further understand racial identity and the way in which it is formed and negotiated with others. Future research should move beyond simply identifying factors shaping racial identity to better understanding the processes by which these factors influence identity. Reflected appraisals, social interactions, social comparisons, and identity work are identified here, but more research is needed on these and other processes.

Future research should also examine how biraciality is viewed within the African American community—in particular, how black Americans view their biracial counterparts. As black? As biracial? And why? Biracial respondents in this study report that blacks often categorize them as black, but in some cases, their black identities are openly challenged (especially for biracial women who find their blackness challenged by black women). The present study looks at this issue from the perspective of these biracial respondents, but future work should more directly examine opinions about biraciality from blacks themselves. Moreover, future work should also look at whether there is a difference between whites and blacks regarding the acceptance of a biracial category. In a Pew Research Center poll, 53 percent of whites said Barack Obama was mixed race, while only 24 percent said he was black. Quite the reverse, 55 percent of blacks said Obama was black and 34 percent said he was mixed race (Washington 2010). While whites appear more accepting of calling Obama mixed race than are blacks, it remains to be seen if there is a racial difference regarding the acceptance of biraciality.

Moreover, this study focused on black-white biracial Americans. While this population is important because of the historically strained relations between blacks and whites in the United States and is a useful starting point to examine racial identity, future work should compare and contrast various biracial groups to further our general understanding of racial identity. According to Miri Song (2003), "There is a need to go beyond the dualities of black and white, not only because it is important to validate the existence of other kinds of mixed people, but also because nuanced theorizing on multiracial people cannot progress without considering the peculiarities of different mixed experiences" (83). Different historical circumstances and structural situations faced by different biracial groups (e.g., black-Asian, Asian-white, Native American-white) no doubt influence identities in different ways, but researchers should investigate the commonalities they share (as well as those differences) regarding identity formation in order to develop a more generalizable theory of racial identity.

Finally, this book has explored identity, and how and why people identify the way they do. Recent research has also begun to move the field forward by looking at the *effects* of multiracial identity, and more work is needed in this area. For instance, recent studies have examined the consequences of multiraciality and these individuals' identity choices on their psychological well-being (Binning et al. 2009; Cheng and Lively 2009; Phillips 2004; Suzuki-Crumly and Hyers 2004), self-esteem (Bracey, Bamaca, and Umana-Taylor 2004; Phillips 2004; Townsend, Markus, and Bergsieker 2009), anxiety and depression (Coleman and Carter 2007), substance use (Choi et al. 2006; Sakai, Wang, and Price 2010), political and racial attitudes (Masuoka 2011), perceptions of racism (Brackett et al. 2006), socioeconomic attainment (Huyser, Sakamoto, and Takei 2010), school attachment (Cheng and Klugman 2010), academic performance (Herman 2009), and even their friendship networks and choices (Doyle and Kao 2007b; Quillian and Redd 2009). Clearly, this is an ever-growing area for new exploration. Understanding how people identify is important, but future work should press forward in answering the latest question: Why does understanding identity matter?

At the beginning of this book, I suggested that identity has implications for both the individual and the larger racial communities to which he or she belongs. Future work should further examine the implications of the racial identity choices that biracial and multiracial people make, not only for the individuals themselves, but also for society at large: Are more and more people identifying as biracial today? If yes, what effect is this having on their respective racial communities and on American society as a whole? The body of research in the area of biracial and multiracial identity, while it has grown exponentially since the 1990s, is still quite young. A better understanding of identity among this population will undoubtedly help illuminate the complexities of identity and provide us with a unique lens with which to more broadly examine race relations in the United States today.

Appendix A

Interview Schedule

BACKGROUND QUESTIONS

1. Gender: ____ Female
   ____ Male
   ____ Other
2. Age: _____
3. Where do you currently live? (city and state) _____
   Have you always lived in X?
   _____ Yes
   _____ No
   What other places have you lived? _____
4. What is your current educational level?
   _____ Less than high school
   _____ High school
   _____ Some college
   _____ College
   _____ Some professional/graduate school (specify _____)
   _____ Professional/graduate school (specify _____)
5. The educational level you expect to achieve?
   _____ Less than high school
   _____ High school
   _____ Some college
   _____ College
   _____ Some professional/graduate school (specify _____)
   _____ Professional/graduate school (specify _____)

6. Are you currently employed?
   _____ Yes (occupation) _____
   _____ No, I'm currently unemployed
   _____ No, I'm currently in school
   (program/school) _____
7. Please describe your ethnic & racial background. _____
   What is the race of your mother? _____
   What is the race of your father? _____
8. Were you raised by both biological parents? [If yes: Are they still married?]
   _____ Yes, I was raised by both parents
   _____ No, I was raised by my mother
   _____ No, I was raised by my father
   _____ No, I was raised by another family member (specify_____)
   _____ No, I was adopted
9. Have you had contact with both sides of your extended family? [Explain]. _____
   _____
   _____ Yes
   _____ Mostly with my white relatives
   _____ Mostly with my non-white relatives
   _____ Other (specify _____)
10. What is/was your mother's educational background?
    Occupation? _____
    _____ Less than high school
    _____ High school
    _____ Some college
    _____ College
    _____ Some professional/graduate school (specify _____)
    _____ Professional/graduate school (specify _____)
11. What is/was your father's educational background?
    Occupation? _____
    _____ Less than high school
    _____ High school
    _____ Some college
    _____ College
    _____ Some professional/graduate school (specify _____)
    _____ Professional/graduate school (specify _____)

GENERAL RACIAL IDENTITY QUESTIONS

12. Have you ever had people ask you about your racial background (e.g., "What are you?")?
    How do you tend to identify yourself to others?

13. How strongly would you say you identify with being black? ____
    Would you say very strongly, somewhat, very little, or not at all?
    [Why?]
14. How strongly would you say you identify with being white? ____
    Would you say very strongly, somewhat, very little, or not at all?
    [Why?]
15. Is there a racial group with which you most identify (black or white)?
    [Explain.]
16. Does how you identify yourself to others differ according to who is
    asking or who you are with? [whites vs. blacks?] Why?
17. So you say you tend to identify as ----, do you think your racial identity
    has changed as you've gotten older?
    Have you ever identified yourself differently than you do today?
    Why do you think that is?
18. Do you feel that others (other blacks & other whites) have been sup-
    portive of this identity (black/white/biracial)?
19. Can you think of a situation in which that identity was not supported?
20. In general, how important is race to you?
    Would you say it has been pretty important, somewhat important,
    or not important at all? [Explain.]
    Are there any experiences that you could describe, in which race
    seemed to be pretty important?

IDENTITY CONSTRAINTS

21. Okay, so you told me that your racial background is white and black.
    Even though you tend to identify as X, do you feel that you can identify
    however you choose?
22. Questions about your parents: What messages, if any, have you re-
    ceived from your parents about your race?
    How was race addressed in your household growing up (if at all)?
    [Explain.]
    Have your parents influenced how you think about yourself racially?
    How so? Mom? Dad?
    Have they ever directly told you how you should identify yourself?
    [Explain.]
    What about other family members? (Grandparents, siblings, aunts/
    uncles, etc.)
23. What messages, if any, have you received from ____ about how you
    should or should not identify?
    From other blacks in general?
    From other whites in general?
    How do you think this has impacted your identity?

24. How would you describe your social networks growing up? Today?
    Were you primarily surrounded by other blacks, whites, another
    group altogether, or by diverse racial groups?
    What about in your neighborhood? Church? At school? College?
    How do you think growing up in this environment has impacted
    you? Your identity?
25. Do you feel as if you made a conscious choice to surround yourself by
    a specific racial group or groups? (Or has this been by chance?)
    Have you ever made a conscious choice to surround yourself by a
    specific group?
    [If yes, why?]
26. Have you ever experienced hostility or negative treatment by other
    blacks because of your multiracial background (DIRECTLY OR INDI-
    RECTLY)?
    Because of your looks?
    What about because of your white background?
27. Have you ever experienced hostility or negative treatment by other
    whites because of your multiracial background?
    Because of your looks?
    What about because of your black background?

AGENCY AND IDENTITY WORK

28. Have you ever tried to hide (or at least downplay) your multiracial
    background, or highlight one racial background over another? Why?
    At any point in your life? When you were younger?
29. Do you ever or have you ever presented yourself differently when you
    were with whites versus when you've been with other blacks?
    How so?
    Why?
30. Are you currently married or in a long-term relationship?
    What is the race/ethnic background of your partner?
    If not, what are the race/ethnic backgrounds of previous dating
    partners?
    Has race ever played a role in who you selected to date/marry?
31. In terms of your friends today, would you describe them as belonging
    primarily to one race or another, or are they varied in terms of racial
    background?
    Has race ever played a role in who you choose/chose to become
    friends with? Why or why not? [Please explain.]

INCONGRUITY OF RACIAL IDENTITY

32. How do you think other people (who may not know you) would classify you according to race based on your looks? [What have people told you?]

    How does this compare to how you see yourself?

33. Do you think that how you look has played a role in how you identify? How so? [Explain.]

34. Do you feel like others (blacks or whites or others) try to (or ever have tried to) categorize you or label you racially (put you into one group)?

    How does this make you feel?

    Your response?

    What about by parents or other family members?

    What about by friends, peers, coworkers?

35. Can you recall a specific situation or instance in which someone challenged your identity (or how you think of yourself)? [Please explain].

    How did this situation make you feel?

    What was your response? How did you deal with this?

WRAP-UP QUESTIONS

36. All in all, how would you characterize your experience of having a multiple racial background? Would you characterize it as a positive or negative experience? [Please explain.]

    Has your experience changed over time? Has it gotten better or worse?

    Why do you think that is? [Please explain.]

37. You mentioned that you lived in X, Y, Z, has your experience differed in these different contexts? [Please explain.]

38. Is there anything we haven't covered that you want to talk about or add before we finish?

39. Do you have any questions about the interview, the study, or myself?

Appendix B

Profile of the Research Sample

		Sex	Age	Education	Public Identity	Internalized Identity	Network Type
1	John	M	29	College	Biracial	Black	Mixed
2	Grant	M	22	Some college	Multiracial	Biracial	White
3	Natalie	F	27	Some graduate school	Biracial	Biracial	White
4	Samantha	F	19	Some college	Mixed	Black	Mixed
5	Nicole	F	42	Some graduate school	Multiracial	White	Mixed
6	Denise	F	19	Some college	Black	Black	Mixed
7	Michael	M	23	Some college	Mixed/Biracial	Black	Mixed
8	Anthony	M	21	Some college	Mixed	Black	Black
9	Nick	M	24	Some graduate school	Mixed	Black	Mixed
10	Stephanie	F	19	Some college	Biracial	Black	Black
11	Michelle	F	29	College	Biracial	Black	Mixed
12	Kendra	F	20	Some college	Black	Black	Mixed
13	Beth	F	32	Some graduate school	Black	Black	Mixed
14	Isabel	F	18	Some college	Multiracial	White	White
15	Julie	F	21	Some college	Mixed	Black	Black
16	Natasha	F	20	Some college	Black	Black	Mixed
17	Olivia	F	45	College	Multiracial	Biracial	Mixed
18	Caroline	F	25	Some graduate school	Biracial/ Interracial	White	White
19	Monique	F	28	Some college	Biracial	Biracial	Mixed
20	Kate	F	23	Some graduate school	White	White	White
21	Alicia	F	18	Some college	Mixed	Black	Mixed
22	Angie	F	25	Some college	Black	Black	White
23	Kim	F	21	Some college	Biracial	Biracial	Mixed
24	Carrie	F	21	Some college	Biracial	White	White
25	Lisa	F	19	Some college	Biracial	Black	Mixed
26	Stacey	F	33	College	Biracial	Biracial	Mixed
27	Jack	M	22	Some college	Biracial	White	White
28	Leslie	F	19	Some college	Mixed	Black	Mixed
29	Sarah	F	25	College	Biracial	Black	Mixed
30	Charlotte	F	20	Some college	Biracial	White	Mixed
31	Georgia	F	21	Some college	Mixed	Black	Black
32	Allison	F	19	Some college	Mixed	White	White
33	Kristen	F	19	Some college	Biracial	Black	Mixed
34	Chris	M	18	Some college	Biracial	White	White
35	Sheryl	F	19	Some college	Mixed	Black	White
36	Jackie	F	42	College	Biracial	Black	White
37	Lauren	F	37	College	Biracial	Black	Mixed
38	Blake	M	18	Some college	Biracial	Black	Mixed
39	Cherise	F	18	Some college	African American	Black	Mixed
40	Shane	M	26	Some college	Mixed/Biracial	Biracial	Mixed

Appendix C

Further Reading

SOCIAL SCIENCE/PSYCHOLOGY/HISTORY

Azoulay, Katya Gibel. 1997. *Black, Jewish, and Interracial: It's Not the Color of Your Skin, but the Race of Your Kin, and Other Myths of Identity.* Durham, NC: Duke University Press.

Bird, Stephanie Rose. 2009. *Light, Bright, and Damned Near White: Biracial and Triracial Culture in America.* Westport, CT: Praeger.

Bost, Susan. 2005. *Mulattas and Mestizas: Representing Mixed Identities in the Americas, 1850–2000.* Athens, GA: University of Georgia Press.

Brown, Ursula. 2001. *The Interracial Experience: Growing Up Black/White Racially Mixed in the United States.* Westport, CT: Praeger.

Brunsma, David L., ed. 2006. *Mixed Messages: Multiracial Identities in the "Color-Blind" Era.* Boulder, CO: Lynne Rienner Publishers.

Caplan, Lionel. 2001. *Children of Colonialism: Ango-Indians in a Postcolonial World.* Oxford: Berg.

Chiong, Jane Ayers. 1998. *Racial Categorization of Multiracial Children in Schools.* Westport, CT: Bergin & Garvey.

Christian, Mark. 2000. *Multiracial Identity: An International Perspective.* New York: St. Martin's Press.

Colker, Ruth. 1996. *Hybrid: Bisexuals, Multiracials, and Other Misfits under American Law.* New York: New York University Press.

Coombes, Annie, and Avtar Brah. 2000. *Hybridity and Its Discontents: Politics, Science, Culture.* New York: Routledge.

DaCosta, Kimberly. 2007. *Making Multiracials: State, Family, and Market in the Redrawing of the Color Line.* Stanford, CA: Stanford University Press.

Dalmage, Heather M., ed. 2004. *The Politics of Multiracialism: Challenging Racial Thinking.* Albany, NY: State University of New York Press.

Daniel, G. Reginald. 2002. *More Than Black? Multiracial Identity and the New Racial Order*. Philadelphia: Temple University Press.

Davis, F. James. 1991. *Who Is Black? One Nation's Definition*. University Park, PA: Pennsylvania State University Press.

Downing, Karen, ed. 2005. *Multiracial America: A Resource Guide on the History and Literature of Interracial Issues*. Lanham, MD: The Scarecrow Press, Inc.

Elam, Michelle. 2011. *The Souls of Mixed Folk: Race, Politics, and Aesthetics in the New Millennium*. Palo Alto, CA: Stanford University Press.

Forbes, Jack D. 1993. *Africans and Native Americans: The Language of Race and the Evolution of Red-Black Peoples*. Urbana, IL: University of Illinois Press.

Foster, Martha Harroun. 2006. *We Know Who We Are: Metis Identity in a Montana Community*. Norman, OK: University of Oklahoma Press.

Ifekwunigwe, Jayne O., ed. 2004. *"Mixed Race" Studies: A Reader*. London: Routledge.

Johnson, Kevin, ed. 2003. *Mixed Race America and the Law: A Reader*. New York: New York University Press.

Katz, William Loren. 1997. *Black Indians: A Hidden Heritage*. New York: Aladdin.

Kennedy, N. Brent, and Robyn Vaughan Kennedy. 1997. *The Melungeons: The Resurrection of a Proud People*. Macon, GA: Mercer University Press.

Kennedy, Randall. 2003. *Interracial Intimacies: Sex, Marriage, Identity, and Adoption*. New York: Vintage Books.

Kilson, Marion. 2001. *Claiming Place: Biracial Young Adults of the Post–Civil Rights Era*. Westport, CT: Bergin and Garvey.

Kilson, Marion, and Florence Ladd. 2009. *Is That Your Child? Mothers Talk about Rearing Biracial Children*. Lanham, MD: Lexington Books.

Klein, Sybil, ed. 2000. *Creole: The History and Legacy of Louisiana's Free People of Color*. Baton Rouge, LA: Louisiana State University Press.

Korgen, Kathleen. 1998. *From Black to Biracial: Transforming Racial Identity among Biracial Americans*. New York: Praeger.

——, ed. 2010. *Multiracial Americans and Social Class; The Influence of Social Class on Racial Identity*. New York: Routledge.

Kwan, SanSan, and Kenneth Speirs. 2004. *Mixing It Up: Multiracial Subjects*. Austin, TX: University of Texas Press.

McCubbin, Hamilton, Krystal Ontai, Lisa Kehl, Laurie McCubbin, Ida Strom, Heidi Hart, Barbara Debaryshe, Marika Ripke, and Jon Matsuoka, eds. 2010. *Multiethnicity and Multiethnic Families: Development, Identity, and Resilience*. Honolulu, HI: Le' a Publications.

McKelvey, Robert S. 1999. *The Dust of Life: America's Children Abandoned in Vietnam*. Seattle, WA: University of Washington Press.

Menchaca, Martha. 2002. *Recovering History, Constructing Race: The Indian, Black, and White Roots of Mexican Americans*. Austin, TX: University of Texas Press.

Nakazawa, Donna Jackson. 2003. *Does Anybody Else Look Like Me? A Parent's Guide to Raising Multiracial Children*. Cambridge, MA: Perseus Publishing.

Nash, Gary. 1999. *Forbidden Love: The Secret History of Mixed-Race America*. New York: Henry Holt.

Parker, David, and Miri Song, eds. 2001. *Rethinking "Mixed Race."* London: Pluto.

Perlmann, J., and Mary Waters, eds. 2002. *The New Race Question: How the Census Counts Multiracial Individuals*. New York: Russell Sage Foundation.

Renn, Kristen A. 2004. *Mixed Race Students in College: The Ecology of Race, Identity, and Community on Campus.* Albany, NY: State University of New York Press.

Reynolds, Henry. 2005. *Nowhere People.* Camberwell, Australia: Penguin Books.

Rockquemore, Kerry Ann, and David L. Brunsma. 2002. *Beyond Black: Biracial Identity in America.* Thousand Oaks, CA: Sage Publications.

———. 2008. *Beyond Black: Biracial Identity in America,* Second Edition. Lanham, MD: Rowman & Littlefield.

Rockquemore, Kerry Ann, and Tracey Laszloffy. 2005. *Raising Biracial Children.* Lanham, MD: AltaMira Press.

Root, Maria P. P., ed. 1992. *Racially Mixed People in America.* Newbury Park, CA: Sage Publications.

———, ed. 1996. *The Multiracial Experience: Racial Borders as the New Frontier.* Thousand Oaks, CA: Sage Publications.

Russell, Kathy, Midge Wilson, and Ronald E. Hall. 1992. *The Color Complex: The Policies of Skin Color among African Americans.* New York: Harcourt Brace Jovanovich.

Sharfstein, Daniel J. 2011. *The Invisible Line: Three American Families and the Secret Journey from Black to White.* New York: The Penguin Press.

Sollors, Werner, ed. 2000. *Interracialism: Black-White Intermarriage in American History, Literature, and Law.* Oxford: Oxford University Press.

Spencer, Jon Michael. 1997. *The New Colored People: The Mixed Race Movement in America.* New York: New York University Press.

Spencer, Rainier. 1999. *Spurious Issues: Race and Multiracial Identity Politics in the United States.* Boulder, CO: Westview Press.

———. 2006. *Challenging Multiracial Identity.* Boulder, CO: Lynne Rienner Publishers.

———. 2010. *Reproducing Race: The Paradox of Generation Mix.* Boulder, CO: Lynne Rienner Publishers.

Spickard, Paul. 1989. *Mixed Blood: Intermarriage and Ethnic Identity in Twentieth Century America.* Madison, WI: University of Wisconsin Press.

Spickard, Paul, and W. Jeffrey Burroughs. 2000. *We Are a People: Narrative and Multiplicity in Constructing Ethnic Identity.* Philadelphia: Temple University Press.

Squires, Catherine R. 2007. *Dispatches from the Color Line: The Press and Multiracial America.* Albany, NY: State University of New York Press.

Tizard, Barbara, and Ann Phoenix. 2002. *Black, White, or Mixed Race? Race and Racism in the Lives of Young People of Mixed Parentage.* New York: Routledge.

Walker, Clarence E. 2009. *Mongrel Nation: The America Begotten by Thomas Jefferson and Sally Hemmings.* Charlottesville, VA: University of Virginia Press.

Williams, Kim M. 2006. *Mark One or More: Civil Rights in Multiracial America.* Ann Arbor, MI: The University of Michigan Press.

Williams-Leon, Teresa, and Cynthia L. Nakashima, eds. 2001. *The Sum of Our Parts: Mixed Heritage Asian Americans.* Philadelphia: Temple University Press.

Williamson, Joel. 1980. *New People: Miscegenation and Mulattoes in the United States.* New York: The Free Press.

Winters, Loretta I., and Herman L. Debose, eds. 2003. *New Faces in a Changing America: Multiracial Identity in the 21st Century.* Thousand Oaks, CA: Sage Publications.

Zack, Naomi. 1993. *Race and Mixed Race.* Philadelphia: Temple University Press.

———, ed. 1995. *American Mixed Race: The Culture of Microdiversity.* Lanham, MD: Rowman & Littlefield.

Ziv, Alon. 2006. *Breeding between the Lines: Why Interracial People Are Healthier and More Attractive.* Fort Lee, NJ: Barricade Books, Inc.

AUTOBIOGRAPHY/MEMOIR/BIOGRAPHY

Arboleda, Teja. 1998. *In the Shadow of Race: Growing Up as a Multiethnic, Multicultural and "Multiracial" American.* Mahwah, NJ: Lawrence Erlbaum Associates.
Ball, Edward. 1999. *Slaves in the Family.* New York: Random House.
Broyard, Bliss. 2007. *One Drop: My Father's Hidden Life—A Story of Race and Family Secrets.* New York: Back Bay Books.
Cross, June. 2007. *Secret Daughter: A Mixed-Race Daughter and the Mother Who Gave Her Away.* New York: Penguin.
Derricotte, Tio. 1997. *The Black Notebooks: An Interior Journey.* New York: W. W. Norton.
Frazier, Sundee Tucker. 2002. *Check All That Apply: Finding Wholeness as a Multiracial Person.* Downers Grove, IL: InterVarsity Press.
Haizlip, Shirlee Taylor. 1994. *The Sweeter the Juice: A Family Memoir in Black and White.* New York: Simon and Schuster.
Hall, Wade. 1997. *Passing for Black: The Life and Careers of Mae Street Kidd.* Lexington, KY: University Press of Kentucky.
Hugel-Marshall, Ika. 2001. *Invisible Woman: Growing Up Black in Germany.* New York: Continuum.
Jacobs, Harriet A. 1987. *Incidents in the Life of a Slave Girl.* Cambridge, MA: Harvard University Press.
Jones, Lisa. 1994. *Bulletproof Diva: Tales of Race, Sex and Hair.* New York: Doubleday.
Lazarre, Jane. 1996. *Beyond the Whiteness of Whiteness: Memoir of a White Mother of Black Sons.* Durham, NC: Duke University Press.
Lee, Vicky. 2004. *Being Eurasian: Memories across Racial Divides.* Seattle, WA: University of Washington Press.
Lewis, Elliot. 2006. *Fade: My Journeys in Multiracial America.* New York: Carroll & Graf Publishers.
McBride, James. 1997. *The Color of Water: A Black Man's Tribute to His White Mother.* New York: Riverhead.
Minerbrook, Scott. 1996. *Divided to the Vein: A Journey into Race and Family.* New York: Harcourt Brace.
Nissel, Angela. 2006. *Mixed: My Life in Black and White.* New York: Villard.
Obama, Barack. 1995. *Dreams from My Father: A Story of Race and Inheritance.* New York: Random House.
Scales-Trent, Judy. 1995. *Notes of a White Black Woman.* University Park, PA: Pennsylvania State University Press.
Stone, Judith. 2007. *When She Was White: The True Story of a Family Divided by Race.* New York: Miramax Books.
Talalay, Kathryn. 1995. *Composition in Black and White: The Life of Philippa Schuyler.* New York: Oxford University Press.
Walker, Rebecca. 2001. *Black, White, and Jewish: Autobiography of a Shifting Self.* New York: Riverhead.

Williams, Gregory Howard. 1996. *Life on the Color Line: A True Story of a White Boy Who Discovered He Was Black.* New York: Plume.

ESSAY/INTERVIEW COMPILATIONS

Camper, Carol, ed. 1994. *Miscegenation Blues: Voices of Mixed Race Women.* Toronto: Sister Vision.

D.A., Adebe, and Andrea Thompson, eds. 2010. *Other Tongues: Mixed-Race Women Speak Out.* Toronto: Inanna Publications.

Funderburg, Lise. 1994. *Black, White, Other: Biracial Americans Talk about Race and Identity.* New York: William Morrow.

Gaskins, Pearl Fuyo, ed. 1999. *What Are You? Voices of Mixed-Race Young People.* New York: Henry Holt.

Gay, Kathlyn. 1995. *"I Am Who I Am": Speaking Out about Multiracial Identity.* New York: Franklin Watts.

O'Hearn, Claudine Chiawei, ed. 1998. *Half + Half: Writers on Growing Up Biracial and Bicultural.* New York: Pantheon Books.

Penn, William S., ed. 1997. *As We Are Now: Mixblood Essays on Race and Ethnicity.* Berkeley, CA: University of California Press.

Tauber, Mike, and Pamela Singh. 2010. *Blended Nation: Portraits and Interviews of Mixed-Race America.* Berkeley, CA: Publishers Group West.

References

Albelda, Randy, Robert W. Drago, and Steven Shulman. 2001. *Unlevel Playing Fields: Understanding Wage Inequality and Discrimination.* Cambridge, MA: Economic Affairs Bureau.

Allen, Walter, Edward Telles, and Margaret Hunter. 2000. "Skin Color, Income, and Education: A Comparison of African Americans and Mexican Americans." *National Journal of Sociology* 12: 129–80.

Angier, Natalie. 2000. "Does Race Differ? Not Really, DNA Shows." *New York Times,* August 22.

Arana, Marie. 2008. "He's Not Black." *Washington Post,* November 30.

Aspinall, P. J. 2003. "The Conceptualisation and Categorisation of Mixed Race/Ethnicity in Britain and North America: Identity Options and the Role of the State." *International Journal of Intercultural Relations* 27(3): 269–96.

Backman, Carl W., Paul F. Secord, and Jerry R. Pierce. 1963. "Resistance to Change in the Self-Concept as a Function of Perceived Consensus among Significant Others." *Sociometry* 26: 102–11.

Binning, Kevin R., Miguel M. Unzueta, Yuen J. Huo, and Ludwin E. Molina. 2009. "The Interpretation of Multiracial Status and Its Relation to Social Engagement and Psychological Well-Being." *Journal of Social Issues* 65(1): 35–49.

Blake, John. 2010. "Arab- and Persian-American Campaign: 'Check It Right' on Census." *CNN,* April 1. http://articles.cnn.com/2010-04-01/us/census.check .it.right.campaign_1_arab-american-leaders-census-form-persian?_s=PM:US (accessed March 14, 2011).

Blumer, Herbert. 1969. *Symbolic Interactionism: Perspective and Method.* Englewood Cliffs, NJ: Prentice Hall.

Bond, Selena, and Thomas Cash. 1992. *The Black Community: Diversity and Unity.* New York: HarperCollins.

Bracey, Jeana R., Mayra Y. Bamaca, and Adriana J. Umana-Taylor. 2004. "Examining Ethnic Identity and Self-Esteem among Biracial and Monoracial Adolescents." *Journal of Youth and Adolescence* 33(2): 123–32.

Brackett, Kimberly P., Ann Marcus, Nelya J. McKenzie, Larry C. Mullins, Zongli Tang, and Annette M. Allen. 2006. "The Effects of Multiracial Identification on Students' Perceptions of Racism." *Social Science Journal* 43(3): 437–44.

Bradshaw, Carla K. 1992. "Beauty and the Beast: On Racial Ambiguity." In *Racially Mixed People in America*, edited by Maria P. P. Root, 77–88. Newbury Park, CA: Sage Publications.

Bratter, Jenifer. 2007. "Will 'Multiracial' Survive to the Next Generation?: The Racial Classification of Children of Multiracial Parents." *Social Forces* 86(2): 821–49.

———. 2010. "The One-Drop Rule through a Multiracial Lens: Examining the Roles of Race and Class in Racial Classification of Children of Partially Black Parents." In *Multiracial Americans and Social Class: The Influence of Social Class on Racial Identity*, edited by Kathleen Odell Korgen, 184–204. London: Routledge.

Brown, Ursula. 2001. *The Interracial Experience: Growing Up Black/White Racially Mixed in the United States*. Westport, CT: Praeger.

Brunsma, David L. 2005. "Interracial Families and the Racial Identification of Mixed-Race Children: Evidence from the Early Childhood Longitudinal Study." *Social Forces* 84: 1131–57.

———. 2006. "Public Categories, Private Identities: Exploring Regional Differences in the Biracial Experience." *Social Science Research* 35: 555–76.

Brunsma, David L., and Kerry Ann Rockquemore. 2001. "The New Color Complex: Appearance and Biracial Identity." *Identity: An International Journal of Theory and Research* 1: 225–46.

Cahill, Spencer E. 1989. "Fashioning Gender Identity." *Symbolic Interaction* 12: 281–98.

Campbell, Mary E. 2007. "Thinking Outside the (Black) Box: Measuring Black and Multiracial Identification on Surveys." *Social Science Research* 36: 921–44.

Campbell, Mary E., and Melissa R. Herman. 2010. "Politics and Policies: Attitudes towards Multiracial Americans." *Ethnic and Racial Studies* 33(9): 1511–36.

Chang, Elizabeth. 2010. "Why Obama Should Not Have Checked 'Black' on His Census Form." *Washington Post*, April 29.

Cheng, Simon, and Joshua Klugman. 2010. "School Racial Composition and Biracial Adolescents' School Attachment." *Sociological Quarterly* 51(1): 150–78.

Cheng, Simon, and Kathryn J. Lively. 2009. "Multiracial Self-Identification and Adolescent Outcomes: A Social Psychological Approach to the Marginal Man Theory." *Social Forces* 88(1): 61–98.

Choi, Yoonsun, Tracy W. Harachi, Mary Rogers Gillmore, and Richard F. Catalano. 2006. "Are Multiracial Adolescents at Greater Risk? Comparisons of Rates, Patterns, and Correlates of Substance Use and Violence between Monoracial and Multiracial Adolescents." *American Journal of Orthopsychiatry* 76(1): 86–97.

Christian, Mark. 2000. *Multiracial Identity: An International Perspective*. New York: St. Martin's Press.

Coakley, Jay J. 1998. *Sport in Society: Issues and Controversy*. St. Louis, MO: Mosby.

Cockerham, William C. 2007. *Social Causes of Health and Disease*. Cambridge: Polity Press.

Coleman, Victoria H., and M. M. Carter. 2007. "Biracial Self-Identification: Impact on Trait Anxiety, Social Anxiety, and Depression." *Identity: An International Journal of Theory and Research* 7(2): 103–14.

Collins, Michael F. 2003. *Sport and Social Exclusion*. London: Routledge.

Cooley, Charles H. 1902. *Human Nature and the Social Order*. New York: Scribner's.

Cornell, Stephen, and Douglas Hartmann. 1998. *Ethnicity and Race: Making Identities in a Changing World*. Thousand Oaks, CA: Pine Forge Press.

Cose, Ellis. 2000. "What's White, Anyway?" *Newsweek*, September 18.

Courtney, Susan. 2005. *Hollywood Fantasies of Miscegenation: Spectacular Narratives of Gender and Race*. Princeton, NJ: Princeton University Press.

DaCosta, Kimberly McClain. 2003. "Multiracial Identity: From Personal Problem to Public Issue." In *New Faces in a Changing America: Multiracial Identity in the 21st Century*, edited by Loretta I. Winters and Herman L. DeBose, 68–84. Thousand Oaks, CA: Sage Publications.

Daniel, G. Reginald. 1992. "Passers and Pluralists: Subverting the Racial Divide." In *Racially Mixed People in America*, edited by Maria P. P. Root, 91–107. Newbury Park, CA: Sage Publications.

———. 1996. "Black and White Identity in the New Millennium: Unsevering the Ties That Bind." In *The Multiracial Experience*, edited by Maria P. P. Root, 121–39. Thousand Oaks, CA: Sage Publications.

———. 2002. *More Than Black? Multiracial Identity and the New Racial Order*. Philadelphia: Temple University Press.

———. 2003. "Multiracial Identity in Global Perspective: The United States, Brazil, and South Africa." In *New Faces in a Changing America: Multiracial Identity in the 21st Century*, edited by Loretta I. Winters and Herman L. DeBose, 247–86. Thousand Oaks, CA: Sage Publications.

Davis, F. James. 1991. *Who Is Black? One Nation's Definition*. University Park, PA: Pennsylvania State University Press.

———. 2006. "Defining Race: Comparative Perspectives." In *Mixed Messages: Multiracial Identities in the "Color-Blind" Era*, edited by David L. Brunsma, 15–31. Boulder, CO: Lynne Rienner.

Day, C. B. 1932. *A Study of Some Negro-White Families in the United States*. Cambridge, MA: Peabody Museum of Harvard University.

Dixon, Thomas. [1902] 1994. *The Leopard's Spots*. Newport Beach, CA: Noontide Press.

Douglass, Ramona. 1996. "Multiracial People Must No Longer Be Invisible." *New York Times*, July 12.

Doyle, Jamie Mihoko, and Grace Kao. 2007a. "Are Racial Identities of Multiracials Stable? Changing Self-Identification among Single and Multiple Race Individuals." *Social Psychology Quarterly* 70(4): 405–23.

———. 2007b. "Friendship Choices of Multiracial Adolescents: Racial Homophily, Blending, or Amalgamation?" *Social Science Research* 36(2): 633–53.

Eason, O. 1997. "Biracial Classifications: History Forgotten?" *New Pittsburgh Courier*, August 30.

Edwards, Ozzie L. 1972. "Skin Color as a Variable in Racial Attitudes of Black Urbanites." *Journal of Black Studies* 3: 473–83.

England, Sarah. 2010. "Mixed and Multiracial in Trinidad and Honduras: Rethinking Mixed-Race Identities in Latin America and the Caribbean." *Ethnic and Racial Studies* 33(2): 195–213.

Espiritu, Yen. 1992. *Asian-American Panethnicity.* Philadelphia: Temple University Press.

Farley, Reynolds. 1999. "Racial Issues: Recent Trends in Residential Patterns and Intermarriage." In *Diversity and Its Discontents: Cultural Conflict and Common Ground in Contemporary American Society,* edited by Neil J. Smelser and Jeffrey C. Alexander, 85–128. Princeton, NJ: Princeton University Press.

Felson, Richard B. 1981. "Social Sources of Information in the Development of the Self." *Sociological Quarterly* 22: 69–79.

———. 1985. "Reflected Appraisal and the Development of Self." *Social Psychology Quarterly* 48: 71–78.

Fernandez, Carlos A. 1992. "La Raza and the Melting Pot: A Comparative Look at Multiethnicity." In *Racially Mixed People in America,* edited by Maria P. P. Root, 126–43. Newbury Park, CA: Sage Publications.

———. 1996. "Government Classification of Multiracial/Multiethnic People." In *The Multiracial Experience,* edited by Maria P. P. Root, 15–36. Thousand Oaks, CA: Sage Publications.

Festinger, Leon. 1954. "A Theory of Social Comparison Processes." *Human Relations* 7: 117–40.

Fiske, Susan T., and Shelley E. Taylor. 1991. *Social Cognition.* New York: McGraw-Hill.

Frazier, E. Franklin. 1957. *Black Bourgeoisie.* New York: Collier Books.

Freeman, Howard E., J. Michael Ross, Davis Armor, and Thomas F. Pettigrew. 1966. "Color Gradations and Attitudes among Middle-Income Negroes." *American Sociological Review* 31: 365–74.

Funderburg, Lise. 1994. *Black, White, Other: Biracial Americans Talk about Race and Identity.* New York: William Morrow.

———. 1996. "Boxed In." *New York Times,* July 10.

Gans, Herbert. 1979. "Symbolic Ethnicity." *Ethnic and Racial Studies* 2: 1–20.

Gardner, LeRoy. 2000. *Black/White Race Mixing: An Essay on the Stereotypes and Realities of Interracial Marriage.* St. Paul, MN: Paragon House.

Gartrell, C. David. 1987. "Network Approaches to Social Evaluation." *Annual Review of Sociology* 13: 49–66.

———. 2002. "The Embeddedness of Social Comparison." In *Relative Deprivation,* edited by Iain Walker and Heather J. Smith, 164–84. New York: Cambridge University Press.

Gecas, Victor, and Michael L. Schwalbe. 1983. "Beyond the Looking-Glass Self: Social Structure and Efficacy-Based Self-Esteem." *Social Psychology Quarterly* 46: 77–88.

Gibbs, Jewelle Taylor. 1987. "Identity and Marginality: Issues in the Treatment of Biracial Adolescents." *American Journal of Orthopsychiatry* 57: 265–78.

Gibbs, Jewelle Taylor, and Alice M. Hines. 1992. "Negotiating Ethnic Identity: Issues for Black-White Biracial Adolescents." In *Racially Mixed People in America,* edited by Maria P. P. Root, 223–38. Newbury Park, CA: Sage Publications.

Goethals, George R., and William M. P. Klein. 2000. "Interpreting and Inventing Social Reality: Attributional and Constructive Elements in Social Comparison." In *Handbook of Social Comparison*, edited by Jerry Suls and Ladd Wheeler, 23–44. New York: Kluwer Academic/Plenum.

Goethals, George R., D. Messick, and S. T. Allison. 1991. "The Uniqueness Bias: Studies of Constructive Social Comparison." In *Social Comparison: Contemporary Theory and Research*, edited by Jerry Suls and Thomas Ashby Wills, 149–73. Hillsdale, NJ: Lawrence Erlbaum.

Goffman, Erving. 1963. *Stigma: Notes on the Management of Spoiled Identity*. Englewood Cliffs, NJ: Prentice Hall.

Goodman, Alan H. 2001. "Biological Diversity and Cultural Diversity: From Race to Radical Bioculturalism." In *Cultural Diversity in the United States: A Critical Reader*, edited by Ida Susser and Thomas Carl Patterson, 29–45. Oxford and Malden, MA: Blackwell.

Gould, Stephen Jay. 1994. "The Geometer of Race." *Discover* 15: 64–69.

———. 1996. *The Mismeasure of Man*. New York: Norton.

Grant, Madison. 1923. *The Passing of the Great Race, or the Racial Basis of European History*. New York: Charles Scribner's Sons.

Graves, Joseph L. 2004. *The Race Myth: Why We Pretend Race Exists in America*. New York: Plume.

Hall, Christine. 1980. "The Ethnic Identity of Racially Mixed People: A Study of Black-Japanese." PhD diss., University of California, Los Angeles.

Hall, Ronald. 1995. "The Bleaching Syndrome: African Americans' Response to Cultural Domination vis-à-vis Skin Color." *Journal of Black Studies* 26: 172–85.

Hao, Lingxin. 2007. *Color Lines, Country Lines: Race, Immigration, and Wealth Stratification in America*. New York: Russell Sage Foundation.

Harris, Art. 1983. "Louisiana Court Sees No Shades of Gray in Woman's Request." *Washington Post*, May 21.

Harris, Cherise A. 2004. "In a Space No One Could Share: Race, Class, and Identity among the New Black Middle Class." PhD diss., University of Georgia, Athens.

Harris, Cherise A., and Nikki Khanna. 2010. "Black Is, Black Ain't: Biracials, Middle-Class Blacks, and the Social Construction of Blackness." *Sociological Spectrum* 30: 639–70.

Harris, David R., and Jeremiah Joseph Sim. 2002. "Who Is Multiracial? Assessing the Complexity of Lived Race." *American Sociological Review* 67: 614–27.

Harrison, Roderick J., and Claudette E. Bennett. 1995. "Racial and Ethnic Diversity." In vol. 2 of *State of the Union: America in the 1990s*, edited by Reynolds Farley, 141–210. New York: Russell Sage Foundation.

Herman, Melissa. 2004. "Forced to Choose: Some Determinants of Racial Identification in Multiracial Adolescents." *Child Development* 75: 730–48.

———. 2009. "The Black-White-Other Achievement Gap: Testing Theories of Academic Performance among Multiracial and Monoracial Adolescents." *Sociology of Education* 82(1): 20–46.

———. 2010. "Do You See What I Am? How Observers' Backgrounds Affect Their Perceptions of Multiracial Faces." *Social Psychology Quarterly* 73(1): 58–78.

Herring, Cedric. 2004. "Skin Deep: Race and Complexion in the 'Color-blind' Era" in *Skin Deep: How Race and Complexion Matter in the "Color-Blind" Era*, edited by Cedrick Herring, Verna M. Keith, and Hayward Derrick Horton, 1–21. Urbana: University of Illinois Press.

Herring, Cedric, Verna M. Keith, and Hayward Derrick Horton, eds. 2004. *Skin Deep: How Race and Complexion Matter in the "Color-Blind" Era*. Chicago: University of Illinois Press.

Hill, Mark E. 2002. "Skin Color and the Perception of Attractiveness among African Americans: Does Gender Make a Difference?" *Social Psychology Quarterly* 65: 77–91.

Holloway, Steven R., Richard Wright, Mark Ellis, and Margaret East. 2009. "Place, Scale, and the Racial Claims Made for Multiracial Children in the 1990 Census." *Ethnic and Racial Studies* 32(3): 522–47.

Hughes, Michael, and Bradley Hertel. 1990. "The Significance of Color Remains: A Study of Life Chances, Mate Selection, and Ethnic Consciousness among Black Americans." *Social Forces* 69: 1105–20.

Hunter, Margaret L. 1998. "Colorstruck: Skin Color Stratification in the Lives of African American Women." *Sociological Inquiry* 68: 517–35.

———. 2005. *Race, Gender, and the Politics of Skin Tone*. New York and London: Routledge.

Huyser, Kimberly R., Arthur Sakamoto, and Isao Takei. 2010. "The Persistence of Racial Disadvantage: The Socioeconomic Attainments of Single-Race and Multi-Race Native Americans." *Population Research and Policy Review* 29(4): 541–68.

Ignatiev, Noel. 1995. *How the Irish Became White*. New York: Routledge.

Israel, Joachim. 1956. *Self-Evaluation and Rejection in Groups*. New York: Wiley.

Jayaratne, Toby Epstein, and Abigail J. Stewart. 1991. "Quantitative and Qualitative Methods in the Social Sciences: Current Feminist Issues and Practical Strategies." In *Beyond Methodology: Feminist Scholarship as Lived Research*, edited by Mary Margaret Fonow and Judith A. Cook, 85–106. Bloomington, IN: Indiana University Press.

Johnson, James H., Elisa Jayne Bienenstock, and Jennifer A. Stoloff. 1995. "An Empirical Test of the Cultural Capital Hypothesis." *Review of Black Political Economy* 23: 7–27.

Kahn, Jack S., and Jacqueline Denmon. 1997. "An Examination of Social Science Literature Pertaining to Multiracial Identity." *Journal of Multicultural Social Work* 6: 117–38.

Karthikeyan, Hrishi, and Gabriel J. Chin. 2002. "Preserving Racial Identity: Population Patterns and the Application of Anti-Miscegenation Statutes to Asian Americans, 1910–1950." *Asian Law Journal* 9: 1–29.

Keith, Verna M., and Cedric Herring. 1991. "Skin Tone and Stratification in the Black Community." *American Journal of Sociology* 97: 760–78.

Kennedy, Randall. 2000. "The Enforcement of Anti-Miscegenation Laws." In *Interracialism: Black-White Intermarriage in American History, Literature, and Law*, edited by Werner Sollors, 140–62. Oxford: Oxford University Press.

———. 2003. *Interracial Intimacies: Sex, Marriage, Identity, and Adoption*. New York: Vintage Books.

Khanna, Nikki. 2004. "The Role of Reflected Appraisals in Racial Identity: The Case of Multiracial Asians." *Social Psychology Quarterly* 67(2): 115–31.

———. 2010a. "'If You're Half Black, You're Just Black': Reflected Appraisals and the Persistence of the One-Drop Rule." *Sociological Quarterly* 51(1): 96–121.

———. 2010b. "Country Clubs and Hip-Hop Thugs: Examining the Role of Social Class and Culture in Shaping Racial Identity." In *Multiracial Americans and Social Class: The Influence of Social Class on Racial Identity*, edited by Kathleen Korgen, 53–71. New York: Routledge.

———. 2011. "Ethnicity and Race as 'Symbolic': The Use of Ethnic and Racial Symbols in Asserting a Biracial Identity." *Ethnic and Racial Studies*, 34(6): 1049–67.

Khanna, Nikki, and Cathryn Johnson. 2010. "Passing as Black: Racial Identity Work among Biracial Americans." *Social Psychology Quarterly* 73(4): 380–97.

Kibria, Nazli. 2000. "Race, Ethnic Options, and Ethnic Binds: Identity Negotiations of Second-Generation Chinese and Korean Americans." *Sociological Perspectives* 43: 77–95.

———. 2002. *Becoming Asian American: Identities of Second-Generation Chinese and Korean Americans*. Baltimore, MD: Johns Hopkins University Press.

Kich, George Kitahara. 1996. "In the Margins of Sex and Race: Difference, Marginality, and Flexibility." In *The Multiracial Experience*, edited by Maria P. P. Root, 263–76. Thousand Oaks, CA: Sage Publications.

Kiecolt, K. Jill, and Anna F. LoMascolo. 2003. "Roots of Identity: Family Resemblances." In *Advances in Identity Research*, edited by Peter J. Burke, Timothy J. Owens, and Peggy A. Thoits, 27–40. New York: Kluwer Academic/Plenum.

Killian, Lewis M. 1985. "The Stigma of Race: Who Now Bears the Mark of Cain?" *Symbolic Interaction* 8: 1–14.

Kilson, Marion. 2001. *Claiming Place: Biracial Young Adults of the Post–Civil Rights Era*. Westport, CT: Bergin and Garvey.

King, James C. 1981. *The Biology of Race*. Berkeley: University of California Press.

Korgen, Kathleen. 1998. *From Black to Biracial: Transforming Racial Identity among Americans*. New York: Praeger.

Kusow, Abdi M. 2004. "Contesting Stigma: On Goffman's Assumptions of Normative Order." *Symbolic Interaction* 27: 179–97.

Lakoff, Robin Tolmach, and Raquel Scherr. 1984. *Face Value: The Politics of Beauty*. Boston, MA: Routledge and Kegan Paul.

Lareau, Annette. 2003. *Unequal Childhoods: Class, Race, and Family Life*. Berkeley: University of California Press.

Lee, Jennifer, and Frank D. Bean. 2004. "America's Changing Color Lines: Immigration, Race/Ethnicity, and Multiracial Identification." *Annual Review of Sociology* 30: 221–42.

———. 2007. "Reinventing the Color Line: Immigration and America's New Racial/ Ethnic Divide." *Social Forces* 86(2): 561–86.

Lee, Sharon M. 1993. "Racial Classification in the US Census: 1890–1990." *Ethnic and Racial Studies* 16: 75–94.

Lewis, Elliot. 2006. *Fade: My Journeys in Multiracial America*. New York: Carroll and Graf.

Lewontin, R. C., Steven Rose, and Leon J. Kamin. 1984. *Not in Our Genes: Biology, Ideology, and Human Nature*. New York: Pantheon.

Lieberson, Stanley, and Mary Waters. 1986. "Ethnic Groups in Flux: The Changing Ethnic Responses of American Whites." *Annals of the American Academy of Political and Social Science* 487: 79–91.

Mahtani, Minelle. 2001. "'I'm a Blonde-Haired, Blue-Eyed Black Girl': Mapping Mobile Paradoxical Spaces among Multiethnic Women in Toronto, Canada." In *Rethinking "Mixed Race,"* edited by David Parker and Miri Song, 173–90. Sterling, VA: Pluto Press.

Makalani, Minkah. 2003. "Rejecting Blackness, Claiming Whiteness: Anti-Black Whiteness and the Creation of a Biracial Race." In *Whiteout: The Continuing Significance of Racism,* edited by Woody Doane and Eduardo Bonilla-Silva, 81–94. New York: Routledge.

Marger, Martin N. 2006. *Race and Ethnic Relations: American and Global Perspectives.* 7th ed. Belmont, CA: Wadsworth.

Marriott, Michael. 1996. "Multiracial Americans Ready to Claim Their Own Identity." *New York Times,* July 20.

Marvasti, Amir. 2005. "Being Middle Eastern American: Identity Negotiation in the Context of the War on Terror." *Symbolic Interaction* 28: 525–47.

Masuoka, Natalie. 2011. "The 'Multiracial' Option: Social Group Identity and Changing Patterns of Racial Categorization." *American Politics Research* 39(1): 176–204.

McCall, George J. 2003. "The Me and the Not-Me: Positive and Negative Poles of Identity." In *Advances in Identity Theory and Research,* edited by Peter J. Burke, Timothy J. Owens, Richard T. Serpe, and Peggy A. Thoits, 11–25. New York: Plenum.

Mead, George Herbert. 1934. *Mind, Self, and Society.* Chicago: University of Chicago Press.

Mensh, Elaine, and Harry Mensh. 1991. *The IQ Mythology.* Carbondale and Edwardsville: Southern Illinois University Press.

Morning, Ann. 2003. "New Faces, Old Faces: Counting the Multiracial Population Past and Present." In *New Faces in a Changing America: Multiracial Identity in the 21st Century,* edited by Loretta I. Winters and Herman L. DeBose, 41–67. Thousand Oaks, CA: Sage Publications.

Murphy-Shigematsu, Stephen. 2001. "Multiethnic Lives and Monoethnic Myths: American-Japanese Amerasians in Japan." In *The Sum of Our Parts: Mixed Heritage Asian Americans,* edited by Teresa Williams-Leon and Cynthia L. Nakashima, 207–16. Philadelphia: Temple University Press.

Nagel, Joanne. 1994. "Constructing Ethnicity: Creating and Recreating Ethnic Identity and Culture." *Social Problems* 41(1): 152–76.

———. 1995. "American Indian Ethnic Renewal: Politics and the Resurgence of Identity." *American Sociological Review* 60: 947–65.

Nakashima, Cynthia L. 1992. "An Invisible Monster: The Creation and Denial of Mixed-Race People in America." In *Racially Mixed People in America,* edited by Maria P. P. Root, 162–78. Newbury Park, CA: Sage Publications.

Nash, Gary. 1995. "The Hidden History of Mestizo America." *Journal of American History* 82(3): 941–64.

Nixon, Howard L., and James H. Frey. 1996. *A Sociology of Sport.* Belmont, CA: Wadsworth.

Nobles, Melissa. 2000. *Shades of Citizenship: Race and the Census in Modern Politics.* Stanford, CA: Stanford University Press.

Oikawa, Sara, and Tomoko Yoshida. 2007. "An Identity Based on Being Different: A Focus on Biethnic Individuals in Japan." *International Journal of Intercultural Relations* 31(6): 633–53.

Oliver, Melvin, and Thomas Shapiro. 2006. *Black Wealth, White Wealth: A New Perspective on Racial Inequality.* New York: Routledge.

Omi, Michael, and Howard Winant. 1994. *Racial Formation in the United States: From the 1960s to the 1990s.* New York: Routledge.

Oware, Matthew. 2008. "Status Maximization, Hypodescent Theory, or Social Identity Theory? A Theoretical Approach to Understanding the Racial Identification of Multiracial Adolescents." *Research in Race and Ethnic Relations* 15: 225–53.

Park, Robert E. 1928. "Human Migration and the Marginal Man." *American Journal of Sociology* 33: 881–93.

———. 1931. "Mentality of Racial Hybrids." *American Journal of Sociology* 36: 534–51.

Parker, David. 2001. "'We Paved the Way': Exemplary Spaces and Mixed Race in Britain." In *The Sum of Our Parts: Mixed Heritage Asian Americans,* edited by Teresa Williams-Leon and Cynthia L. Nakashima, 185–96. Philadelphia: Temple University Press.

Patterson, Orlando. 2007. "The New Black Nativism." *Time,* February 8.

Perlmann, J., and Mary Waters. 2002. *The New Race Question: How the Census Counts Multiracial Individuals.* New York: Russell Sage Foundation.

Phillips, Layli. 2004. "Fitting In and Feeling Good: Patterns of Self-Evaluation and Psychological Stress among Biracial Adolescent Girls." *Women & Therapy* 27(1–2): 217–36.

Pitts, Leonard. 2007. "Psst: Obama's a Black Man." *Seattle Times,* February 4.

Qian, Zhenchao. 2004. "Options: Racial/Ethnic Identification of Children of Intermarried Couples." *Social Science Quarterly* 85(3): 746–65.

Quillian, Lincoln, and Rozlyn Redd. 2009. "The Friendship Networks of Multiracial Adolescents." *Social Science Research* 38(2): 279–95.

Ransford, Edward H. 1970. "Skin Color, Life Chances, and Anti-White Attitudes." *Social Problems* 18: 164–78.

Reinharz, Shulamit. 1992. *Feminist Methods in Social Research.* New York: Oxford University Press.

Roberts, Sam, and Peter Baker. 2010. "Asked to Declare His Race, Obama Checks 'Black.'" *New York Times,* April 2.

Roberts-Clarke, Ivory, Angie C. Roberts, and Patricia Morokoff. 2004. "Dating Practices, Racial Identity, and Psychotherapeutic Needs of Biracial Women." *Women & Therapy* 27(1–2): 103–17.

Rockquemore, Kerry Ann. 1999. "Between Black and White: Exploring the 'Biracial' Experience." *Race & Society* 1(2): 197–212.

———. 2002. "Negotiating the Color Line: The Gendered Process of Racial Identity Construction among Black-White Biracials." *Gender and Society* 16: 485–503.

Rockquemore, Kerry Ann, and Patricia Arend. 2003. "Opting for White: Choice, Fluidity, and Racial Identity Construction in Post–Civil-Rights America." *Race & Society* 5: 49–64.

Rockquemore, Kerry Ann, and David L. Brunsma. 2002a. *Beyond Black: Biracial Identity in America*. Thousand Oaks, CA: Sage Publications.

——. 2002b. "Socially Embedded Identities: Theories, Typologies, and Processes of Racial Identity among Black/White Biracials." *Sociological Quarterly* 43: 335–56.

——. 2004. "Negotiating Racial Identity: Biracial Women and Interactional Validation." *Women & Therapy* 27(1–2): 85–102.

Rockquemore, Kerry Ann, David L. Brunsma, and Daniel J. Delgado. 2009. "Racing to Theory or Re-Theorizing Race? Understanding the Struggle to Build a Multiracial Identity Theory." *Journal of Social Issues* 65(1): 13–34.

Rockquemore, Kerry Ann, and Tracey A. Laszloffy. 2003. "Multiple Realities: A Relational Narrative Approach in Therapy with Black-White Mixed-Race Clients." *Family Relations* 52: 119–28.

Rondilla, Joanne L., and Paul Spickard. 2007. *Is Lighter Better? Skin Tone Discrimination among Asian Americans*. Lanham, MD: Rowman and Littlefield.

Root, Maria P. P. 1990. "Resolving 'Other' Status: Identity Development of Biracial Individuals." *Women & Therapy* 9: 185–205.

——. 1992. *Racially Mixed People in America*. Newbury Park, CA: Sage Publications.

——. 1996. *The Multiracial Experience: Racial Borders as the New Frontier*. Thousand Oaks, CA: Sage Publications.

——. 1998. "Experiences and Processes Affecting Racial Identity Development: Preliminary Results from the Biracial Sibling Project." *Cultural Diversity and Mental Health* 4: 237–47.

——. 2001. "Factors Influencing the Variation in Racial and Ethnic Identity of Mixed-Heritage Persons of Asian Ancestry." In *The Sum of Our Parts*, edited by Teresa Williams-Leon and Cynthia L. Nakashima, 61–70. Philadelphia: Temple University Press.

Roth, Wendy D. 2003. "Creating Racial Options: Labeling of Multiracial Children in Black Intermarriages in the 1990 Census." Paper presented at the Harvard Color Lines Conference, Cambridge, MA, August 30–September 1.

——. 2005. "The End of the One Drop Rule? Labeling of Multiracial Children in Black Intermarriages." *Sociological Forum* 20: 35–67.

Russell, Kathy, Midge Wilson, and Ronald E. Hall. 1992. *The Color Complex: The Politics of Skin Color among African Americans*. New York: Harcourt Brace Jovanovich.

Saenz, Rogelio, Sean-Shong Hwang, and Robert Anderson. 1995. "Persistence and Change in Asian Identity among Children of Intermarried Couples." *Sociological Perspectives* 38: 175–94.

Sakai, Joseph T., Cynthia Wang, and Rumi Kato Price. 2010. "Substance Use and Dependence among Native Hawaiians, Other Pacific Islanders, and Asian Ethnic Groups in the United States: Contrasting Multiple-Race and Single-Race Prevalence Rates from a National Survey." *Journal of Ethnicity in Substance Abuse* 9(3): 173–85.

Sanchez, Diana T., and Courtney M. Bonam. 2009. "To Disclose or Not to Disclose Biracial Identity: The Effect of Biracial Disclosure on Perceiver Evaluations and Target Responses." *Journal of Social Issues* 65(1): 129–49.

Scales-Trent, Judy. 2001. "Racial Purity Laws in the United States and Nazi Germany." *Human Rights Quarterly* 233: 259–307.

Schlenker, Barry R. 1980. *Impression Management: The Self-Concept, Social Identity, and Interpersonal Relationships*. Monterey, CA: Brooks/Cole.

Shapiro, Thomas. 2004. *The Hidden Cost of Being African American*. New York: Oxford University Press.

Shih, Margaret, and Diane T. Sanchez. 2005. "Perspectives and Research on the Positive and Negative Implications of Having Multiple Racial Identities." *Psychological Bulletin* 131: 569–91.

———. 2009. "When Race Becomes Even More Complex: Toward Understanding the Landscape of Multiracial Identity and Experiences." *Journal of Social Issues* 65(1): 1–11.

Sickels, Robert J. 1972. *Race, Marriage, and the Law*. Albuquerque, NM: University of New Mexico Press.

Smedley, Audrey. 1993. *Race in North America: Origin and Evolution of a Worldview*. Boulder, CO: Westview Press.

Smolowe, Jill. 1993. "Intermarried with Children." *Time*, December 2.

Snow, David A., and Leon Anderson. 1987. "Identity Work among the Homeless: The Verbal Construction and Avowal of Personal Identities." *American Journal of Sociology* 92: 1336–71.

———. 1993. *Down on Their Luck: A Study of Homeless Street People*. Berkeley and Los Angeles: University of California Press.

Sollors, Werner. 2000. *Interracialism: Black-White Intermarriage in American History, Literature, and Law*. Oxford: Oxford University Press.

Song, Miri. 2003. *Choosing Ethnic Identity*. Malden, MA: Blackwell.

———. 2010. "Is There 'a' Mixed Race Group in Britain? The Diversity of Multiracial Identification and Experience." *Critical Social Policy* 30(3): 337–58.

Song, Miri, and Ferhana Hashem. 2010. "What Does 'White' Mean? Interpreting the Choice of 'Race' by Mixed-Race Young People in Britain." *Sociological Perspectives* 53(2): 287–92.

Spencer, Jon Michael. 1997. *The New Colored People: The Mixed Race Movement in America*. New York: New York University Press.

Spencer, Rainier. 1999. *Spurious Issues: Race and Multiracial Identity Politics in the United States*. Boulder, CO: Westview Press.

———. 2004. "Assessing Multiracial Identity Theory and Politics." *Ethnicities* 4(3): 357–79.

———. 2006a. *Challenging Multiracial Identity*. Boulder, CO: Lynne Rienner.

———. 2006b. "New Racial Identities, Old Arguments: Continuing Biological Reification." In *Mixed Messages: Multiracial Identities in the "Color-Blind" Era*, edited by David L. Brunsma, 83–102. Boulder, CO: Lynne Rienner.

———. 2010. *Reproducing Race: The Paradox of Generation Mix*. Boulder, CO: Lynne Rienner.

Spickard, Paul. 2003. "Does Multiraciality Lighten? Me-Too Ethnicity and the Whiteness Trap." In *New Faces in a Changing America: Multiracial Identity in the 21st Century*, edited by Loretta I. Winters and Herman L. DeBose, 289–300. Thousand Oaks, CA: Sage Publications.

Stephan, Cookie White. 1992. "Mixed-Heritage Individuals: Ethnic Identity and Trait Characteristics." In *Racially Mixed People in America*, edited by Maria P. P. Root, 50–63. Newbury Park, CA: Sage Publications.

Stone, Gregory. 1962. "Appearance and the Self." In *Human Behavior and Social Processes: An Interactionist Approach*, edited by Arnold M. Rose, 86–118. Boston: Houghton Mifflin.

Stonequist, Everett. [1937] 1961. *The Marginal Man*. New York: Russell and Russell.

Storrs, Debbie. 1999. "Whiteness as Stigma: Essentialist Identity Work by Mixed-Race Women." *Symbolic Interaction* 23: 187–212.

———. 2006. "Culture and Identity in Mixed-Race Women's Lives." In *Mixed Messages: Multiracial Identities in the "Color-Blind" Era*, edited by David L. Brunsma, 327–47. Boulder, CO: Lynne Rienner.

Streeter, Caroline A. 2003. "The Hazards of Visibility: 'Biracial' Women, Media Images, and Narratives of Identity." In *New Faces in a Changing America: Multiracial Identity in the 21st Century*, edited by Loretta I. Winters and Herman L. DeBose, 301–22. Thousand Oaks, CA: Sage Publications.

Sullivan, Harry S. 1947. *Conceptions of Modern Psychiatry*. Washington, DC: W. H. White Psychiatric Foundation.

Sullivan, Michael. 2008. "Why Is Obama Black?" *Burlington Free Press*, October 5.

Suls, Jerry, and Ladd Wheeler. 2000. "A Selective History of Classic and Neo-Social Comparison Theory." In *Handbook of Social Comparison: Theory and Research*, edited by Jerry Suls and Ladd Wheeler, 3–19. New York: Kluwer Academic/Plenum.

Suzuki-Crumly, Julie, and Lauri L. Hyers. 2004. "The Relationship among Ethnic Identity, Psychological Well-Being, and Intergroup Competence: An Investigation of Two Biracial Groups." *Cultural Diversity and Ethnic Minority Psychology* 10(2): 137–50.

Swarns, Rachel L., and Jodi Kantor. 2009. "In First Lady's Roots, a Complex Path from Slavery." *New York Times*, October 7.

Sweet, Frank W. 2005. *Legal History of the Color Line: The Notion of Invisible Blackness*. Palm Coast, FL: Backintyme.

Tashiro, Cathy J. 2002. "Considering the Significance of Ancestry through the Prism of Mixed-Race Identity." *Advances in Nursing Science* 25: 1–21.

Tatum, Beverly. 1997. *"Why Are All the Black Kids Sitting Together in the Cafeteria?": And Other Conversations about Race*. New York: Basic Books.

Telles, Edward E., and Christina A. Sue. 2009. "Race Mixture: Boundary Crossing in Comparative Perspective." *Annual Review of Sociology* 35: 129–46.

Teo, Thomas. 2004. "The Historical Problematization of 'Mixed Race' in Psychological and Human-Scientific Discourses." In *Defining Difference: Race and Racism in the History of Psychology*, edited by Andrew S. Winston, 79–108. Washington, DC: American Psychological Association.

Thornton, Michael C. 2009. "Policing the Borderlands: White- and Black-American Newspaper Perceptions of Multiracial Heritage and the Idea of Race, 1996–2006." *Journal of Social Issues* 65(1): 105–27.

Tizard, Barbara, and Ann Phoenix. 2002. *Black, White, or Mixed Race? Race and Racism in the Lives of Young People of Mixed Parentage*. New York: Routledge.

Townsend, Sara S. M., Hazel R. Markus, and Hilary B. Bergsieker. 2009. "My Choice, Your Categories: The Denial of Multiracial Identities." *Journal of Social Issues* 65(1): 185–204.

Tuan, Mia. 1998. *Forever Foreigners or Honorary Whites?* New Brunswick, NJ: Rutgers University Press.

Tucker, William H. 1994. *The Science and Politics of Racial Research*. Urbana and Chicago: University of Illinois Press.

———. 2004. "'Inharmoniously Adapted to Each Other': Science and Racial Crosses." In *Defining Difference: Race and Racism in the History of Psychology*, edited by Andrew S. Winston, 109–28. Washington, DC: American Psychological Association.

Twine, France Winddance. 1996a. "Heterosexual Alliances: The Romantic Management of Racial Identity." In *The Multiracial Experience*, edited by Maria P. P. Root, 291–304. Thousand Oaks, CA: Sage Publications.

———. 1996b. "Brown Skinned White Girls: Class, Culture, and the Construction of White Identity in Suburban Communities." *Gender, Place, and Culture* 3(2): 205–24.

———. 2000. "Racial Ideologies and Racial Methodologies." In *Racing Research, Researching Race*, edited by France Winddance Twine and Jonathan W. Warren, 1–34. New York: New York University Press.

———. 2004. "A White Side of Black Britain: The Concept of Racial Literacy." *Ethnic and Racial Studies* 27(6): 878–907.

———. 2006. "Racial Logics and (Trans)Racial Identities: A View from Britain." In *Mixed Messages: Multiracial Identities in the "Color-Blind" Era*, edited by David L. Brunsma, 217–32. Boulder, CO: Lynne Rienner.

Udry, J. Richard, Karl E. Bauman, and Charles Chase. 1971. "Skin Color, Status, and Mate Selection." *American Journal of Sociology* 76: 722–33.

Valdez, Norberto, and Janice Valdez. 1998. "The Pot That Called the Kettle White: Changing Racial Identities and US Social Construction of Race." *Identities* 5: 379–413.

Van Ausdale, Debra, and Joe R. Feagin. 1996. "Using Racial and Ethnic Concepts: The Critical Case of Very Young Children." *American Sociological Review* 61: 779–93.

Van Tuyl, Loraine Y. 2001. "The Racial Politics of Being *Dogla* and of 'Asian' Descent in Suriname." In *The Sum of Our Parts: Mixed Heritage Asian Americans*, edited by Teresa Williams-León and Cynthia L. Nakashima, 217–30. Philadelphia: Temple University Press.

Washington, Jesse. 2010. "Black or Biracial? Census Forces a Choice for Some." *ABC News*, April 19. http://abcnews.go.com/US/wireStory?id=10411659 (accessed March 14, 2011).

Waters, Mary C. 1990. *Ethnic Options: Choosing Identities in America*. Berkeley: University of California Press.

———. 1991. "The Role of Family Lineage in Identity Formation among Black Americans." *Qualitative Sociology* 14: 57–76.

———. 1996. "Optional Ethnicities: For Whites Only?" In *Origins and Destinies: Immigration, Race, and Ethnicity in America*, edited by Silvia Pedraza and Rubén Rumbaut, 444–54. Belmont, CA: Wadsworth Press.

———. 1999. "The Costs of a Costless Community." In *Race and Ethnic Relations in the United States*, edited by Christopher G. Ellison and W. Allen Martin, 197–203. Los Angeles: Roxbury.

White, Jack E. 1997. "I'm Just Who I Am." *Time*, May 5.

Williams, Garth. 1958. *The Rabbits' Wedding*. New York: HarperCollins.

Williams, Kim M. 2005. "Multiracialism & the Civil Rights Future." *Daedalus* 134: 53–60.

Williams, Teresa Kay. 1996. "Race as a Process: Reassessing the 'What Are You?' Encounters of Biracial Individuals." In *The Multiracial Experience*, edited by Maria P. P. Root, 191–210. Thousand Oaks, CA: Sage Publications.

Williamson, Joel. 1980. *New People: Miscegenation and Mulattoes in the United States.* New York: Free Press.

Winant, Howard. 1994. *Racial Conditions.* Minneapolis: University of Minnesota Press.

Wolf, Naomi. 1991. *The Beauty Myth: How Images of Beauty Are Used Against Women.* New York: Doubleday Books.

Wood, Joanne V. 1996. "What Is Social Comparison and How Should We Study It?" *Personality and Social Psychology Bulletin* 22: 520–37.

Wright, Lawrence. 1994. "One Drop of Blood." *New Yorker*, July 25.

Wright, Richard, Serin Houston, Mark Ellis, Steven Holloway, and Margaret Hudson. 2003. "Crossing Racial Lines: Geographies and Multiraciality in the United States." *Progress in Human Geography* 27(4): 457–74.

Xie, Yu, and Kimberly Goyette. 1997. "The Racial Identification of Multiracial Children with One Asian Parent: Evidence from the 1990 Census." *Social Forces* 76: 547–70.

Zabel, William D. 2000. "Interracial Marriage and the Law." In *Interracialism: Black-White Intermarriage in American History, Literature, and Law*, edited by Werner Sollors, 54–60. Oxford: Oxford University Press.

Zack, Naomi. 1993. *Race and Mixed Race.* Philadelphia: Temple University Press.

———. 1995. "Mixed Black and White Race and Public Policy." *Hypatia* 10: 120–32.

———. 1996. "On Being and Not Being Black and Jewish." In *The Multiracial Experience*, edited by Maria P. P. Root, 140–52. Newbury Park, CA: Sage Publications.

———. 1998. *Thinking about Race.* Belmont, CA: Wadsworth.

Index

organizations, identity work and,
133–34

paper bag test, 34
Park, Robert, 109
passing, 36, 43n6, 138, 142
Patterson, Orlando, 59
perceptions: of acceptance, 72–74; of
discrimination and rejection, 66–70;
of race, 52–58
Persian Americans, xiin6
phenotype (appearance): comparisons
regarding, 7–90; laws and, 32;
manipulation of, as identity work,
116–22; Obama and, 2; and racial
identity, one drop rule and, 61–62,
62f; and reflected appraisals, 46
Phipps, Susie Guillory, x
Pinchback, Pinckney, 34
Pitts, Leonard, 2, 154–55
Plessy, Homer, 31–32
Plessy v. Ferguson, 31–32
private identity, 15
privilege, experiences of, comparisons
regarding, 95–97
Project RACE, 4, 39
psychology, further reading on, 165–68
public identity, 15; of respondents, 48,
49t
public opinion: on interracial marriage,
39; on Obama's racial identity, 155
pull factors: and identity formation,
65–84; term, 65
push factors: and identity formation,
65–84; term, 65

Qian, Zhenchao, 40–41

race: as constructed, ix, 8; terminology
on, ix–xii
racial classification, resistance to, 116,
129–30, 147n3
racial identity, 1–24, 149–56;
Census and, 4–7, 22n2, 23n5,
24n9; defining and measuring,
14–16; factors affecting, 65–84;
formation of, 11, 45–46; further

reading on, 165–69; history of,
25–43; identity work and, 113–47;
as multidimensional, 151–52;
phenotype and, one drop rule and,
61–62, 62f; reflected appraisals
and, 45–64; research directions for,
155–56; research on, 7–12; selective
disclosure of, 126–29; as situational,
97–99; social comparisons and,
87–99; social networks and,
99–107, 107t, 111f; validation of,
116, 153–54
racial identity study, 12–20; author
identity and, 19–20; interviews in,
13–14, 157–61; limitations of,
18–20; participants in, 16–18, 48,
49t, 163–64; rationale for, 3–4;
sample population in, 12–13
racial purity, 3, 27, 35, 38
realistic social comparisons, 100–101;
definition of, 99
Reconstruction, 30–36
reflected appraisals, 45–64; and
multiracial individuals, 46; and
racial identity, 49–52
Reinharz, Shulamit, 13
rejection: gender and, 70–72, 75–81;
perceptions of, 66–70
Rockquemore, Kerry Ann: on
advantages, 143; on constraint
of racial identity, 114; on
discrimination, 68; on gendered
rejection, 77; on one drop rule,
153; research by, 10–11; on self-
identification types, 41; on social
context, 52; on social interactions,
65; on validation, 116
romantic partners, identity work and,
132–33
Root, Maria, xi, 8, 52
Roth, Wendy, 41
Russell, Kathy, 28

Sawyer, Thomas C., 5
science, and racism, 30
segregation: among black community,
34; history of, 30–36

CPSIA information can be obtained at www.ICGtesting.com
Printed in the USA
BVOW030714250113

311325BV00001B/6/P